LEGISLATING THE
HOLOCAUST

Photo of Bernhard Loesener, 1933

Photo by D. Beamter, Ministerialrat im Reichsministerium des Innern

LEGISLATING THE
HOLOCAUST

*The Bernhard Loesener Memoirs
and Supporting Documents*

EDITED BY

KARL A. SCHLEUNES

University of North Carolina at Greensboro

*Memoirs translated by
Carol Scherer*

Westview
PRESS
A Member of the Perseus Books Group

Copyright © 2001 by Westview Press, A Member of the Perseus Books
Group

Published in 2001 in the United States of America by Westview Press,
5500 Central Avenue, Boulder, Colorado 80301-2877,
and in the United Kingdom by Westview Press,
12 Hid's Copse Road, Cumnor Hill, Oxford OX2 9JJ

Find us on the World Wide Web at www.westviewpress.com

Library of Congress Cataloging-in-Publication Data
Legislating the Holocaust: the Bernhard Loesener memoirs and
supporting documents / edited by Karl A. Schleunes ; memoirs
translated by Carol Sherer.
      p.   cm.
   Includes bibliographical references (p.) and index.
   ISBN 0-8133-3775-5 (pbk.)
   1. Jews—Legal status, laws, etc.—History—20th century.   2.
Holocaust, Jewish (1939–1945)—Germany.   3. National Socialism.
4.Lèsener, Bernhard,   5. Lawyers—Germany—Biography.   I.
Schleunes,   Karl A.
KK928 .L44 2001
346.4301'3—dc21   2001026070

Text design in 10-point Palatino by Cynthia Young

10   9   8   7   6   5   4   3   2   1

For Brenda

CONTENTS

ACKNOWLEDGMENTS

A number of people have made important contributions to the comple-
tion of this project. First and foremost, I am grateful to Carol Scherer,
the translator of the Bernhard Loesener memoir, who came forward after
a lecture at Northwestern University several years ago and said she
would be willing to work on the translation. Her offer pushed me to suggest this project to Rob Williams, then the history editor at Westview
Press. Special gratitude is also due to my good friend Jack Hoffmann,
whose knowledge of this period in history stems not only from academic
study for his M.A. in European history under my direction but also from
having lived in Vienna at a time when the effects of Bernhard Loesener's
work were imposed upon him, his sister, and his parents. Jack's critical
historical eye and his native fluency in German have been immensely
helpful.

Jack Hoffmann has saved me from many an infelicitous rendering of
the German into English, especially in the translations of the decrees that
supplemented the Nuremberg legislation. In addition, his critical reading
of my essay on Loesener forced me to confront issues that I might otherwise have approached more indirectly. The sharp editorial eye of another
friend and former student, Cheryl Junk, removed from that same essay a
series of syntactically confused constructions.

Christopher R. Browning of the University of North Carolina at Chapel
Hill read an earlier version of the Loesener essay and offered useful suggestions, all of which I incorporated into its final version. His advice and
friendship have been important to this project and to many others. Clau-
dia Koonz of Duke University, who is also interested in Loesener, located
and then shared with me an out-of-the-way newspaper article on him.
Our hopes that it would offer new information about Loesener were disappointed, but her generosity and advice is greatly appreciated. I also
want to thank Hans Mommsen for calling my attention to Cornelia Ess-

ner's unpublished *Habilitationsschrift* and sharing his copy of it with me, and, of course, Dr. Essner for allowing me to cite her work.

Thanks are due the *Institut für Zeitgeschichte* in Munich and Professor Peter Hoffmann of McGill University for giving me their encouragement in undertaking this project. Finally, I wish to thank the faculty friends of the German Roundtable at my university for listening patiently to my lecture, "Loesener and the Nuremberg Laws," on a beautiful fall Friday afternoon when more uplifting outdoor activities must have beckoned all of them.

Karl A. Schleunes

INTRODUCTION

Bernhard Loesener is a difficult person to characterize. For ten years, from 1933 to 1943, he was the "Jewish expert" in the Nazi Interior Ministry and played an important role in creating anti-Jewish legislation. He is best known for his role in drafting the infamous Nuremberg Laws of September 1935. These laws robbed Germany's Jews of their citizenship rights and became the backbone of the Nazi legislative assault upon their position in German society. Loesener must, therefore, be counted among the perpetrators in the Nazis' search for a solution to what they called the "Jewish question." That search eventually led to the establishment of gas chambers and death camps in Eastern Europe. Not that Loesener was involved in establishing either gas chambers or death camps. On the contrary, he claims to have fought hard to limit the number of people victimized by the laws he helped to write. And when he finally did learn about the gas chambers and death camps, he says he turned his back on his career as "Jewish expert." Indeed, he may even have become a member of the resistance against Hitler and his regime. He tells us in his memoir that he joined resistance circles as early as 1936 and that in 1944 he gave refuge to someone closely involved in the plot to assassinate the *Führer*.

As a perpetrator of Nazi horrors, Loesener ranks somewhere on the third level, far below top Nazi leaders such as Hitler, Goering, or Himmler and well beneath such second-level officials as Ribbentrop, Speer, or his own boss in the Reich Interior Ministry, Wilhelm Frick. Loesener was never involved in plans to kill anyone, never sent anyone to a death camp, and never profited from the seizure of anyone's property.

What he did was draft laws that enabled the Nazi government to speed the process by which it undid a century and more of Jewish assimilation into German society and culture. These laws robbed Jews of their rights of citizenship; their rights to marry, to practice in the professions, to engage in business and commerce, to move about freely; and, ultimately, their right to reside in Germany. Nonetheless, as a closet resister in the early years of the Reich, Loesener claims to have drafted these laws in ways that exempted large numbers of people from their provisions. He did so, he tells us, by defining as narrowly as possible the legal definition of a Jew. He wanted the so-called half Jews, those with one Jewish and one Aryan *parent,* to be excluded from the definition. His efforts met fierce opposition. Nazi radicals insisted that anyone with even one Jewish *grandparent* be defined as a Jew. The most rabid Nazis went further, insisting that "one drop of Jewish blood" was sufficient to make any person Jewish.

Loesener's activities as a "Jewish expert" raise questions that form the heart of this book—questions about historical evidence, about moral ambiguity, and about Loesener's reliability as his own witness. This volume offers the reader a variety of sources in which to look for answers: Loesener's memoir of his years as the "Jewish expert" in the Reich Interior Ministry answers important questions about how the Nazi system functioned, but not without raising others; his testimony after the war delivered to the Nuremberg Military Tribunal raises questions of its own, but it can also be helpful in assessing the memoir itself; and the appendix contains laws and decrees that mark the major milestones of the legislative assault upon German Jewry, the most important of which Loesener helped put in place.

How does one make sense of such a man? Was he a liar? Was he a hero? If we situate him somewhere in between, where on the continuum should he be placed? The purpose of this book is to provide the materials that make such a judgment possible.

1

THE ENIGMA OF BERNHARD LOESENER—NAZI BUREAUCRAT

KARL A. SCHLEUNES

For ten years, from April 1933 to March 1943, Bernhard Loesener was the *Judenreferent* (Jewish expert) in the Third Reich's Ministry of the Interior. His position gave him a critical role in shaping Nazi policy toward the Jews. He was charged with overseeing, coordinating, and often drafting the discriminatory legislation the Nazi regime directed against the Jews. He came to that position, he insists, by accident, although his legal training no doubt played a role. He entered the employ of the Interior Ministry thinking his appointment was to its Desk for Citizenship and Naturalization, an area in which he had some experience. Instead, he found himself assigned, temporarily he thought, to clear his superior's desk of the mountain of proposals and petitions for solving what the Nazis called the "Jewish question" *(Judenfrage)*. These proposals, all of them unsolicited, had been pouring in from across Germany since Hitler had become German chancellor three months earlier, on January 30, 1933. Loesener's new chief, Secretary of State Hans Pfundtner, instructed him to reply to these petitioners, but to do so evasively. Perhaps the new regime had not yet decided how to address what it called the "Jewish question." Perhaps it did not welcome advice from outsiders.

Loesener's "temporary" assignment proved to be permanent. Rather than returning him to the citizenship and naturalization section, his superior named him head of an entirely new department, one responsible for "Legislation in the Jewish Question." His charge was to oversee and coordinate the drafting of laws directed at removing Jews from what the Nazis believed to be their unduly influential positions in German life and culture. During the early years of his tenure, Loesener played a vital role in shaping Nazi policy toward the Jews. After 1935–1936, the importance of legislation receded in the face of more violent anti-Jewish measures. Nonetheless, Loesener remained, even from the sidelines, a witness at the very least to the roles of other important Nazi policymakers such as Adolf Eichmann, Hermann Goering, and Joseph Goebbels.

Loesener produced a memoir of his experiences as a "Jewish expert."[1] Written in 1950, it was published in a German scholarly journal in 1961, nine years after his death. The memoir has become a major, if controversial, source for scholars trying to understand Jewish policy in the Third Reich. Loesener's account of the drafting of the notorious Nuremberg Laws in 1935, for example, has shaped historical understanding of this milestone event in the Nazi persecution of the Jews. At the heart of the controversy, however, is his claim that he worked in numerous ways to mitigate the severity of these laws by, among other things, wording legislation in such a way as to limit the number of people affected. Memoirs are by definition self-serving, and Loesener's is no exception. Yet it is also true that for ten years, he was near the center of the legislative process and occasionally, as in 1935, at its very core. We gain insight from his account into the making of Jewish policy, into the tensions within the Nazi system, and into the process by which the persecutions grew steadily more extreme. For those reasons alone, Loesener's memoir remains one of the most important surviving documents we have on the inner workings of the National Socialist regime of terror.

The Jewish question Loesener was assigned to address lay at the heart of the National Socialist worldview. The perception of a "Jewish question" was by no means a Nazi invention. The term itself had been coined early in the nineteenth century—as a shorthand reference to the search for the most effective ways of facilitating the assimilation of Jews into the larger European culture.[2] From that point forward, however, its meaning went through a series of transmutations. By the end of the century, the term was co-opted by anti-Semitic racists who raised the two-fold charge that Jews were both an unassimilable element in German society and dangerous to its well-being. During the 1920s, German anti-Semites, with the Nazis in the forefront, took to blaming all the evils besetting Germany on the machinations of an alleged worldwide Jewish conspiracy.[3] They blamed this conspiracy for Germany's defeat in the Great War of 1914–1918, a conflict the Nazis believed had been engineered by the Jews to topple the country from its rightful place in world leadership. They likewise blamed the Jews for inflicting upon Germany the humiliating Treaty of Versailles in 1919, for the hyperinflation of 1923, and then, later in the decade, for the Great Depression. Some of Germany's preexisting social problems were similarly laid at the feet of Jewish conspirators. Of these, the most serious to many Germans was the seeming alienation of the working classes from the larger German identity. This alienation was manifested in the large socialist party that emerged late in the nineteenth century and was then reinforced after the Great War by the formation of a German communist party. Undergirding both of these parties was an ideological commitment to revolutionary Marxism, a doctrine the Nazis were certain was Jewish-inspired and concocted to destroy German strength and unity.

The Nazis insisted that the essence of the problem lay in the Jews' racially inferior makeup. The idea that they (or other nationalities, for that matter) constituted a racial group was a product of late nineteenth-century pseudo-science.[4] Racial theorists in Germany and elsewhere, heavily influenced by Social Darwinism, fabricated theories that divided ethnic groups into pseudo-biological entities they called races. The divisions of race, they claimed, determined human difference. For them, race was far more fundamental than the divisions of nationality, religion, or social class. In addition to biology, race theorists borrowed heavily from late eighteenth-century linguistic theories about language families. Racists combined biology and linguistic theory to construct pseudo-scientific explanations of human difference. The synthesis of their borrowings became the familiar racist categories used by the Nazis—"Aryan" (Germanic) and "Semitic" (Jewish), taken from terms initially used for language families.[5]

Central to all race theories was the proposition that the different races were by any measure unequal, be it physically, socially, intellectually, or morally. Some were innately superior, others innately inferior. German racial theorists ranked their own Aryan race above all others, although they also included the English, Dutch, and Scandinavian peoples in the Aryan category. Jews, on the other hand, were almost always placed at the bottom of the scale, deemed not only inferior but also innately evil. German racists almost universally saw them as an immoral and parasitic race that, through deceit and superficial cleverness, managed to exercise a unique penchant to do evil. Thus, when evil deeds needed to be explained, as they did for many Germans in the aftermath of the Great War, the evildoers were already among them.

Because the Jews' inferiority supposedly resided in biological makeup (most racists called it inferior "blood"), the most evil of their machinations was their perverse desire for infusing that inferior blood into that of the superior Aryan race. By this means, every marriage and every act of sexual intercourse between Jew and Aryan served to defile Aryan purity. Thus did every such act dilute the purity of the superior Aryans and weaken them in the face of their racial enemies. So heinous was this act of race mixing that in *Mein Kampf,* Hitler had called it "the original sin"[6] through which Aryan man had fallen from the original Eden of racial purity.

Paradoxically, these theories assigned extraordinary power to a very small number of people. The German census of 1925 showed less than 1 percent (568,000) of its population was Jewish. Moreover, during the course of the nineteenth century, German Jews had been emancipated from the castelike restrictions medieval traditions had imposed upon them and had become enthusiastic and patriotic citizens. By late in the century, their assimilation into German life and culture seemed virtually complete. Few would have thought it reversible. Law, medicine, journalism, the arts, the economy—all benefited from the contributions of Jews. So high were the rates of intermarriage between Jewish and non-Jewish Germans that by 1900 Jewish religious leaders expressed concern about the possible disappearance of Jews as a distinct people.[7] It was a setting in which Jews, and many Germans, could dismiss the race theorists and their followers as remnants of an unenlightened past.

Germany's sacrifices in the Great War and its defeat in November 1918 transformed the national consciousness—a transformation whose impact can hardly be overestimated. Germans had believed in their country's innocence when the war broke out in 1914; they had expected a quick victory, probably by Christmas. During the war, they had made extraordinary sacrifices on the battlefield and on the home front; they had been told for four years that they were winning the war. And then, seemingly overnight, they were told they had been defeated, this while German armies were still deep in enemy territory. The loss shattered the framework within which most Germans understood their world. An additional blow came in the form of the Treaty of Versailles, in which Germany was forced to admit responsibility for starting the war and was therefore commanded to pay for a major portion of its damages. Confusion and resentment fed upon each other in the popular mind, creating the venomous climate in which the likes of Hitler and the Nazis could flourish.

Some of the clouds of what is often called the "poisoned politics" of the postwar era had begun to gather even before the war ended. As the demands for sacrifice upon the home front increased, anti-Semites raised questions about whether the burdens were being equitably shared. In 1916, the army leadership, suspicious that Jews might not be contributing their fair share to the war effort, ordered a secret census of their numbers in the military.[8] When the census revealed that Jews were probably proportionally overrepresented in the ranks of the military, the results were hushed up. By the early 1920s, right-wing racist politicians were blaming Germany's Jews for having "stabbed" the army in the back by calling for peace when victory was, they claimed, just around the corner. Extremists, Hitler among them, went further, charging not merely that Jews had brought on the defeat but that a worldwide Jewish conspiracy had plotted the war itself. Thus, contrary to the dictates of the Versailles Treaty, the Nazis claimed that Jews, not Germans, had caused the war. And they had done so in order to enable the Jewish race to prevail over that of the superior Aryans. Suddenly the "Jewish question," long lurking in the wings of the German political stage, was thrust into its center.

Bernhard Loesener was among the hundreds of thousands of young men who fought for Germany during all four and a half years of the war. He had enlisted in the army in October 1913 as a "one-year volunteer," a privileged form of military service reserved for young men of social standing and educational achievement. These volunteers were expected to pay their own expenses but after a year were given a commission in the army reserves. In Loesener's case, however, the war broke out before his year was over, and he wound up serving to its end. Upon his demobilization, he returned to his legal studies and in 1920 passed his doctoral examinations in law at the ancient University of Tübingen. He began his formal career in the bureaucratic service soon thereafter by taking a position in the Berlin Revenue Office of the Prussian Customs Union. From there, he was eventually moved to several posts in Silesia, where, in 1931, by his account, he joined a local branch of the National Socialist German Workers' Party. He did so, he wrote, because "I wrongly assumed that only this party could succeed in rescuing Germany from the not-so-rosy-situation in which it found itself back then."[9]

He gave no indication in his memoir about whether the party's position on the "Jewish question" was a factor in his decision. Earlier, however, in 1947 (the memoir was written in 1950), he had testified under oath at Nuremberg that he had joined for two reasons. First, he said, "because I found National Socialist propaganda believable and, above all, because I hoped to see a reconciliation of the conflict between [German] nationalists and the communists [working class]";[10] and second, because "conditions had developed in Germany wherein an overly large number of people had their positions not because of their abilities, but because of their connections to Jewry."[11] Widespread as these attitudes were among Germany's educated conservatives, they by no means required joining the Nazi Party. Nonetheless, the longing in conservative circles for reattaching the working classes to the nation's social fabric was often tinged with anti-Semitism, leaving many of them vulnerable to the promises of National Socialism. Whatever Loesener's underlying attitudes toward National Socialism and the Jews might have been, his membership in the party would have been officially frowned upon by the Weimar government. In Prussia, in fact, it should have led to his dismissal.[12]

All that changed on January 30, 1933, when Adolf Hitler became the German chancellor. Suddenly, Nazi Party members with bureaucratic experience were in great demand. If there was to be a National Socialist "revolution," it would have to be carried out by civil servants committed to the goals of the new regime. Loesener recalls being summoned to the Reich Finance Ministry in April 1933 and being offered a position as chief staff aide to State Secretary Fritz Reinhardt. The nature of the position was not to his liking, especially after learning that the Interior Ministry was also interested in him. Here he was already acquainted with its state secretary, Hans Pfundtner. Loesener asked Reinhardt's permission to follow this lead and within days, on April 27, accepted the Interior Ministry position, presumably to work in its citizenship and naturalization section. The fact that Pfundtner assigned Loesener first to work through the pile of correspondence on Jewish matters proved fateful. But it was not the citizenship and naturalization division that Loesener was bound for; Pfundtner's assignment led to his being put in charge of the Interior Ministry's new desk for "Legislation in the Jewish Question."

Because Loesener had not joined the Interior Ministry staff until late April 1933, he was too late to play a role in what was the new regime's most important piece of anti-Jewish legislation in the first two and a half years of its existence. This was the April 7, 1933 "Law for the Restoration of the Professional Civil Service" to which was attached, four days later, a so-called Aryan Paragraph. The civil service law empowered the new regime to expel from government service those it deemed politically undesirable, mainly Communists, Socialists, and liberals. The Aryan Paragraph, by defining who and what a non-Aryan was, added Jews to the expulsion list. Henceforth, any person with "one parent or one grandparent who adheres to the Jewish religion" was deemed to be "non-Aryan." (Obviously, anyone with *more* than one such parent or grandparent was likewise non-Aryan.) This "one-quarter" Jewish principle became the Nazi standard for defining non-Aryans until the Nuremberg legislation in 1935. For many Nazis, however, the Aryan Paragraph was still far too lenient. The more radical of them would have preferred to go back to the generation of the *great-grandparents* and to stipulate as non-Aryan anyone with one Jewish great-grandparent, the "one-eighth" principle. At the extreme end were Nazis like the notoriously disreputable Julius Streicher, the publisher of *Der Stürmer,* a vicious scandal sheet that laced its anti-Semitism with pornography. For them, as Streicher put it, "one drop of Jewish blood" was sufficient to exclude a person from the Aryan race. In his view, an Aryan woman who had sex, even once, with a Jewish male would be so contaminated by his sperm that she would never again be able to bear a pure Aryan child. Hardly less radical in his anti-Semitism was Propaganda Minister Joseph Goebbels, whose sporadic forays into Jewish policy always reflected ideological extremism.

Loesener, on the other hand, who had no part in drafting the Aryan Paragraph, thought it far too extreme. He believed, he tells us, that it was detrimental to Germany's self-interest to exclude so many racially valuable persons from the German national community. After all, someone who was one-quarter Jewish was at the same time three-quarters Aryan. Indeed, the theme he sounds in his memoir is that for his entire tenure as the Interior Ministry's "Jewish expert," he tried to mitigate the severity of the regime's anti-Semitic measures. His goal, he writes, "was to influence legislation so that the largest possible number of people would, from the outset, be spared the clutches of anti-Semitic legislation."[13] His memoir is largely a catalog of those efforts.

During the months following its promulgation, the Aryan Paragraph led to the dismissal of thousands of Jewish professionals in government service, including lawyers, judges, doctors, dentists, professors, teachers, artists, musicians, and so on. To the regime's delight, private agencies and associations quickly adopted it to suit their own purposes and used it to eliminate Jews from their membership lists. The first was the German Boxing Association, which expelled Eric Seelig,[14] Germany's non-Aryan middleweight and light-heavyweight boxing champion. The German Davis Cup team dropped its tennis champion Daniel Press for the same reason. Dozens of sports associations followed suit. By the end of 1933, virtually every German sports club had expelled its Jewish members.[15] And sports clubs were not alone. In September, the Professional Association of Composers applied the Aryan Paragraph to limit its membership to those of Aryan extraction.[16] Businesses, too, followed suit. The huge Dresdener Bank used it to justify the dismissal of hundreds of Jewish employees.[17]

Loesener speaks of being appalled by the Aryan Paragraph, both because of its epidemic-like spread and its reach into the ranks of those of "mixed race." The first task he took upon himself, he claims, was "to attack on the most marginal front by trying to improve the position of the one-quarter Jews."[18] His first opportunity to do this came in September 1935 in connection with the promulgation of the infamous Nuremberg Laws. These two pieces of legislation became the backbone of the Nazi assault upon the legal position of Jews in German society. The first, the Reich Citizenship Law, deprived German Jews of their citizenship, relegating them to the second-class status of "state subjects" (*Staatsangehöriger*). It also became the basis for a series of thirteen supplementary decrees that gradually expelled Jews from the professions and virtually all business enterprises. Two months later, the first of these supplementary decrees reconfigured the definition of the non-Aryan, or Jew, that had been established in the Aryan Paragraph of 1933. The thirteenth and final supplementary decree of July 1, 1943, placed Germany's small Jewish remnant outside the bounds of all legal protection, passing its fate entirely into the arbitrary hands of the Nazi police. A second Nuremberg measure, the Law for the Protection of German Blood and German Honor (often called the "Blood Protection Law"), prohibited the race mixing the Nazis so despised. Thenceforth, Jews and Aryans were forbidden to marry or engage in sexual intercourse outside of marriage. Violators of this prohibition were liable to the charge of "racial treason."

Loesener tells us of his central role in drafting these Nuremberg Laws. His is the most detailed account we have of the major milestones in the escalation of the Nazi persecution of the Jews. The setting in which the laws were promulgated was appropriately dramatic: the Nazi Party Rally held annually in Nuremberg since 1929. After the Nazi seizure of power in 1933, these rallies attracted hundreds of thousands of the party faithful. The 1935 rally, scheduled for the week of September 9–15, was titled the "Reich Party Rally of Freedom"—to celebrate Germany's unilateral snubbing earlier in the year of the Versailles Treaty's restrictions on German rearmament.[19] To symbolize the breaking of this hated treaty, Hitler planned to announce at the rally's end a law to make the Nazi Party flag the official emblem of the new German Reich. The change was likely to offend those in conservative circles, especially the officer corps that had fought under the tradition-laden black, white, and red imperial banner. Hitler believed there was wide popular support for a new national symbol. Accordingly, he had summoned the *Reichstag* to Nuremberg to ratify the new flag law. And then, as Loesener tells it, on the spur of the moment, late in the afternoon of Friday, September 13, only two days before the scheduled *Reichstag* meeting, Hitler apparently decided he needed something more dramatic, in addition to the flag law, to justify the pomp and pageantry that would surround such an occasion. Among party officials, rumors were also afloat that the *Führer* wanted the additional legislation "because the conflict between Streicher and Schacht [over how Jews were to be treated] was becoming worrisome" and he wanted it resolved.[20]

That same Friday, Loesener and several of his colleagues were spending the evening in a Berlin wine bar to celebrate his recent promotion to the rank of ministerial counselor. It had been an easy week. Because of the party rally, official Berlin was virtually shut down for the week. Everyone who was "anybody" was in Nuremberg, including Loesener's superiors, Hans Pfundtner and Wilhelm Stuckart, and, of course, Interior Minister Frick. It was at the wine bar that Loesener received a telephone message, probably from Stuckart, ordering him to fly to Nuremberg early the next morning. He was told only that it had to with preparing a Jewish law and that he should bring along documents relevant to that subject. At 7:00 A.M. the next morning, Loesener and his colleague Franz Albrecht Medicus caught a plane to Nuremberg. Upon their arrival at the airport, a driver whisked them off to the municipal police headquarters in the city center. Here they were greeted by Stuckart and Pfundtner, who informed them of Hitler's sudden decision the previous afternoon. What the *Führer* had in mind, Stuckart explained, was legislation to cover "the entire complex of questions" relating to a prohibition on marriages and extramarital relations between Aryans and Jews, including restrictions on the employment of Aryan women as household servants in Jewish homes. The matter of Aryan women working in the service of Jews was a particularly sensitive issue for the Nazis. The sexual symbolism alone violated their racial sensitivities. Without further instruction, Loesener and his team were asked to draft laws to regulate these matters and to submit them for the *Führer*'s approval. With the *Reichstag* session scheduled for early the next evening, they had fewer than thirty-six hours to complete their work.

The challenge to Loesener under these circumstances was daunting, but it was also, he claims, an opportunity to limit the number of people who would be affected by such legislation. His objective was to formulate the laws so that they would apply solely to "full Jews," that is, persons with two Jewish parents (or four Jewish grandparents). Convincing Hitler to drop the "one-quarter" Jewish principle of the Aryan Paragraph would be no simple task. Loesener may have thought it went too far, but party radicals were convinced that it did not go far enough. Indeed, later that morning a delegate from the party's Munich headquarters, Dr. Walter Sommer, arrived at Nuremberg's police headquarters to represent the party's position to the drafting team. Sommer had been instructed by his boss, the rabidly anti-Semitic Reich physicians' leader, Dr. Gerhard Wagner, to press for laws that, in addition to prohibiting new marriages between Jews and Aryans, would allow mixed-race couples to dissolve existing marriages. Wagner himself advocated the "one-eighth" principle for defining Jewishness. Fortunately, Loesener recalls, Sommer took little interest in the proceedings and spent most of his time playing with a souvenir trinket produced especially for the rally, a windup toy tank that spewed sparks and climbed over documents he piled on the floor. The situation with Wagner was more dangerous. He, along with Streicher, was part of Hitler's inner circle and now, here in Nuremberg, constantly in his company.

Loesener and his team worked furiously throughout the day and into the evening hours. Draft after draft was delivered across town to Hitler's quarters for the *Führer*'s approval. One by one they were returned as insufficient. Finally, at midnight, Interior Minister Frick himself came over to police headquarters to inform the exhausted team that Hitler wanted to have four different versions of the marriage law, ranging from "mild" to "harsh," by the next morning. He, Hitler, would then select one of these to present that evening to the *Reichstag*. The four versions were quickly compiled, labeled "A" through "D," and handed to Frick, who was to deliver them to Hitler. To the mildest one of them, version "D,"

Loesener appended the stipulation, "This law applies only to full Jews." It was 1:30 in the morning when Frick suddenly added another task—oh yes, he said, the *Führer* also wanted a new citizenship law to present to the *Reichstag* that evening. Would Loesener and his colleagues please come up with something quickly? Before tomorrow morning! A few meaningless words would do, he hinted. And so they went back to work. Within an hour they managed to fashion a proposal that would elevate Germans to the status of "Reich citizens" *(Reichsbürger)* and classify non-Aryans as "state subjects" *(Staatsangehöriger).* What these words meant was left to be determined later.

Loesener did not learn until the *Reichstag* session that evening that Hitler had chosen to present the delegates with the mildest of the four versions. His initial elation ended abruptly, however, when he learned that Hitler had crossed out the critical sentence about this law applying only to "full Jews." But then, as if deliberately to confuse the issue, Hitler ordered the sentence restored to the version sent to the newspapers for publication in their morning editions. However, when the law was published in the official legal gazette later that day, the sentence was once again missing. Without that sentence it was not at all clear to whom the law applied. Neither was it clear how a "Reich citizen" was to be identified or to be distinguished from a "state subject." The crucial, and controversial, question of how to define the Jews to whom these laws applied was once again wide open. Until its resolution, there was no hope of alleviating the "complete chaos" Loesener describes as prevailing in official circles about "who was to be regarded as a Jew, what exactly was to be the definition of a Jewish offspring or non-Aryan, and where the line between them and Aryans was to be drawn."[21] It would take another two months of protracted and bitter bargaining between Interior Ministry officials, led by Loesener and Stuckart, and Munich party officials, led by the likes of Gerhard Wagner and Julius Streicher, to resolve the issues the Nuremberg laws left unsettled.

Loesener's account of the making of the Nuremberg Laws has been an invaluable source to historians seeking to understand the origins of these laws and, by extension, the way the Nazi system functioned. Nearly all historians of the Nazis make some use of Loesener's account in their own analyses. Nonetheless, their reactions range widely. The most unequivocally positive assessment of Loesener's endeavors comes from British historian Jeremy Noakes, who has done extensive work on the Nazis and the *Mischling* (a "hybrid," or person of mixed race) question. Loesener's

efforts on behalf of *Mischlinge* leads Noakes to conclude that Loesener
was "[t]he key figure among the officials who were endeavoring to protect the *Mischlinge*" and that he represents "one of the few instances
where the notorious excuse used by so many after 1945—'I stayed in office in order to prevent worse things from happening'—would have a
good deal of justification."[22] Christopher R. Browning concurs, crediting
Loesener with waging "a long and successful struggle to prevent the legal equalization of half-Jews with full Jews, which ultimately saved the
former from deportation and death."[23] Noakes's and Browning's views
are not universally shared. Many scholars of the Third Reich question the
reliability of Loesener as a witness to the events he describes. Two aspects of his story seem particularly jarring. Is it possible that so major an
escalation of Jewish persecutions should have come about so haphaz-
ardly, as if it had been, as he puts it, "shaken out of someone's sleeve"?
Similarly, how credible is his claim that the goal of his career as a "Jewish
expert" was to limit the reach of Nazi discriminatory legislation, the
Nuremberg Laws included?

The list of Loesener's critics is long and eminent. The German historian Reinhard Rürup dismisses the account as "legend" in the service of
the author's self-interest.[24] Kurt Pätzold, Rürup's colleague, is equally
dismissive. He finds Loesener's memoir entirely self-serving and argues
that the anti-Jewish laws promulgated at Nuremberg had long been in
preparation. The only question he sees is in the timing of their announcement. Loesener, he says, was covering his own culpability by claiming it
was a matter of Hitler's sudden decision.[25] Essentially the same argument is forwarded by Werner Jochmann, who dismisses Loesener's story
and calls the Nuremberg Laws "long-planned and intensely prepared."[26]

No less skeptical is Israeli historian David Bankier, a leading expert on
public opinion in the Third Reich. Bankier labels Loesener's memoir "a
dubious source" and rejects the idea that the Nuremberg Laws could
have been produced on the spur of the moment. Nazi intentions on matters of citizenship, he notes, were signaled as early as 1920 in the Party
Program. Point Four of that program clearly stipulated that only "members of the nation may be citizens of the state" and that only "those of
German blood, whatever their creed, may be members of the nation."[27]
No Jew could, therefore, be a member of the nation. Bankier's mentor,
Otto Dov Kulka, has been even more critical of Loesener's story. Kulka
contends that Interior Minister Frick had given a direct announcement of
the upcoming Nuremberg legislation nearly a month before it was pro-

mulgated.[28] The setting for his announcement, says Kulka, was an August 20, 1935 conference of leading government and party officials chaired by the then minister of economics, Hjalmar H.G. Schacht. Representing the Interior Ministry were Stuckart and Loesener, with Loesener taking the minutes. Schacht had convened the meeting to discuss the "heavy damage" being done to Germany's rearmament program by the party's "exaggerated and outrageous anti-Semitic propaganda" and by its "lawless hooliganism."[29] At that meeting Frick did indeed mention that his ministry was preparing legislation to deal with these problems, but rather than sending signals about the Nuremberg legislation, he spoke only of a decree that would initiate strong police measures against the perpetrators of excesses against Jews.[30]

New doubts about the details and thrust of Loesener's memoir are raised by Cornelia Essner in her 1999 habilitation thesis, "The System of the 'Nuremberg Laws' (1933–1945)."[31] In subjecting Loesener's memoir to a systematic critique, she cites evidence that questions many of his assertions. Some are quite minor, such as the date when he joined the Nazi Party, and might be attributed to memory lapses. Loesener said it was December 1930; Essner believes it was in September.[32] She raises other, more serious questions, however. She doubts, for example, that Loesener's becoming *Judenreferent* in the Interior Ministry was as "accidental" as he claims. She has discovered a speech titled "Races and the Jewish Question" that he gave in the summer of 1931 to a public audience in Neisse in the province of Silesia. The speech suggests to her that he came to the Interior Ministry in 1933 with a "reputation as a specialist in the race and Jewish question."[33] She has also been able to establish that he had been a member of the Storm Troopers (SA) since 1931 and that in the local elections of March 1933 (shortly before coming to Berlin), he was among the Nazi officials elected to the Neisse City Council. As for Loesener's portrayal of the drafting of the Nuremberg Laws, Essner casts doubt about the suddenness with which they were produced and the claim that in drafting them he and his colleagues were practicing a kind of resistance to the evil party radicals.[34] It is the latter claim that leads her to ask why Loesener neglected to provide any specific details about the contents of versions A through D. Despite what she calls the "fictional aspects" of Loesener's memoir, she concludes that "the value of his document for the researcher should not be underestimated."[35] Far less dismissive of Loesener's account than most of his critics is Saul Friedlander, who, in his recent study of Nazi Germany and the Jews in the 1930s, finds "no reason for Loesener to offer a false picture" of how the Nuremberg Laws were drafted, "except for his suppression of the fact that much preliminary work had been accomplished before then."[36]

The nature of that preliminary work needs to be added to our understanding of Loesener's role in the making of the Nuremberg Laws. Loesener himself tells us that the summons he received that Friday evening to come to Nuremberg included instructions to bring along certain documents relating to the Jewish question. He spent the next several hours rummaging through his own office and those of his superiors to collect documents. He does not say what they included, except that they were "records, files, and the ministry's document registry."[37] Likely to have been among them, however, was a thick file from Pfundtner's office, one recently discovered in the German archives by Frick's biographer Günter Neliba.[38] Pfundtner's file contained drafts and reworkings of legislative proposals regarding race and citizenship questions. If Loesener did take this file, his likening of the production of the Nuremberg Laws to having been decided upon "without a moment's notice" and then suddenly shaken out of someone's sleeve is at best misleading.[39] To have been so shaken out, they must also have been "up someone's sleeve" for some time beforehand.

It should occasion no surprise that the Nazis would restrict the citizenship rights of Jews or their right to marry non-Jews. The surprise is that it took them until September 1935, more than two and a half years after their seizure of power, to do so. Something resembling the Nuremberg legislation had been "up the sleeve" of virtually every anti-Semitic German (and European) since the latter part of the previous century. From 1879 forward, when Wilhelm Marr coined the term "anti-Semitism," racists had insisted on the need to halt the mixing of the Germanic and Jewish "races."[40] Likewise, their calls for expelling the Jews from the community of German citizens often went far beyond reducing them merely to the "state subject" status stipulated in the Reich Citizenship Law. Thus, even in 1920, the drafters of the Nazi Party Program were inventing nothing new in declaring that "no Jew may be a member of the nation."

Had Loesener been looking for more up-to-date models upon which to pattern the Nuremberg Laws, he would have needed to look no further than the legislative proposals made by the Nazi party's *Reichstag* delegates in 1930. The leader of that delegation, moreover, had been the same Wilhelm Frick who was now the Interior Minister. In March 1930, Frick had introduced a ten-paragraph bill entitled the "Law for the Protection of the Republic," paragraph five of which dealt directly with the question of race mixing. Accordingly, "[a]nyone who endeavors to undermine the natural fertility of the German people or who fosters the same through words, writings, or by means of other pressures, or by way of mixing with members of the Jewish blood community or the colored races and thereby contributes to the same, will be punished with a prison sentence for the crime of racial treason."[41] In early 1930, with a party delegation of only twelve members, the Nazis could harbor no hope of getting their bill approved. Nonetheless, its propaganda value was not to be underestimated, especially when another of the bill's paragraphs required the death sentence for any person suggesting that in 1914 Germany had borne any responsibility for initiating the Great War.[42] The publicity Frick's bill received let the Germans know where the Nazis stood. Moreover, the Nazi position on race mixing was for the first time couched in legal terms. Loesener could not possibly have been unaware of its existence.

Frick's proposal, along with many others, had been prepared by a small planning staff at the party's Munich headquarters, popularly known as the Brown House. Gregor Strasser, the party's organizational chief, had brought this staff together in 1929 for the purpose of "preparing for the construction of a future National Socialist state."[43] Most of the records of these planners were destroyed by Allied bombing raids over Munich late in the war. From what has survived, however, it is clear that they had addressed both the questions of citizenship for Jews and the "problems" of race mixing long before Loesener and his team faced them at Nuremberg in September 1935. On race mixing, Helmut Nicolai, then the head of the planning staff's domestic section and later, in 1934, Loesener's immediate superior in the Interior Ministry, had proposed a "clear separation between the two peoples [Jews and Germans]" on grounds that "the Jews are racially a totally separate people from the Germans."[44] For that reason, he concluded, Jews and Germans were to be prohibited from marrying each other and from engaging in sexual intercourse.

The Brown House planners were equally adamant on the question of citizenship for Jews. Chief among them was Achim Gercke, the party's genealogical expert and a passionate anti-Semite, whose main job was to weed out racially undesirable applicants for party membership.[45] In 1932, he drafted a policy proposal to which he gave the startling title "Should German-Jewish Bastards Be Given Reich Citizenship?"[46] The

draft itself is lost. Only the title remains, but it is not hard to guess his answer. Nicolai's staff in the domestic section produced citizenship proposals of its own. In 1932, they recommended dividing the German population into "Reich Germans" *[Reichsdeutsche]* and "Reich aliens"
[Reichsfremden]. Naturally, the "aliens" were to be deprived of their German citizenship. Obviously, Loesener did not need to search far to find
models for a citizenship law. The sleeves of National Socialism were
stuffed with them.

Loesener mentions none of these possible models. Perhaps, as Friedlander suggests, he suppressed all of the preliminary proposals that
pointed to the Nuremberg Laws. It is hard to believe he had forgotten
them. Possibly, he found their mention unnecessary, taking his reader's
acquaintance with them for granted. Certainly, by 1935, it took no great
act of imagination to draft the outline of what became the Nuremberg
Laws. Any Nazi worth his salt should have been up to the task. And as
Loesener points out, there were plenty eager to try.

Loesener, of course, recognized that the proposals he and his team submitted to Hitler early on the morning of September 15, 1935, were little
more than outlines for action. When Hitler penciled out the sentence that
applied these laws only to "full Jews," it was no longer clear to whom
they might apply. The essential problem still had to be faced. Where was
the line between Aryan and Jew to be drawn? To draw that line clearly
required a new definition of who was to be counted as a Jew. Had Loesener's definition been accepted, it would have required four Jewish
grandparents (or both parents) for a person to be classified as a Jew. Even
the person with three Jewish grandparents would have been exempted.
One possibility, of course, was to return to the definition set in the Aryan
Paragraph of 1933 whereby one Jewish grandparent was sufficient to render a person non-Aryan. We know, if we accept Loesener's word, that he
was eager to limit the number of people these laws affected, hence his
narrow conception of who counted as Jewish. Stuckart and Pfundtner
must have been at least in tacit agreement or they would not have allowed him to submit the "full Jews only" version to Hitler.

The issue of defining Jewishness took two months to settle. Loesener
tells us that there were some thirty negotiating sessions between Interior
Ministry officials, mainly himself, Stuckart, and party representatives led
by Dr. Gerhard Wagner. Joining them on occasion were Hjalmar Schacht,
the economics minister, and Franz Gürtner, the minister of justice. Wagner was an especially inflexible negotiator. He held to the position that

anyone with one Jewish *great*-grandparent should be classified as non-Aryan. Eventually, and with great reluctance, he agreed to limit the definition to persons who were one-half Jewish (two Jewish grandparents or one Jewish parent), but only if "one-quarter Jews would be defined as Jewish if they were married to an Aryan or to a full- or three-quarters Jew."[47] Cheering him on from the sidelines, of course, were Julius Streicher and his ilk, the advocates of the "one drop of Jewish blood" principle.

Loesener and Stuckart, on the other hand, appear to have been equally tenacious, continuing to insist on a more limited definition. Loesener opposed Wagner's "half-Jewish" principle, arguing that it would unnecessarily raise up a whole new set of political opponents from among those who had heretofore seen themselves as Germans and had been unquestioningly loyal to the German nation. The Aryan relatives of these people would likewise be driven into opposition. Moreover, Loesener pointed out, the classifying of half Jews as non-Aryans would exclude from military service the equivalent of two divisions of young men. Quite aside from its military implications, this would make a bad impression abroad and do harm to Germany's economic interests.

Lobbyists checked in from all sides. Dr. Walter Gross, head of the party's Racial Policy Department and a fanatical anti-Semite, backed Wagner. Absurdity soon piled on top of absurdity. Because questions of heredity were at issue, Dr. Arthur Gütt of the Interior Ministry's public health division, apparently upon someone's request, submitted a memorandum explaining Gregor Mendel's laws of heredity.[48] Thus ensued a discussion of the hereditary determinants of pea-blossom colors and their relevance to gauging the consequences of mixing Aryans and Jews! The conclusion was pessimistic. It would take many generations to restore the German race to something approaching its original purity. Absolute purity, however, would be beyond reach. As with Mendel's peas, the supposedly recessive traits (in this case, those of Jewishness) would inevitably reappear in future generations.

It eventually became clear that only Hitler's intervention could resolve these disagreements. At one point that intervention seemed imminent. In late September 1935, Loesener and Stuckart were summoned to Munich, where Hitler was scheduled to speak to party leaders on the 29th and, they assumed, announce his position on the issue of Jewish definition. Upon arrival at their hotel, they were greeted by a triumphant deputy of Wagner, who informed them that the *Führer* had decided against them and was about to announce that half Jews would be counted as Jews. But Hitler did no such thing. Instead, Loesener recalls, after giving an expert overview of race-mixing questions, he ended by saying that these issues needed further study and would have to be ironed out in negotiations between the party and the Interior Ministry. Had Hitler changed his mind about making an announcement? Had Wagner's deputy been lying? Loesener never knew. And so negotiations continued for another five weeks.

Not until five weeks later, on November 7, did Hitler finally make the decision that a week later allowed for the promulgation of the First Supplementary Decree to the Reich Citizenship Law. Hitler had taken a position somewhere between Loesener and the party radicals. To no one's surprise, persons with three or four Jewish grandparents were to be classified as Jews. Loesener and his allies had never fought on that front. At issue had been those in the middle, the so-called "half Jews" with two Jewish grandparents. These were now deemed to be *Mischlinge* (of mixed race). But even within this category there were to be distinctions. Someone with two Jewish grandparents was to be classified as a *Mischling* of the first degree; someone with one Jewish grandparent, a *Mischling* of the second degree. However, a first-degree *Mischling* could still be classified as Jewish *(Geltungsjude)* if he or she was married to a spouse classified as Jewish or was himself or herself a member of a Jewish religious congregation. Given that both of these were matters of free choice, the Nazi assumption was that the Jewish qualities in that person were predominant over the non-Jewish ones.

Loesener had won at least part of the battle. Half Jews were not automatically classified as Jewish. In an official commentary on the laws, he wrote that "the Jewish question has finally been steered in the direction in which it will find a complete solution *(völlige Lösung)*."[49] To be sure, it was a solution, he added elsewhere, that while providing for a legal separation between Jews and Germans, "on the other hand, also provided Jews with legal protections."[50] Loesener's arguments may have played a role in influencing Hitler's decision, especially the one focusing on the military implications of defining Jewishness. Walter Gross reports a meeting with the *Führer,* while the negotiations were still going on, at which Hitler spoke in favor of assimilating the children of mixed racial marriages into the German bloodstream so as not to weaken Germany's military strength.[51] Two divisions, it appears, may have been worth a few drops of Jewish blood. The radicals were, of course, displeased with the new definitions and their retreat from the standard of the Aryan Paragraph. Gerhard Wagner and Julius Streicher remained adamantly opposed to the compromise. Propaganda Minister Goebbels recorded his disappointment in his diary: "A compromise, [but] probably the best one possible. Quarter Jews now pushed over to our [the German] side. Half-Jews only in an exception."[52] Definitions were not the only problem for the radicals. Their biggest disappointment lay in the failure of both the law and the decree to make so much as a mention of dissolving the mixed marriages already in existence. [To do so would have violated Paragraph 1333 of the German Civil Code and would have created havoc with a whole body of family and inheritance law.]

The inescapable irony in all of this was that the definition of Jewishness, allegedly a racial attribute, was still rooted in the religious background of an individual's forebears rather than in biology. Actually, the Nazis had no other choice. Their expectation that Nazi scientists would identify the biological basis of the differences between Germanness and Jewishness was to remain unfulfilled. As if to cover up this embarrassment, the official language in the Nazi commentaries dropped the reference to Aryans and replaced it with the phrase "German or related blood." At least the vocabulary, if not the fact itself, was now biological.

Scholars have paid closer attention to Loesener's account of the making of the Nuremberg Laws than to any other part of his memoir because of their centrality to the Nazi assault upon German Jewry. However, the memoir provides us with much more than just the story of how the Nuremberg Laws came into being. Loesener gives us an insider's insights into the workings of the decision-making process in the Third Reich. There is no reason to doubt his claim that Hitler's decision to promulgate the Nuremberg Laws was made on the spur of the moment, even if Loesener is guilty of failing to mention the preceding background preparations. We know from other sources that Hitler often worked in this unpredictable fashion. We also know that he was prone to delaying, or even avoiding, decisions, something Loesener and Stuckart learned from his speech to party leaders in Munich on September 29, 1935. They had expected his decision on the Jewish definition question and got none. His failure to act led to another six weeks of protracted and contentious negotiations with party radicals over how the Jew should be defined. Loesener's description of these negotiations provides a perfect illustration of what Hitler's recent biographer Ian Kershaw calls the "dialectic of radicalization" that produced the ratchet-like escalations in the Nazis' persecution of the Jews.[53] The radicals may have been disappointed by not gaining all they had wished for, and yet they had scored heavily against the pragmatists like Loesener who had hoped to limit the law's definition to "full Jews only." Other even more radical players, such as Heinrich Himmler (SS) and Reinhard Heydrich (Security Service of the SS, or SD), would soon join the scramble for solutions to the Jewish question and, as Loesener points out, either eclipse the pragmatists in the Interior Ministry or, as in the case of Stuckart, enlist them into their camp.

Loesener's description of the making of the "Jewish Star Decree" of September 1, 1941, offers another revealing illustration of how the system worked. The decree stipulated that as of September 15, 1941, "all Jews over the age of six are forbidden to appear in public without wearing an identifying Jewish star."[54] [The order affected Jews in Germany, Slovakia, and the Protectorate of Bohemia and Moravia.] The decree played an important role in the escalation of Jewish persecution, although it obviously pales in significance to the much more fateful decisions, taken at roughly the same time, to construct death camps in which to effect a "Final Solution" to the Jewish question. Like the Nazi ban on interracial marriages, the idea of forcing Jews to wear an identifying mark on their clothing had a long history. Jews in the Middle Ages had frequently been forced to wear such a marking, usually a yellow star. In Nazi circles, the idea had been broached in the aftermath to the nationwide Crystal Night *(Kristallnacht)* pogrom of November 1938. SD Chief Heydrich had made the suggestion at the meeting Hermann Goering had convened in his Air Ministry on November 12 to assess the damage, political as well as physical, the pogrom had caused. Loesener was present at this meeting. At that point, the idea of forcing Jews to wear an identifying star was rejected. Hitler, among others, feared that making Jews so immediately identifiable would incite the German population to acts of violence against them. Although he believed such acts quite justifiable in light of Jewish perfidy, Hitler was also still concerned about Germany's image abroad—an image that had been badly damaged as a result of the pogrom.

There the matter stood, Loesener reports, until August 14, 1941, when Interior Ministry officials received from Propaganda Minister Goebbels a summons for the very next day to discuss the matter of an identifying badge for Jews. Being his ministry's "expert" on matters of legislation for Jews, Loesener was sent to the meeting to find out what was going on and, at the very least, to remind the propaganda minister that he was treading onto turf rightly belonging to the Interior Ministry. When he got to the meeting, Loesener found some forty persons in attendance, most of them wearing their brown party uniforms. Among the exceptions was the black-shirted SS lieutenant colonel Adolf Eichmann, chief of the Jewish desk in Heydrich's Security Office.

State Secretary Leopold Gutterer was standing in as chair of the meeting for the absent Goebbels. Gutterer explained that soldiers on furlough from the east had complained to the ministry about the apparent liberties still being allowed to Jews on the home front. Given the racial ideals these soldiers were fighting for, he said, they took offense at the sight of Jews still walking the streets, free and unmolested. Public order, for which the Propaganda Ministry bore responsibility, was at issue. Measures to address these objections needed to be taken immediately. As a start, he proposed, Jews needed to made more easily identifiable. To this Eichmann raised a procedural point, noting that after the Crystal Night pogrom, Hitler had designated Hermann Goering to be the coordinator of Jewish policy. Any proposal such as the one Gutterer was making would first have to be submitted to the *Führer.* At this point Loesener acknowledged that, yes, he knew all measures regarding the Jewish question had to be cleared by Goering, but he said he also needed to remind the assembly that measures of this sort needed to be prepared in the Interior Ministry, not in the Propaganda Ministry. Gutterer responded coolly by claiming that the pressures of public opinion were forcing his ministry to take the lead. Moreover, he added, Goebbels was planning to speak to Hitler on this matter at an early opportunity.

Loesener quite rightly judged Goebbels's initiative to be nothing more than an attempt to assert himself in a policy area from which he had largely been excluded. He had for some time been in Hitler's disfavor, both for his philandering and for his role in initiating the Crystal Night pogrom—a disaster not only for Jews but also for the regime's finances and for its image abroad. It had forced Hitler to name an overseer for Jewish policy, to insure a degree of coordination. That overseer, Hermann Goering, also happened to be one of Goebbels's most bitter rivals. Goebbels's voice in the making of Jewish policy was for the time being silenced. Now, however, largely because of his brilliant engineering of Nazi propaganda during the war's early stages, he was back in Hitler's favor. Within days of the meeting, Gutterer informed Loesener that Goebbels had met with Hitler and that he had agreed that the Jews should be forced to wear an identifying yellow star. The requisite order was issued on September 1, 1941, by Heydrich's Security Police (the RSHA). The Interior Ministry was able to save some face. As a police official, Heydrich was technically subject to the authority of the Interior Ministry. However, "[i]n practice," Loesener recalls, "he did not pay the least regard to such niceties."[55]

Loesener's proudest accomplishment, it seems, was his success in April 1939 in attaching an exclusionary clause to a Goering decree designed to force Jews into ghetto-like buildings or neighborhoods.[56] Without giving details, Loesener again directed his efforts, he claims, in favor of half Jews. He managed to add an exclusionary clause (Paragraph 7) that created a category of "privileged mixed marriages" (*Mischehe*), whose members were exempted from Goering's decree. Two types of marriages qualified as "privileged": first, those in which a Jew (as defined by the Nuremberg legislation) had married a spouse from the "German blood community"—a marriage in which the children were by the Nuremberg standard seen as non-Jewish *Mischlinge*; and, second, childless marriages in which the wife was Jewish and the husband of German blood. Loesener's argument was that simple justice should prevent racially German spouses and their half-German children from being stuck into a ghetto for Jews.

The effect of the "privileged mixed marriage clause," Loesener claims, was to render "privileged" by far "the great majority of mixed marriages [in Germany]."[57] By his estimate, some 100,000 people may have come under protection of the "privileged marriage" clause, although his figures refer also to some of the territories occupied by the Germany army. He goes on to list another ten pieces of legislation to which the privileged clause would be applied, ranging from the Tenth Supplementary Decree to the Reich Citizenship Law of 1939 to the "Jewish Star Order" of 1941. The most important "success" for the clause came later, he claims, outside the boundaries of legislation, when Jews living in privileged marriages were largely spared deportation to Auschwitz or the other killing centers. Their exact number is impossible to determine, though it is likely to have been considerable.

What are we to make of all this? How reliable is Loesener's memoir? He was, after all, not only a witness to the Nazi persecutions of the Jews; he was also a participant in them. But was he, as he claims, a brake on the machinery of that brutal persecution? It seems the answer must be at least a partial yes, while at the same time recognizing that his account is self-serving. How useful is his memoir as a source for understanding this most complicated, confusing, and controversial epoch in German history? The evidence does not allow for absolute answers.

The enigma of Loesener's career is mirrored in the enigma of his person. He was a man of great contradictions. His early career, for someone born into his class and station in the 1890s, followed a predictably traditional pattern, at least until 1931 when he joined the Nazi Party. His father had been a local court judge, and young Bernhard himself studied law before taking up his one-year military service in 1913. Like virtually every young man of his generation, he fought in the Great War and was, no doubt, devastated by the German defeat in 1918. Upon completing his legal studies after the war, he entered the Prussian bureaucratic service, once again a traditional move for man of his rank. His politics most certainly were conservative. Indeed, his friendship with Hans Pfundtner, which predated his tenure in the Interior Ministry, suggests he might have been, along with Pfundtner, a member of the arch-conservative and antirepublican German National People's Party. As such, he would have been anti-Semitic, though moderately so compared to most Nazis. On the other hand, it seems quite plausible that he might have wanted to spare "less than full Jews" the privations of Nazi discrimination. Equally plausible is his claim to have been horrified by the regime's wartime brutalities against the Jews and to have made that his reason, in 1943, for leaving the Interior Ministry. Not all anti-Semites approved of mass murder.

Greater stretches of the imagination may be required to accept his claim of involvement in the underground resistance to Hitler. By 1936, he tells us, his aversion to Nazi excesses led him into the circles of Carl Goerdeler and Hans Gisevius, two men deeply involved in the conspiracy to overthrow Hitler and the Nazi regime. At first glance, the claim sounds preposterous: The "Jewish expert" in the Nazi Interior Ministry and a drafter of the Nuremberg Laws involved in the resistance to Hitler? But the claim cannot be so easily dismissed. First of all, Loesener limits his claim to having been involved only on the outer fringes of resistance. Moreover, in November 1944, after leaving the employ of the Interior Ministry, because, he says, of his extreme discomfort at learning of the mass murder of Jews in the East, he was indeed arrested by the *Gestapo* for an act of service to the resistance. In August 1944, only a few weeks after the dramatic failure of the plot on July 20 to assassinate Hitler, he had given refuge in his home to Captain Ludwig Gehre, an intelligence officer in the army's counterintelligence service *(Abwehr)* and a major operative in the assassination plot.[58] Gehre was later arrested by the *Gestapo* and under torture named Loesener as someone who had hidden him. Loesener claims no advance knowledge of the assassination plot, but he does claim to have been known by the conspirators as someone they could trust.

Loesener remained imprisoned until the last days of the war in April 1945, when the Soviets, upon their conquest of Berlin, opened all the city's prisons. He had, in the meantime, been expelled from the Nazi Party for, as Martin Bormann's expulsion letter read, "treason against the *Führer* and the German people."[59] His immediate postwar circumstances proved to be as chaotic as they were for most other Germans. Very early in the occupation of Berlin, believing that the Soviets might need experienced bureaucrats to restore the city to order, he sought an interview with the Russian occupation command. Here, he says, he was interrogated "Russian-style" and then, instead of being given a job, was arrested, only to be released eight days later without explanation. From there he went to the American occupation zone in the western district of the city, where U.S. military authorities subjected him to "automatic arrest," this time because of his high rank in the Nazi civil service. For the third time within a year, he found himself in prison, this time for fourteen months.

Following his release by the Americans in October 1946, Loesener was able to acquire a "de-Nazification" certificate with the help of exonerating documents from his personal files and with the aid of testimony from people he had assisted during the Nazi years. In August 1947, the American military government stamped his identification papers with the all-important word "Rehabilitated." His memoir ends on June 6, 1950, with the lament that all his efforts to reestablish a civil service career had ended in failure. Actually, as we learn from one of his friends, he had by then been employed in the legal department of the new German Federal Republic's Economic Council in Frankfurt am Main. Why he fails to mention this is puzzling. Later, in October 1950, he would take another government job in the Customs Office in Cologne. There he remained until his death on August 24, 1952, following a gall bladder operation. He was sixty-two years old.

For some reason, Loesener chose to mention only in passing a remarkable episode in his life during the postwar years. In June 1948, he was called upon by the American Military Tribunal in Nuremberg to testify in the trial of his former Interior Ministry boss, Wilhelm Stuckart. Stuckart, along with twenty other high-level Nazi bureaucrats, was charged with six crimes: crimes against the peace; being involved in a conspiracy to plan a war of aggression; war crimes and crimes against humanity; engaging in the plunder and spoliation of peoples and property in German-occupied territories; participating in the enslavement of forced labor; and being a member of a criminal organization, the SS.[60] The charge of war crimes and crimes against humanity had to do with his work relating to the Jewish question in his capacity as a state secretary in the Interior Ministry.

Loesener appeared before the tribunal as a witness for the prosecution against his former chief. Loesener's testimony seems deliberately ambiguous. Stuckart's lawyers had attempted to portray their client as a small fish with a big title. Loesener testified to the contrary, saying that the size of the title was matched by the size of the fish. In an affidavit delivered to the tribunal beforehand, Loesener had characterized Stuckart "as active, able, ambitious and [as someone who had] seized hold of the reins and to an increasing extent become the real Minister of the Interior, due to Frick's weakness and lack of interest in his work."[61] On the other hand, Loesener claimed that Stuckart, at least during his early years in the ministry, had been an ally in his efforts to mitigate the severity of anti-Jewish legislation. Moreover, he portrayed Stuckart's notorious proposal (made at the Wannsee Conference on January 20, 1942) that half Jews be sterilized as a milder alternative to being deported to death camps. The tribunal found Stuckart guilty on three of the six counts, including the one of having committed war crimes and crimes against humanity in his dealings with Jews. He was sentenced to a four-year prison term.

That Loesener should have so thoroughly downplayed his appearance before the American Military Tribunal is surprising. Much more so is his failure to mention a second episode, his brief career between April and September 1949, working in Frankfurt am Main for the German Mission of the Jewish Joint Distribution Committee (JDC), an international Jewish welfare organization assisting Jewish survivors of the Nazi concentration and death camps. What he did for the JDC during these few months is unknown. We know of his work there only because his friend Walter Strauss, who wrote an introduction to the German publication of Loesener's memoir, says Loesener got the job because of the testimony of people whom he helped rescue. The archives for the German Mission contain no record of Loesener's employment, but JDC officials explain that records for this chaotic period in postwar Germany are spotty at best.[62]

Another piece of evidence attaching itself to the Loesener enigma came to public attention through the testimony of the Reverend Heinrich Grüber at the trial in Jerusalem of Adolf Eichmann in 1961, nine years after Loesener's death. Heinrich Grüber (1891–1975) was a German clergyman who in 1937 founded an agency (the *"Büro* Grüber") to aid Protestants who had converted from Judaism and were being victimized by the Nazis. Grüber's agency assisted these people in their efforts to emigrate, to find jobs abroad, and often, to care for the children of those who were arrested. Grüber himself spent much of his time intervening on their behalf with Nazi officials, among them Adolf Eichmann in the Reich Main Security Office (RSHA, or *Gestapo*). Hence his appearance at this trial. When Grüber was asked whether he had contacts with other government officials during these years, he replied that he had been "fortunate to have at least one person in more or less every ministry." In the Interior Ministry, he said,

> [T]here was a certain Government Counselor *(Oberregierungsrat)* Loesener who was a member of the party but who suffered so much, as a matter of conscience, from the whole situation that he often said to us: "If only I could get out of here, but there is only one way I can get out of here, and that is via a concentration camp. He helped us a great deal and later actually did leave his work, and after 1945 he came to see me and asked me to give him a certification for de-Nazification purposes, which I was happy to do."[63]

Exactly how did Loesener help him, the court asked Grüber. "[E]ither to delay things which were planned or already ordered, or to the extent that [he] was able to do so, to moderate them," Grüber replied. Grüber's own integrity and humanitarian credentials are well documented. He was soon to be honored as a "Righteous Gentile" by the Yad Vashem Authority in Jerusalem, Israel's official Holocaust memorial agency, for his role in rescuing Jews from Nazi clutches. In the United States, he would be granted an honorary doctoral degree by the Hebrew Union College in Cincinnati, and in Germany he would serve as honorary president of the German-Israeli Society.[64]

The enigma surrounding Bernhard Loesener does not disappear, even in the face of testimony as exculpatory as that of Pastor Grüber. Questions remain. How does one reconcile the contradictions in a person who, on the one hand, contributed to the escalation of Nazi persecutions, and, on the other, worked to mitigate their effects? Who joined the Nazi Party, served in its government, and also became involved in the effort to overthrow and even assassinate its leader? Who helped the Nazis in their search for a solution to the "Jewish question" and afterward worked for the Jewish Joint Distribution Committee in assisting Jewish refugees whose plight he had helped create? The various possible answers to these questions reflect the dilemma of those who try to understand not only Bernhard Loesener but also the Nazi world in which he functioned.

Notes

1. Bernhard Loesener, "Als Rassereferent im Reichsministerium des Innern," *Vierteljahrshefte für Zeitgeschichte* 9 (1961):264–313.

2. Hannah Arendt, "Privileged Jews," *Jewish Social Studies* 8 (1946):24; Alex Bein, *The Jewish Question: Biography of a World Problem*, trans. Harry Zohn (Rutherford, NJ: Fairleigh Dickenson University Press, 1990), pp. 18–25.

3. Norman Cohn, *Warrant for Genocide: The Myth of the Jewish World-Wide Conspiracy and the Protocols of the Elders of Zion* (Washington, DC: Harper and Row, 1967).

4. Ivan Hannaford, *Race: The History of an Idea in the West* (Washington, DC: The Woodrow Wilson Center Press, 1996), pp. 235–276.

5. Leon Poliakov, *The Aryan Myth: A History of Racist and Nationalist Ideas in Europe*, trans. Edmund Howard (New York: Basic Books, 1974).

6. Adolf Hitler, *Mein Kampf* (Munich: Zentralverlag der NSDAP, Frz. Eher Nachf., 1943), p. 272.

7. Karl A. Schleunes, *The Twisted Road to Auschwitz: Nazi Policy Toward German Jews, 1933–1939* (Urbana: University of Illinois Press, 1970), p. 7.

8. Werner T. Angress, "The German Army's 'Judenzählung' of 1916—Genesis—Consequences—Significance," *Leo Baeck Institute Yearbook* 23 (1978):134–135.

9. Loesener Memoir (see p. [000] here).

10. Nuremberg Document (NG) 1944A, affidavit by Dr. Bernhard Loesener.

11. Loesener's testimony at the Nuremberg Military Tribunal Under Control Council Law No. 10, Interrogation Nr. 2703, Bl. 4342 in Yad Vashem Archives in Jerusalem, File O-53/141.

12. Hans Mommsen, *Beamtentum im Dritten Reich: Mit ausgewählten Quellen zur nationalsozialistischen Beamtenpolitik* (Stuttgart: Deutsche Verlags-Anstalt, 1966), p. 21.

13. Loesener Memoir (see p. [000] here).

14. U.S. Holocaust Museum, "The Nazi Olympics, Berlin 1936," in "Online Exhibitions." See www.ushmm.org/olympics/.

15. *The Yellow Spot: The Outlawing of a Million Human Beings; A Collection of Facts* ... (London: Victor Gallanz, 1936), pp. 204–205.

16. Alan Steinweis, *Art, Ideology, and Economics in Nazi Germany: The Reich Chambers of Music, Theater, and the Visual Arts* (Chapel Hill: University of North Carolina Press, 1993), p. 36.

17. Dieter Ziegler, "Die Verdrängung der Juden aus der Dresdener Bank, 1933–1938," *Vierteljahrshefte für Zeitgeschichte* 47 (1999):204.

18. Loesener Memoir (see p. [000] here).

19. Hamilton T. Burden, *The Nuremberg Party Rallies: 1923–39* (New York: Frederick A. Praeger, 1967), pp. 100–101.

20. See the report dated September 19, 1935, by Dr. Vollguth, a *Gaureferent* (district official) in Saxony, in the archives of the U.S. Holocaust Museum. USHMM, RG-11:00M.01, Reel 5, Folder 343.

21. Loesener Memoir (see p. 54).

22. Jeremy Noakes, "The Development of Nazi Policy Towards the German-Jewish '*Mischlinge*' 1933–1945," *Leo Baeck Institute Yearbook* 34 (1989):353.

23. Christopher R. Browning, "The Government Experts," in *The Holocaust: Ideology, Bureaucracy, and Genocide,* ed. Henry Friedlander and Sybil Milton (Millwood, NY: Kraus International Publications, 1977), p. 191.

24. Reinhard Rürup, "Das Ende der Emanzipation; Die antijüdische Politik in Deutschland von der 'Machtergreifung' bis zum Zweiten Weltkrieg," in *Die Judenfrage im Nationalsozialistischen Deutschland,* ed. Arnold Paucker (Tubingen: J.C.B. Mohr [Paul Siebeck], 1986), pp. 111–112.

25. Kurt Pätzold, *Faschismus, Rassenwahn, Judenverfolgung: Eine Studie zur politischen Strategie und Taktik des faschistischen deutschen Imperialismus (1933–1945)* (Berlin: VEB Deutscher Verlag der Wissenschaften, 1975), pp. 265–271.

26. Werner Jochmann, *Gesellschaftskrise und Judenfeindschaft in Deutschland, 1870–1945* (Hamburg: Christians, 1988), p. 247.

27. David Bankier, *Germans and the Final Solution: Public Opinion Under Nazism* (Oxford: Blackwell, 1992), p. 43.

28. Otto Dov Kulka, "Die Nürnberger Rassengesetze und die deutsche Bevölkerung im Lichte geheimen NS-Lage und Stimmungsberichte," *Vierteljahrshefte für Zeitgeschichte* 32 (1984):615–618.

29. Bundesarchiv R 18/5573 Bl. 3–4 in Yad Vashem Archives, JM 3579.

30. Kulka, "Die Nürnberger Rassengesetze," p. 616.

31. Cornelia Essner, *Das System der "Nürnberger Gesetze" (1933–1945) oder der verwaltete Rassismus* (unpublished Habilitationsschrift) Berlin, 1999. I wish to thank Dr. Essner for allowing me to quote from her thesis and Professor Hans Mommsen for calling it to my attention.

32. Ibid. p. 123.

33. Ibid., p. 129.

34. Ibid., p. 135.

35. Ibid., p. 144.

36. Saul Friedlander, *Nazi Germany and the Jews,* vol. 1, *The Years of Persecution, 1933–1939* (New York: HarperCollins, 1997), p. 147.

37. Loesener Memoir (see p. [000] here).

38. Günter Neliba, *Wilhelm Frick, Der Legalist des Unrechtsstaates; Eine politische Biographie* (Paderborn: Ferdinand Schöningh, 1992), pp. 205–206.

39. Loesener Memoir (see p. [000] here).

40. Moshe Zimmermann, *Wilhelm Marr: The Patriarch of Anti-Semitism* (Oxford: Oxford University Press, 1986), p. 11.

41. Wilhelm Frick, *Die Nationalsozialisten im Reichstag, 1924–1931* (Munich: Verlag Fr. Eher, Nachf., 1932), pp. 63–64.

42. Ibid.

43. Udo Kissenkoetter, *Gregor Strasser und die NSDAP* (Stuttgart: Deutsche Verlags-Anstalt, 1978), p. 50.

44. Helmut Nicolai, *Rasse und Recht (Vortrag gehalten auf den Deutschen Juristentage . . .* (Berlin: Reiner Hobbig, 1933), pp. 64–65.

45. See entry for "Gercke" in *Das Deutsche Führerlexikon, 1934/35* (Berlin: Verlagsanstalt Otto Stolberg, 1934), p. 144.

46. Karl Dietrich Bracher, Wolfgang Sauer, and Gerhard Schulz, *Die Nationalsozialistische Machtergreifung; Studien zur Errichtung des totalitären Herrschaftssystems in Deutschland, 1933/34* (Cologne: Westdeutscher Verlag, 1960), p. 412, n. 147.

47. Loesener Handakten, F/712, p. 193 in the Institut für Zeitgeschichte in Munich.

48. Bundesarchiv, R 18/5246 ("Grundsätze der Mendelschen Erbregel"), Bl. 33–45 in Yad Vashem Archives.

49. Bernhard Loesener and Friedrich August Knost, *Die Nürnberger Gesetze mit den Durchführungsverordnungen und den sonstigen einschlägiger Vorschriften* (Berlin: F. Vahlen, 1939), p. 18.

50. Bernhard Loesener, "Die Hauptprobleme der Nürnberger Gesetze und ihrer Ersten Ausführungsverordnungen," *Reichsverwaltungsblatt* 56 (1935):88.

51. Saul Friedlander, "Die Genese der 'Endlösung'; Zur Phillipe Burrins These," *Jahrbuch zur Antisemitismusforschung* 1 (1992):168; Phillipe Burrin, *Hitler and the Jews: The Genesis of the Holocaust*, trans. Patsy Southgate (London: Edward Arnold, 1994), p. 48.

52. Joseph Goebbels, *Tagebücher: Sämtliche Fragmente*, Pt. 1, Vol. 1, ed. Elke Fröhlich (Munich: K. G. Sauer, 1987), pp. 537, 540.

53. Ian Kershaw, *Hitler, 1889–1936: Hubris* (New York: W. W. Norton, 1999), p. 571.

54. For the text of the "Jewish Star Decree," see the Appendix here.

55. Loesener Memoir (see p. [000] here).

56. For the text of the "Law Regulating Rental Relationships with Jews," see the Appendix here.

57. Loesener Memoir (see p. [000] here).

58. On Gehre, see Peter Hoffmann, *The History of the German Resistance, 1933–1945*, trans. Richard Berry (Cambridge: MIT Press, 1977), pp. 246, 271, 282, 530.

59. Loesener Memoir (see p. [000] here).

60. See *Trials of War Criminals Before the Nuernberg Military Tribunal Under Control Council Law No. 10*, vol. 12 (Washington, DC: U.S. Government Printing Office, n.d.), pp. 316–332.

61. Ibid., p. 640.

62. Jewish Joint Distribution Committee letter to author, May 24, 2000.

63. Eichmann Trial Transcripts, Testimony of May 16, 1961, Session 41. See http://nizkor.org/hweb/people/e/eichmann-adolf/transcripts/Sessions/Session-041-04.html. See also Henrich Grüber, *Errinnerungen aus sieben Jahrzehnten* (Cologne: Kiepenheuer and Witsch, 1968), pp. 126–127.

64. Yad Vashem Archives, M-31/75.

2

AT THE DESK FOR RACIAL AFFAIRS IN THE REICH MINISTRY OF THE INTERIOR

(Als Rassereferent im Reichsministerium des Innern)

MEMOIRS OF DR. BERNHARD LOESENER
Carol Scherer, Translator

Introductory Remarks

There is already such an abundance of writings of every kind about the persecution of the Jews during the "Third Reich" that to add yet another piece can only be justified if it reveals something substantially new. The deeds of the persecutors and the sufferings of the persecuted, which have shocked the world, have been preserved in thousands of court records and in numerous first-hand accounts. Less, and in some cases nothing, is known about the persecution in its preparatory stage, how the Hitler regime's measures, behind the curtain of "Party and State," took on the shape—sometimes slowly, sometimes quickly—in which they would later come to light. The trials before the Nuremberg military tribunal[1] did, to be sure, subject these matters to the closest possible examination. What made its way into the press, however, was by necessity incomplete.

Much of it was not included in the protocols, or was taken out of context. The author of this record held the Desk for "Racial Law" (*Referent für "Rassenrecht"*) in the Reich Ministry of the Interior from mid-1933 until late 1942 and personally witnessed most of the early history of the persecution, at least those measures cloaked, albeit scantily, in legality. The only part of his lengthy and detailed testimony as witness at the Nuremberg Trials included in the protocols concerned his statements regarding the conduct of the accused Secretary of State Dr. Stuckart.[2] It seems likely that the large majority of the people who, apart from myself, experienced these proceedings and are still alive today—in other words, my opponents on the Nazi side—feel the urgent need to bury their knowledge of what transpired. In many of the preliminary events, meetings, and confrontations, I was probably the only participant who stood wholeheartedly on the other side. To describe the more remarkable of these experiences has thus, perhaps, a certain value as a contribution to uncovering the truth—provided that it is presented objectively. The fortunate circumstance of being able to save a number of reference files and notes from this time helped me come closer to this goal. Proceedings marked by such ever-escalating atrocity as Hitler's persecution of the Jews tend, perhaps more quickly than others, to give rise to legends and schematic simplifications—in other words, to misjudgments that become seemingly insurmountable obstacles to uncovering the truth, and thus to assigning guilt more justly. It therefore seems incumbent upon me to explain at certain points how I, as a hostile and critical contemporary, personally viewed and judged things during this period.

This record consists of personal memories. Proceedings already part of history, the darkest part of German history, remain inextricably interwoven with one's own experiences. The nature of the subject at hand thus repeatedly forces me to speak of myself as well. In addition, I must also offer a legitimate explanation of just how I came to hold the Desk for Racial Affairs and, perhaps more importantly, why I remained there so long, although I ran the clear risk of exposing myself to the suspicion that, through guilt by association, I was involved in one of the most terrible crimes in recent history. I am prompted not only by what is the understandably human desire to justify myself personally, at the very least to my fellow human beings who are capable of making such judgments. Much more so, I find it necessary to do so if I am to achieve the purpose of this record: that whoever reads it will simultaneously form a judgment of the author's conduct in order to assess the truthfulness of his word and thereby assess the truthfulness of this work.

How I Came to Hold
the Desk for Racial Affairs

Two years prior to the "assumption of power" [*Machtübernahme*] I joined the NSDAP[3] in Glatz, the small Silesian city where I had been posted, because I wrongly assumed that only this party could succeed in rescuing Germany from the not-so-rosy situation in which it found itself back then. I had no other motive for joining the Party. I was a well-qualified higher-ranking official in the civil service, had a family, was earmarked for transfer to the Reich Ministry of Finance and thus had no reason to engage in political gamesmanship to secure for myself a better income or to advance my career prospects. No one could foresee that it would later be impossible to leave the Party without jeopardizing one's entire existence.

Following 30 January 1933, there was an urgent search for higher-ranking civil servants who belonged to the Party. By the end of April 1933 I was summoned by telegraph to see Secretary of State Reinhardt[4] in the Reich Ministry of Finance. While waiting in his outer office I discovered that he intended to make me his personal assistant [*Referent*]. I found this prospect distasteful since I have always been inclined to work on larger policy problems rather than to serve in an assisting capacity with its constant personal dependence upon the daily agenda of the boss, especially one as unstable and explosive as Reinhardt. While I was waiting, the man who was acting as Reinhardt's assistant showed me a request for my file that had just arrived from the Reich Ministry of the Interior [RMdI].[5] In hoping to avoid being assigned to Reinhardt, I told him about the request and after repeated entreaties, he reluctantly agreed to allow me to inquire what the RMdI had in mind. There, Secretary of State Pfundtner,[6] who had known me from earlier encounters, told me that the RMdI urgently needed new officials because the new drive towards centralization was causing its previously limited importance to increase rapidly. In the course of this search, Pfundtner had been made aware of me and welcomed the fact that I was already a Party Comrade [*Parteigenosse*].[7] He was thinking of assigning me to the Desk for Matters Related to Citizenship [*Staatsangehörigkeitsreferat*], which was about to take on significant new duties. I was to help take care of his own overwhelming mass of correspondence. Happy over this turn of events, I asked him to pick up the telephone and pry me free of Reinhardt, something he willingly and successfully accomplished. The next day I started the position in the RMdI (April 27, 1933).

I have detailed the strange linkage of circumstances which gave a surprising turn to my professional life and brought about my transfer to another Ministry because, in retrospect, they affected not only my own existence, but also became significant in a higher context.

Since the Nazis had been at the helm for 3 months, there was already a stack of written demands and "suggestions" [*Anregungen*] for all possible anti-Semitic measures, as well as an array of protests and emergency appeals from Jewish organizations. All were addressed to the Ministry of the Interior, or landed there as coming under its jurisdiction. In order to clear his desk and because there was no designated Desk for such matters, Pfundtner turned these things over to me, along with a bundle of all other sorts of letters, and told me to draft a short reply to each, making the reply, for the time being, as evasive as possible. This I did, as well, or as poorly, as circumstances allowed. Then Pfundtner, who was overrun with visitors and petitioners, started to shove those who were most burdensome and embarrassing off on me, including those who showed up because they had been affected, actively or passively, by the "Jewish Question" [*Judenfrage*]. After a while I came to be seen as having some expertise in this area, and gradually these matters began to cling to me, in addition to my primary responsibilities at the Desk for Matters of Citizenship. I was unable to counter this development effectively, especially because I was, at first, one of the very few Party members from the pre-1933 period in the Ministry, and therefore could hardly claim any aversion to taking care of these matters.

This disinclination, however, was already present. Three weeks prior to my assignment in the Ministry, the "Law for the Restoration of the Professional Civil Service" of April 7, 1933, had been promulgated. Its "Aryan Paragraph"[8] gave me my first severe shock. As everyone knows, this paragraph defined the concept of "non-Aryan" to include one-quarter Jews and subjected anyone at that line or above to severe legal discrimination. This no longer bore the slightest resemblance to what I had imagined, and a foreboding of evil came over me because, all at once and without the least pretext of national necessity, thousands of capable and completely loyal people were being abruptly robbed of their economic underpinnings. And I was supposed to draft responses to their protests, protests that were in line with my own views word for word.

Day after day I read or heard things relating to the entire area of the Jewish Question, things that the press would no longer report at all or, if so, with the greatest caution. My inner reservations grew visibly stronger.

But I also saw from the outset that there was not the least prospect for a government office, let alone a single official, to resist what was intended for the Jews, that is the full Jews, since Hitler and the Party were pushing things ahead with the full force of their influence. I will talk later about Frick's indifference to all these problems. Deep inside himself Pfundtner rejected the harassment of the Jews, but as a former German National[9] he never had any influence with the Party. This he knew, and so he avoided any friction in order not to jeopardize his position. My other superiors were old competent bureaucrats through and through and therefore despised by the Party. For this reason their views on the Jewish Question were from the very beginning of little practical consequence vis-à-vis Party demands.

In contrast to my minor Silesian posting, I now occupied a position from which I had a direct glimpse into the Party's political game. I saw with dismay that all the promises made before the Party assumed power had given a completely wrong picture of a future National Socialist state—not because the Nazi leaders had run up against a very different situation, but because they had had, from the very beginning, intentions other than those they had made public. Of course this insight did not dawn on me all at once, but bit by bit I filled in the picture quickly enough. Naturally my illusions collapsed first in the area that I could observe more closely than others, that is, the Jewish Question. Then came the Church Question,[10] when Hitler, contrary to his program, worked actively against and not for "a positive Christianity" (during the 1933 Protestant Church elections), and so it continued. My inner resistance grew accordingly, first in my area of work, then against everything else that the Party did and aspired to. I became ever more bitter because I felt personally deceived. For someone who has never been in the Party, it is difficult to imagine how anguished upright people felt about learning they had been led to join under false pretenses. As a civil servant, one could not leave the Party without exposing oneself and one's family to personal catastrophe and so, starting in the fall of 1933, and until I was expelled from the Party, I suffered under the sense of an additional affront.

Up Until the Nuremberg Laws

The position of the Ministries during the Hitler years cannot be compared with that of the time either before or after. Everyone knows with what utter contempt Hitler looked down upon government offices, professional civil servants, and especially lawyers. Shortly after the assumption of power, he undermined and destroyed their authority through mockery in his speeches and particularly through his slogan *"The Party dictates to the State,"* a slogan jubilantly echoed by the brown masses.[11] These words bore ripe fruit. Over the course of time, the Reich Ministries dwindled into mere executors of the Party will. As early as 1933, Party members, displaying an unparalleled arrogance, presented themselves at the Ministries. Despite his previous service to the [Nazi] movement, Frick[12] too had much to suffer under Hitler's personal disdain for him as lawyer and civil servant. This was part of the reason why he soon withdrew in a sulk and let things take their course. There is no need to go into the influence Frick's subordinates had under these conditions if they did not acquiesce—as so many of them did—to becoming fawning servants of the Party instead of attempting to confront Party efforts. Fortunately the Ministry of the Interior also had quite a few staff members who fought against the Party with every means at their disposal, and continued to do so until the very end. They all knew each other and helped each other out in every conceivable way in this struggle, a struggle which would, could we add up the sum of its successes, prove itself to have been much more effective than is usually assumed today—even though victory was denied to their tenacious and always dangerous efforts.

I was not responsible for "Jewish Matters" in general, but as a member of Department I of the RMdI only for legislation pertaining to the Jewish Question. There was also a Jewish Desk *(Judenreferat)* in the Medical Affairs Department of the Ministry (under Gütt,[13] later under the notorious Conti),[14] as well as "Jewish Desks" in the Ministry of Propaganda, Ministry of Economics, Ministry of Justice, Ministry of Education, and later in the Foreign Office, but most important of all in the Police Affairs Department of the "Main Office Security Police" *(Hauptamt Sicherheitspolizei,* or *Gestapo),* later named "Reich Security Main Office" *(Reichssicherheitshauptamt,* or RSHA), directed by Himmler. This last office was technically tied to the RMdI, but in point of fact completely independent of it. It was the Reich Security Main Office that eventually carried out the most vicious persecution of the Jews, and it had no intention of involving Department I of the RMdI, as had been formally specified. Nor did the Ministry of Propaganda or even the Brown House,[15] the Party Chancellery. In contrast, the others, the old Ministries, did involve us by sending over draft proposals and inviting us to meetings in advance; thus I often had the opportunity to make my efforts felt.

My authority was confined to attempting to influence the decisions of my superiors by gathering material, making suggestions, and presenting contrary views. Had I ever made any suggestions aimed at intensifying the pressure on the Jews, however, they would have fallen on the most fertile soil, and I would have quickly won the goodwill of the mighty.

The question of the responsibility of Department I of the RMdI for developments in the Jewish Question and for the formulation of anti-Semitic laws (the fewest of which, incidentally, were initiated by our offices), along with Hitler's instructions in these matters and the absolute necessity of adhering to them, eventually played a leading role in the proceedings against Secretary of State Dr. Stuckart ("Wilhelmstrasse Trial") before the military tribunal at Nuremberg. All this was taken into account but figured little in mitigating the sentences of the accused. It will be clear to anyone who takes an objective look at the conditions after 1933 and judges them in an unbiased way, how little influence in the decision making process a single person, even the brightest and boldest, could have wielded against the Party, especially in an area so central to its "satanic drive" [satanische Dynamik] as the "Jewish Question." Absolutely no one succeeded in this.

It was clear from the very beginning that the Jewish Question in its narrower sense, that is for the full Jews, was as unmovable as a mountain. In terms of tactics, to try and change things here would have been the most futile thing I could have done, since this would from the very beginning have foreclosed every other possibility of achieving anything at all.

The precise area where my efforts in the Jewish Question could be implemented suggested itself. With the Aryan Paragraph in the Law for the Restoration of the Professional Civil Service of April 7, 1933, the Party had come to regard half- and one-quarter Jews as its certain victims and [had] begun to cast a threatening eye on mixed marriages. Here there was a possibility for me to act. My effort to keep these circles, highly endangered from the start, from experiencing the Jewish fate runs like a red thread through my entire work in the RMdI, stretching from early 1933 to my resignation.

Over and over again, my personal and political friends, as well as those seeking advice from among the ranks of the affected, persuaded me to remain in my position even as disgust threatened to choke me. Starting in 1936, when I joined the Goerdeler[16] circles, specifically that of Dr. Gisevius himself, purely political motives of another sort also played a role.

In the face of the rapidly growing system of violence, countering measures could not be those of open opposition. Nor could I use the only real arguments of basic humanity, ethics, and above all religion, which for upright individuals would have been persuasive, because my opponents were not upright individuals. Any such attempt and I would have been thrown out of the saddle. I thus had to limit myself to arguments that might make an impression on people of this sort. The first task was to attack on the most marginal front by trying to improve the position of the *one-quarter* Jews. The only still-existing example from that first period is the following text of a position paper I presented to Frick dated October 30, 1933. Whoever today might take exception to turns of phrase that seem to sanction measures against the full Jews, is not putting himself into the general situation, or my personal one, in the year 1933, and is forgetting that this tone was necessary in order to save that which was *perhaps* still possible to save.

To Herr Minister dutifully submitted

Memorandum regarding the application of the Aryan provisions to the offspring of mixed marriages.

Since its introduction six months ago, the Aryan legislation has given rise to repercussions of such general significance that it seems necessary to examine them in more detail.

First, it has become apparent that through this legislation—introduced with § 3 of the Law for the Restoration of the Professional Civil Service and the provisions related to its implementation (requirement that all grandparents are of pure blood)—*the children and grandchildren of mixed marriages are affected more strongly than full Jews.* The full Jews, with some exceptions, are affected economically and burdened emotionally chiefly through the difficulties resulting from the fact that they must give up their previous influence and look for another accommodation or place of residence. The children, however, and particularly the grandchildren of mixed marriages, face both these difficulties and the emotional burden of being placed in the same category as Jews. In other words, they feel defamed and forcibly deprived of their German national identity *(deutsches Volkstum),* even though they feel they belong exclusively to the German nation. In addition, it is almost impossible for them to start a new life outside German borders because other countries see them not as Jews but as Germans, and because the Jews want nothing to do with them.

Special rigor is called for to cleanse the German professional civil service of all foreign influence, because these people are the immediate servants and keepers of the State. In many cases, however, the uncritical *application of the "Aryan Paragraph" to almost every area of life* has led to a grave situation, particularly because it means that the offspring of mixed marriages, who are being forced out of the civil service, are thereby excluded from professional employment of any kind. This applies to professions demanding a university degree as well as for all others, even for athletics and all kinds of physical activity (labor service, military associations, civil air defense, even tennis clubs, rowing clubs, etc.). To mention a specific example, the Reich Minister of Finance has ordered that employees of business and commercial firms must submit a declaration of Aryan descent if they want to make customs declarations or obtain customs information for their firms.

Another factor is that German-Jewish *Mischlinge* ("hybrids" or those of mixed race) and their children become social outcasts. This affects them emotionally more than full Jews, especially since most *Mischlinge* are, unfortunately, found in families whose members are in the military officer corps or have a high number of university degrees. Given their current scope, the Aryan provisions will also remove from the "national community" *(Volksgemeinschaft)*[17] descendents of men who have done great service to German science or to the renewal of Germany (Privy Counselor Bering, who discovered the antitoxin serum therapy, particularly for diphtheria and tetanus; also Otto von Gierke, who pioneered in developing the German conceptions of rights and laws). The majority of other similar petitions show that the individuals in question have likewise performed great service in their positions, be it as soldiers on the battlefront or in the early development of National Socialist ideology. Most of the petitions do not necessarily aim at being granted permission to resume their professions, but rather arise from concern about the future of their children.

There are several reasons for reexamining the *Mischling* problem, particularly in connection with those who have only one Jewish grandparent:

1. The decision not to consider particularly important services to the German people seems out of proportion to whatever success can be expected from removing the descendents of such men [from the national community].
2. The number of persons in question is apparently so high that it encompasses a significant portion of the total population.

3. The provisions regarding *Mischlinge* primarily affect those who otherwise stand firmly on the side of the government, and whose upbring-
   ing and intelligence make them valuable to the German nation.
4. The enormous pressure on the persons in question, and which for now is
   expressed only in petitions, must gradually lead to more forceful reactions.
   This would present an additional burden, if not danger [to the state].

Should a reexamination of the question seem in order, it might be worth-
while to consider whether the government should publish some kind of decision or programmatic statement before the elections[18] so as to exert a favorable influence on the election outcome, a measure which would,
however, seem out of step with the government's authority.
   Possible ways to mitigate the situation include the *following:*

1. If it is decided that the advantage of removing those Germans who are
   burdened with one Jewish grandparent does not outweigh the disadvantages of their removal, it would be useful to seek to apply § 3 *of the
   Law* for the Restoration of the Professional Civil Service *in its original
   sense.* In other words, this regulation should apply in its full severity
   only to civil servants in the narrower sense, but not to those in positions
   that merely resemble those of the civil service, be they accountants,
   customs officials, and the like, and under no circumstances to positions
   that have nothing whatsoever to do with the professional civil service
   (artisans, Red Cross, the German Labor Front,[19] etc.).
2. Another way would be to limit the Aryan Paragraph in its existing version to *political civil servants in the actual sense of the word.* Even if there
   can be no question of reversing measures already taken on the basis of
   this paragraph, one could *for the future* consider allowing so-called
   three-quarter Aryans to enter non-political careers in the civil service,
   as attorneys, etc. This step would not present any new threat to how
   these persons view their offices, or to the racial composition of the German people, because [in the latter case] government measures to date
   have already taught the German people the severe lesson about avoiding mixed marriages from this point on. In addition, such a measure
   would be *in accord with the legislation regarding institutions of higher
   learning.* This legislation does not recognize children from mixed marriages as Aryans, but it does allow grandchildren from mixed marriages to study at the university. It would for this reason be difficult for
   the same State after passing this regulation to then bar a candidate who

had passed the qualifying examinations from entering the legal professions, teaching at the university, etc.

3. Should it prove impossible to carry out the suggestions to 1 and 2, the
question would arise as to whether to *prohibit*, by law or other means,
the spread of the provisions against three-quarter Aryans to all areas of
life. All such provisions, even those already enacted, would be made
dependent on the approval of the Reich Minister of the Interior.

4. One suggestion is to provide exceptions for descendents of *particularly
worthy Germans* (von Bering, von Gierke) or men who distinguished
themselves during the war or the German revolution, perhaps in the form
of a *general "hardship paragraph," [Härteparagraph]* whose application
would be defined by the guidelines of the Reich Minister of the Interior.

signed *Loesener*
October 30, 1933

Another draft I submitted to Frick led the Ministry to issue a circular
ordinance *[Runderlass]* based on my proposal. It read:

Reich Minister of the Interior	Berlin,
I 6071/30.12.	January 17, 1934

To The Highest Offices of the Reich,
The Reich Governors *[Reichsstatthalter]*,
The Governments of the Federal States
(for Prussia: the Prime Minister and all other Ministers).

The German Aryan legislation is necessary for the good of the ethnic nation and state politics. Nonetheless, the Reich government itself sets certain
bounds that likewise need to be adhered to. The German Aryan legislation
would be judged more accurately, both here and abroad, if these bounds
were to be heeded without exception. It is particularly inappropriate, indeed
harmful, for the principles of § 3 of the Law for the Restoration of the Professional Civil Service, the so-called "Aryan Paragraph" (which has become the
model for countless other laws and decrees) to be extended to areas for
which they were never intended. This holds particularly true, as the National Socialist government has repeatedly expressed its support for a free
market economy.

I therefore repeat my request to resist such encroachments resolutely, and
also to emphasize to subordinate offices that they are to reach decisions and

take measures in accordance *with current laws only.* On the one hand, government officials must carry out official acts (for example, the performing of marriages or taking protective police measures) without delay when the conditions for such are met according to current regulations. On the other hand, they must refrain from interfering with business enterprises, associations, etc. beyond what is stipulated by law or decree. *According to the Enabling Act,*[20] *only the Reich government is permitted to suspend, alter, or extend existing Reich laws,* and not the organs charged with carrying out these laws. The latter are charged only with the application of these laws as long as they are in force, and are not to contradict them even if the laws do not appear to correspond fully to National Socialist views.

In the interest of maintaining a unified procedure I also request that I be involved at the earliest possible moment in the preparation of any measures aimed at the special treatment of non-Aryans. Should intentions or suggestions of this sort already exist, I request to be informed of them immediately, along with the grounds for them, with supporting materials, and the like so that I can comment upon them at the appropriate juncture.

Signed *Dr. Frick*

I will return to my continued efforts along these lines when I describe the Nuremberg legislation below.

It goes without saying that I was not completely alone in this struggle, and that I cannot claim sole credit for any achieved and lasting successes. I had first to secure the support of superiors in my own Ministry, since I was only in charge of a Desk and did not have the authority even to sign important communications to other offices at the same level in the State or Party, to say nothing of reports to the "Führer." It was necessary to flood the departmental chiefs and the State Secretary, and (through him) the Minister, with a steady stream of written and verbal arguments to get them to sign what I drafted, so that my own superiors would not immediately compromise me when meetings turned heated. Otherwise, all my efforts would have remained a spear without a point. It was also necessary to have helpful colleagues in other government offices. The most passionate and important of them was my friend Dr. Killy[21] in the Reich Chancellery, with whom I discussed these things throughout this period, devising and implementing measures to counter every new wave of dangers. In these endeavors Killy played an indispensable role. In addition, I always found understanding and help in the Ministry of Economics, and, during the initial years, also in the Ministry of Justice. In my own Department I, the constant consultations with Dr. Globke[22] were invaluable. On the basis of the powers vested in my Desk, however, I remained the pivotal point around which everything else turned. Without my persistent efforts, the superiors mentioned above would hardly have begun to think of resisting, or at least they would have quickly abandoned such ideas. The longer the Hitler Reich, contrary to expectations, persisted with its merciless methods, the more difficult it became to keep these gentlemen in line. Killy and Globke, my allies and comrades in thought and deed, were not authorized to prepare, suggest, or initiate official measures in this area. That was up to me.

Although I in no way want to claim that whatever successes we did achieve were solely of my doing, I may nonetheless claim that they would never have been achieved without me. A zealous party member in my place would have brought additional and untold misfortune to countless people.

The year 1934 was relatively inhospitable to my goals. After the departure of departmental chief Ministerial Director Dammann, the position was filled by a younger Party comrade, Dr. Nicolai.[23] Although I could speak somewhat openly with him, he was little inclined to come around to my views. Fortunately, around this time the Jewish Question became less pressing for the Party. The situation did not improve for me until early 1935, when, after the disappearance of Nicolai, Secretary of State Dr. Stuckart took over the position as Chief of Department I. Dr. Stuckart was even younger (as I recall, not much over 30 at the time) and likewise an ardent National Socialist. But he was a most enterprising man and of a completely different stature than the run-of-the-mill upstarts of that time. Above all, he was receptive to different views if they were well founded, and did not cling narrow-mindedly to preconceived notions when forced to recognize that they were wrong. As he requested of all his subordinates, I too presented an initial report after he assumed office so that he could gain a general overview of the various problems under his jurisdiction. My presentation probably lasted 40 minutes, during which time he never once interrupted me, but listened intently. This gave me the courage to risk bringing everything out into the open and detailing my complete set of goals regarding the *"Mischlinge"* and "mixed marriages" questions, including even the ethical reasons for my position. At the end of my presentation he simply said, "Herr L., I approve of every word you have said," and dismissed me with every sign of his personal goodwill.

This marked the start of a more favorable turn, the significance of which would quickly become apparent.

The Origin of the
"Nuremberg Laws" of 15 September 1935

On the occasion of the "Reich Party Congress of Freedom," which started on 8 September 1935 in Nuremberg, Hitler had called for the convening of the Reichstag in the city on the 15th, the concluding Sunday, in order to pass a Reich Flag Law.[24] This law had been drafted in the Reich Ministry of the Interior. The Berlin Ministries had in effect stopped working since Monday, the 8th of September, because everyone of name and rank was in Nuremberg. Those of us who had stayed home were enjoying the peace and quiet. On Friday the 13th we met for a long and leisurely twilight drink to celebrate the fact that I had two weeks previously been promoted to Ministerial Counselor. It went well into the night. Around 11 P.M. I was called to the telephone: my wife informed me that the Ministry had just informed her that at 7 o'clock the next morning I had to fly from Tempelhof airport [in Berlin] to Nuremberg. It concerned a Jewish Law (*Judengesetz*), she was told; I needed to take along my files. Shortly after this call, Kettner, who held the Desk as personal assistant to Secretary of State Stuckart, was also called to the telephone and passed along the same orders in Stuckart's name. Accompanied by a colleague, Kettner as I recall, I hastily made my way to the dark RMdI, at that time still housed at the Königsplatz in the same building as the General Staff, in order to pick up some notes, drafts, the document registry, and other writings from my office and the offices of my various superiors. Because everything was locked, we woke up the concierge [*Bürodirektor*], Stoppel, who lived in the building and who proceeded to help us. I also had to alert my forwarding clerk, Culmsee, and have him come from Spandau to the Ministry because I could not recall the whereabouts of some papers that might have been important. Around 2:30 A.M. I finally returned home, slept for two hours, left Tempelhof around 7, together with Medicus,[25] and was in Nuremberg at 9, the day before the Reichstag session. (A car was waiting and drove us immediately to police headquarters, where Secretaries of State Pfundtner and Stuckart greeted us in a small office.) Ministerial Counselor Seel from the RMdI was also present, as well as a stenographer from the police headquarters. The gentlemen revealed to us that the day before, on Friday, the "Führer" had ordered them to submit an immediate draft for a Jewish Law. This was to be passed the next day by the Reichstag "to top off the program" because, Hitler believed, the Flag Law alone seemed "too meager" to suit the grandeur of a Reichstag meeting in Nuremberg. In 1935 the Party propaganda had, with increasing volume, raised a great uproar surrounding certain issues: the prohibition of marriages between Jews and Aryans, the prohibition of extramarital sexual relations between them, and the employment [in Jewish households] of Aryan female domestic servants—and now Hitler, they said, had passed on to Frick the order that this entire complex of questions be settled by legislative measures. After five days of Party doings, however, these gentlemen were rather exhausted. They had come up with some written drafts, but were still dissatisfied. It was clear to me that here was a great opportunity to formulate the draft so as to achieve certain goals, something that until that point the constant back-and-forth with the Party had prevented. Hitler himself wanted to sign the law (the so-called Blood Protection Law) and this, or so we then thought, would finally create a legal foundation, however unsatisfactory, and settle things in this area. On both days, Saturday and Sunday, discussions with the two Secretaries of State were free of any constraints, personal or professional—as though among comrades. What was disagreeable was the task itself. There was no changing Hitler's strict orders about the three points mentioned above, but perhaps there was something to wrest out of the Party slogan about "Jews and Jewish offspring" (*Juden und Judenstämmlinge*), which were always mentioned in the same breath. Here we could undermine the party's position by drawing a clear legal boundary between the two [Jews and Jewish offspring] and make it clear that the Führer's directives would apply exclusively to full Jews. Through my countless written and verbal presentations, the two Secretaries of State knew and approved of my ongoing efforts in this direction, and they energetically supported the attempt to draft legislation to this effect, which, given all the fanfare surrounding a meeting of the Reichstag, was likely to have lasting significance. In the course of the morning, Sommer,[26] then Ministerial Counselor from the Brown House in Munich, joined us as Party envoy. (Sommer later became Ministerial Director in the Party Chancellery, and eventually served for a time as President of the Reich Administrative Court.) He announced the Party demand that the law would, as a "matter or course," include Jewish offspring and must either dissolve already existing mixed marriages or stipulate that Aryan partners of Jews would be treated exactly like Jews. He came in the name of

Dr. Gerhard Wagner,[27] the "Leader of Reich Physicians" *(Reichärzteführer)* and one of the most vehement forces behind measures related to the Jewish Question. Throughout the hours leading up to the opening of the Reichstag, Wagner, in order to secure the most ruthless law possible, kept close to Hitler's side. Herr Sommer himself turned out to be less of an obstacle, because he found "the whole writing bit simply too stupid." He withdrew to another room where he spent hours with the new "hit" of the Reich Party Congress, a little wind-up tank that could spit sparks and climb over piled up files.

When the first draft (which ignored Party demands) was ready, I was told to take it to Frick so that he could be informed about the reasons behind our version and represent them to Hitler. Frick was staying far away from police headquarters, in the Häberlein Villa in the eastern part of the city. It took me a long time to make my way through the city. Twice I had to cross the endless processions of all kinds of party organizations, marching in their rows of twelve. I was doing something that was strictly forbidden, and it caused me considerable unpleasantries with the police and SS cordons because I was not in uniform. Frick was gone by the time I arrived. I lost a great deal of time before I reached him. He took the draft, but politely declined to hear any explanation and proceeded to present it to Hitler. What happened then would repeat itself over and over again. Gerhard Wagner, who was with Hitler, would raise objections and because Frick lacked any background information, he was unable to counter Hitler's faultfinding with any convincing arguments. He could not even present the draft effectively. Nevertheless, Frick insisted every time that he go to Hitler by himself, and coolly declined taking along Pfundtner or Stuckart. Naturally there was never any question that I myself would go along. Neither at this point, nor at any other time, did I ever speak with Hitler. Frick's actions, the reasons for which were never clear to me (an absurd craving for recognition?), not only annoyed the Secretaries of State, who already expected as much, and therefore never took the trouble of even attempting to reach him themselves. (With all the marching that day, walking was practically the only way possible of getting through the city.) What Frick did would cause enormous damage. After working for more than two years on what were now burning problems, I had put together so many arguments that, had they been cleverly presented, would have impressed even Hitler—as later events would prove. One would, of course, have needed to know all the complicated issues involved, knowledge that Frick in his incomprehensible and ever-growing indolence never had, or even, for that matter, tried to acquire. He never spent so much as a minute in consultation with us until after the Reichstag assembly. There is no need to give an hour-by-hour account of what then transpired. Nor can I recall all the monotonous details. As Saturday progressed, the following repeated itself over and over again: Frick went with a draft to Hitler, was unable to give any background information, Hitler's objections were prompted by Wagner, Frick came back with Hitler's order to change this or that point. Thus, over the course of the day, there emerged a large number of drafts ranging greatly in severity. That afternoon we betook ourselves, and our work, over to where Frick was staying in order to avoid the disruption of reaching him. It was Saturday afternoon—the weekend—and the stenographer from police headquarters had gone home. With the bustle of the Party Congress at its high point and all the local officials out and about, it was impossible to find a replacement. There was a typewriter in Frick's room and various police officers from his retinue would transcribe our drafts. None of our own stenographers from the Ministry were along since no one had foreseen this kind of work. We all sat crowded together in the music room of the villa; Pfundtner's desk was the piano, Stuckart was on the sofa, Seel, who did not really participate, was off in the corner, and I seated on a chair at the piano or the smoking table. Frick sat in the next room, separated from us by a closed sliding door, conversing with Frau Häberlein and sampling wine and gingerbread. Around midnight he returned from his last meeting with Hitler, our last draft in hand. We had listed the main explanatory points in telegraph form, which Pfundtner had given him, together with the draft (this might have happened sometime that afternoon). Frick informed us that the Führer wished to have fresh copies of 4 drafts by the next morning, ranging from the most severe version A, with two intermediate versions B and C, to the mildest version D, the one we supported. But, he said, the Führer also wished to round out the legislation of the coming day with *another basic law, a law for Reich citizenship (ein Grundgesetz, ein Reichsbürgergesetz)* which he wanted to see immediately. Shocked, Pfundtner asked him in a tone stripped of all politeness what that was supposed to mean; why hadn't he opened the Führer's eyes (or something similar) to the fact that such a law, a basic law for a "Thousand Year Reich" would require careful deliberation and preparations, etc.? Stuckart expressed similar reservations, but Frick, completely unmoved, said it should be simply a few well-chosen words, reflecting the importance of the law, taken perhaps from the relevant chapter of the Führer's book, that produced a kind of legal privileging for those of pure German blood. He then returned to the adjacent room and closed the door. By now it was about 12:30 A.M., and we had reached the limits of our strength, physically and mentally. We had spent the whole day locked in a struggle with our invisible opponent, Gerhard Wagner, hurriedly drafting a work whose enormous importance weighed heavily on our sense of responsibility. We first let loose a few curses and comments otherwise unthinkable in an official meeting of this sort. We were almost in despair and did not have the least notion of what to do with this new caprice of Hitler. Slowly we began to formulate ideas, first of a negative sort. The law, we thought, would have to have as little actual content as possible and thus forestall any immediate practical consequences. All else would have to be left to the future, we thought. Under all circumstances, moreover, we felt that the current law on the status of state subjects *(Staatsangehörigkeitsgesetz)* needed an explicit guarantee: the status of Jews as state subjects needed, above all else, to remain inviolable. The ensuing discussion, which dragged on ever more slowly and arduously, demanded some kind of still foggy concept of Reich citizenship, a kind of "elevated state subject status" *(eine Art gehobener Staatsangehörigkeit).* I no longer know just who in our circle tossed this or that arduously produced notion into the debate. The discussion had ceased to proceed along logical lines, and some even more ridiculous impulses were brought up and tossed aside. At last, because time was running out, a draft was pieced together with a phrase at the core (Article II, Paragraph 1), and at about 1:30 A.M. Frick went over to Hitler. All told we had something like an hour to draft this phantom of a basic law, not to mention the state we were in! Frick returned about an hour later. The Führer had approved the draft; Frick then invited us (2:30 A.M.) to share a bottle of wine, and we sat down at the table with him and Frau Häberlein. Frick said not a word about the "legislation" and the unrelenting strain of the past 15 hours. He uttered a few bored sentences about his duties as Fraction Leader[28] in the Reichstag, scheduled to meet in 12 hours. Finally, about an hour later, we could leave. At 4:30 A.M. I reached the "Bamberger Hof" and fell into bed. At 6:30 A.M., right below my windows, a large police band started to play a birthday serenade for Daluege,[29] who was also staying in the hotel. At 8 A.M. Pfundtner's chauffeur fetched me for a meeting in Pfundtner's room. I had to appear in my pajamas; Pf[undtner] was still wearing his, too. We were supposed to draft a detailed release which Frick wanted for the Party press. It was an impossible assignment because we did not know which of the completely different versions would become law, or what Hitler himself would say in his speech to the Reichstag. Nonetheless we had to start in on it right after breakfast. It was also important to seek out support so that Hitler would be inclined towards version D, and to stem, at least to some extent, the constantly dangerous influence of G. Wagner and his ilk. Because Frick was the wrong man for the job, Pfundtner and Stuckart were to try to win over Ministers Neurath[30] and Gürtner.[31] We thus needed to stay in the Bamberger Hof, and went on with the press release and winning over those sympathetic to our views, surrounded by boisterous morning drinking in the narrow hotel bar. Since it was Sunday and there was no paper to be had, I tried to draft the press releases on old menus and dictate to the hotel porter seated at the typewriter, since there was no other typist to be found, and time was tight. Then the few pieces of paper in the typewriter ran out. In the meantime Pfundtner had worked on Neurath and Gürtner. As far as I know—I was not present—one of them sought out Hitler or at least tried to reach him. Shortly before the Reichstag assembly, we had a hurried meal in the hotel bar. As we ate, Pfundtner dictated another version of the press release to me, which I wrote down on the menus lying on the table. We quickly ran to the car and arrived shortly before the assembly started. The Reichstag assembly was being held in the banquet hall of a large hotel close to the train station. I believe it was the "Fürstenhof." We civil servants had seats behind the speaker's rostrum in the next-to-last row. Following the usual speeches, the legislation was read aloud, the printed text of which the representatives held in their hands as a proposal for consideration by the Reichstag: "Proposal of Frick and Comrades." To our delight we heard that Hitler had chosen our version D. The only thing missing was a key sentence on which I had placed so much weight: "This law applies only to full Jews." As I found out shortly thereafter, Hitler had crossed it out with his own hand, but had ordered that the sentence be included with the laws when they were given to the German press agency *(DNB-Notiz)* for publication. This is also what happened. I also saw the sentence, crossed out, when I finally got hold of the original in Berlin. In contrast, both the sentence and its handwritten deletion were missing from what the *Völkischer Beobachter*[32] printed as the purported facsimile, and from the original texts of the Nuremberg Laws when they were later given ceremoniously to the city of Nuremberg.

Apart from the fact that version D was selected, I accorded particular significance to the ostentatiously furious, scornful face of Julius Streicher,[33] seated across from us in the second or third row of Reichstag delegates, and to those sections of Hitler's speech in which he emphasized that this was a conclusive, final ruling on the position of Jews. When the session was over, and the participants poured out onto the street, a large crowd was roaring over and over again: "What was decided? What was decided?" Because there were plenty of loudspeakers installed out there for them, we did not know what they meant, but we soon found out that Goebbels had permitted the radio broadcast of the session only up to the reading of the Laws, and had then ordered the switch to music. A sudden thunderstorm quickly scattered the crowd, and Hitler and the other bosses fled in their cars.

That evening Frick called again on the phone to have us draft a completely new press release, and we worked on it until 2:30 A.M. But after two nights with almost no sleep and the excessive excitement of the last two days, we did not produce anything useful—nor did we want to. The next morning (Monday), Frick made it known that he had changed his mind and did not want any press release at all. At this point I slipped away with the consent of Pfundtner, who was likewise fed up with everything. Not until two days later did I turn up again in the Berlin Ministry.

The Meaning of the Nuremberg Laws

The first Nuremberg Law, the Reich Flag Law, can be disregarded. In common usage, the Nuremberg Laws are understood to be the Reich Citizenship Law and the Law for the Protection of German Blood and German Honor. The latter was the most important of the laws passed by the Reichstag on 15 September 1935. The popular view today is that the Nuremberg Laws marked the beginning of the actual persecution of the Jews and prepared the ground for all later atrocities.

Today's view rests on a misreading of what transpired and reverses the relationship between cause and effect in the chain of historical events. The events described here followed each other chronologically, but not causally. Nothing could be further from my mind than to excuse or gloss over these laws. I regarded them as an outrage every minute of the two days it took to draft them. But for the historical record they need to be understood correctly, and this demands a closer look at the status of the "Jewish Question" in the third year of the dictatorship.

The first piece of anti-Semitic legislation was the Law for the Restoration of the Professional Civil Service of 7 April 1933 which, with its

"Aryan Paragraph," was promulgated before I was transferred to the Ministry. The Aryan Paragraph came as an abrupt and severe shock to me because it yielded to the Party's harassment of "Jews and Jewish offspring" up to and including those it defined as "one-quarter Jews." Similar Aryan paragraphs followed, but in their aftermath, legislation in the racial question basically came to a standstill. In 1933 the Party's anti-Semitic harassment had been particularly noisy and achieved its first success. To the Party, it now seemed a matter of course, *at the very least,* to classify half Jews together with full Jews in every way. In 1934 the harassment stayed within these existing bounds. I had already prepared a collection of arguments against its spread and presented Frick with several draft proposals to this effect. In his indifferent manner, he paid them little regard, averse as he was to examining a problem in any depth. But the emerging resistance within the Ministry, where I had the full support of my former superior, Assistant Ministerial Director Hering, soon aroused the attention of the Party bosses. In 1934 (the exact date has slipped my mind) Julius Streicher arranged a meeting with Frick in order to reconcile the differences in the opposing views in a "comradely discussion." Frick ordered me to attend. (It was the only time except for a meeting about 6 years later, when a Hungarian diplomat sought his help on behalf of the then Hungarian Minister of the Interior who was lacking the requisite Aryan grandmother. Somehow his problem was solved.) Streicher appeared, accompanied by his photographer. There was no sign of an exchange of views. Streicher was the only one who talked, following the filthy style of the articles in his *"Der Stürmer."* He enlightened Frick as to the dangers of the *Mischling* problem, smacking his lips over stories that a single act of sexual intercourse between a Jewish man and an Aryan woman would, because of his alien semen, so "impregnate" the mucus of her vagina that this woman, even if conception did not occur, would be never again be able to bear pure-blooded Aryan children, even if conceived by an Aryan male. This was the tone of everything he said. I did not say a word. Frick uttered a few insignificant remarks when Streicher finished, something along the lines of not seeing any difficulties. When we got up, the photographer raised his camera and I was able to step quickly aside.

Shortly after this "historic event," the *"Stürmer"* began to direct a new round of attacks upon the "Jews and Jewish offspring" and their sexual drives. Each act of spied-upon sexual intercourse was described and illustrated. The rest of the Party press followed suit, as did Party functionaries of every shade and hue. That was around the beginning of 1935. Throughout the Reich, local Party offices and the SA were pressuring civil registry offices[34] to reject marriage banns between Jewish and Aryan partners; district judges, who were supposed to decide the appeals against the prohibition of marriage banns, were also threatened; there were several cases of lynch justice against people of Jewish blood who wanted to marry "Aryan women" or who had had extramarital relations with them. *Every Gau- or Kreisleiter*[35] was making up his *own definition of a Jew* and extended it at will from full to one-eighth Jews. Each case received full-blown coverage in the press and at Party rallies and was used to whip harassment to new heights. If I recall correctly, the year 1935 was relatively quiet in terms of foreign policy, and so something else had to happen to keep the people "stirred up." In the Ministry of the Interior, appeals for help [from registry officials] were piling up, together with requests from provincial administrative officials asking for guidance on what instructions to give the civil registries. Complete chaos also surrounded the question of just who was to be regarded as [a] Jew, what exactly was to be the definition of a Jewish offspring or non-Aryan, and where the line between them and Aryans was to be drawn. In some areas the state's administration of marriage between Jews and Aryans came to a complete halt. Criminal judges were pressured to punish such alleged "crimes of blood" *(Blutschände)*; in some cases they complied with the vilest distortions of the criminal law code. The Party exercised its own "justice" in the most forcible ways.

This was the situation in September 1935 when Hitler, "without a moment's notice," ordered the promulgation of the Nuremberg Laws. After they became public, they were not always seen exclusively as laws of persecution. Many people who had in no way been adherents of the Nazi system, and even those directly affected, viewed them with a certain relief because they promised to put an end to a state of complete legal disarray. At least one knew now where one stood. A large number of previously threatened individuals drew a deep breath, especially "Jewish offspring" and spouses in mixed marriages, because until this point some extremists had demanded the legal dissolution of mixed marriages. Likewise, civil servants, especially those in the Ministry of the Interior, viewed the Nuremberg Laws in this positive light.

Let me emphasize: in broad circles at that time, these laws were not viewed as something unprecedented and new, or the beginning of a more severe anti-Semitic harassment, but rather as the *conclusion of an epoch of particularly vile harassment.* This conclusion, moreover, had turned out to be much milder than had been feared. Indeed *Hitler* himself, with the volubility he was known for, had announced to everyone that this was *the conclusion of and the solution to the Jewish Question* in Germany. I too regarded this as a great success, one for which I took a certain amount of credit. Evil Party demands had been kept out of the law, including its demand for the classification [of] one-eighth Jewish *Mischlinge* as Jews, the sterilization or the death penalty for "violators of German blood" *("Blutschänder"),* the sterilization of all Jews and half Jews, and the compulsory dissolution of racially mixed marriages. Here after all was a law, announced and signed by Hitler himself in the most conspicuous setting possible; as vile as it was, it at least provided something to hold on to, a solid foundation for the future. This was the widespread opinion, including, at first, my own. In countries outside Germany, where there was less awareness of developments prior to the promulgation of the laws, they seemed to announce the beginning of the actual persecution of the Jews, especially given the tumultuous propaganda with which they had been blared out to the world. This was particularly the case in the USA. From there, this view has forced its way back to Germany and is now no longer questioned. This view is wrong.

It is a misjudgment of historical truth to see all the misery, all the murders and other atrocities committed against the Jews, as simply the result of the Nuremberg Laws—as though they had, in a manner of speaking, unleashed everything Hitler's Germany has on its conscience, or that without them none of this would have happened, or at least taken a less murderous shape. For me, given my knowledge of the facts that never became publicly known, or particularly those that have today slipped from memory, it is a simple statement of objective fact to point out the following: the completely hellish form of the persecution of the Jews in later years became horrible reality *not as a result of, but rather despite the Nuremberg Laws.* Whoever sees it differently does not know the reality of it. All the atrocities were prompted and carried out by the Party, SS, SD, etc. The RMdI was *completely* excluded from them, and all its legal recommendations were disregarded. What was stipulated in the Blood Protection Law, the only one of the two laws with any actual substance? The prohibition of marriage between Jews and those of "German blood"; the prohibition of extramarital sexual relations between them; the prohibition upon Jews to employ female domestic servants of German blood under the age of 45, and the prohibition (which was not likely to have been seen as hardship) for Jews to fly the Hitler flag, along with severe punishments for violating these prohibitions. These four prohibitions, proclaimed by the Führer, the highest authority in the Reich, were meant to bring order into what had become a chaotic situation and to mark the end of the persecution of the Jews. Soon there were signs that the Party (by which I mean not only the Party itself, but particularly the SS, SD, Gestapo, Goebbel's Ministry, etc.) had scorned the Nuremberg Laws from the moment they were announced and had no intention of respecting the limits they imposed. The Nuremberg Laws were a thorn in their flesh. The following years were punctuated by their repeated assaults on the laws and by demands to suspend or sharpen this or that paragraph. While the legal barrier was never really an obstacle to the spiraling terror, its existence nonetheless served as [an] annoying reminder that the continuing persecution was "illegal." From September 1935 on, I thus waged a tough battle to prevent the laws from changing—that is, worsening. Even though I was granted nominal success, developments cancelled it out. In December 1941, when I requested to be removed from my position and transferred, Stuckart reproached me for a lack of "dynamism" and for *stubbornly clinging to the solution of the Nuremberg Laws*, which he called the source of all the difficult tension with Heydrich and the SS (more on this below).

The Two "First Decrees" to the Nuremberg Laws of 14 November 1935

As soon as the Nuremberg Laws were announced, it became clear how disastrous was Hitler's deletion of the sentence that applied the Blood Protection Law to full Jews only, although he had allowed its publication by the German news agency as a comment. As such, the law was almost completely worthless. The first week after passage of the laws, Party representatives appeared at the Ministry to negotiate their implementation with Stuckart and myself. In actuality, the question of how the laws were to be implemented was more important than the laws themselves. The Reich Citizenship Law in particular consisted almost entirely of phrases that lacked any kind of concrete substance. By far the most pressing matter was to find a legal definition of "Jew" and to draw a clear line separating him from the "non-Jews." The real battle had not yet even started. It would last eight weeks, every day, including Sundays, after going well into the night, and it ruined my health for a long time afterwards. Meetings were held at least every other day with representatives from the Brown House who attended in different combinations. Their leader was the "Führer of Reich Physicians," Dr. Gerhard Wagner. The others were Ministerial Counselor Sommer, Dr. Bartels [the "Deputy to the Führer of Reich Physicians"], and Prof. Dr. Gross.[36] Every one of them had a fanatical hatred of the Jews. *At that time* I had brought Stuckart around to the point where he shared almost all of my views about the problems we had to contend with. Without him, I would have soon been thrust aside as a "mere" civil servant. Dr. Globke, who headed the Civil Registry Desk, was often present, and his well-thought-out advice was of great help. Essentially, however, Stuckart and I led the struggle. During this period, Stuckart put aside all other official business. Pfundtner often inquired as to how things stood. Frick did not display the least interest, despite all our efforts to involve him. From the very beginning, in other words, we found ourselves at a tactical disadvantage: the Party representatives constantly had "the ear of the Führer," while we did not. Our written drafts to him had very little effect because Hitler did not read correspondence from ministries. Sometimes we could use Lammers to convey our arguments to Hitler. He also heard about them from Gerhard Wagner, whenever Wagner complained about our obstinacy and was compelled to repeat our views, however much he perverted them.

At the very first meeting, the Party representatives put forth their maximum demands: first and foremost, to extend the definition of Jew to include one-quarter Jews (at first Wagner had demanded the inclusion of one-eighth Jews); the compulsory dissolution of mixed marriages; the sterilization of those with various degrees [of Jewishness], etc. We fought back with an array of collected arguments. We could not use the only genuine argument, that of basic humanity or even of "positive Christianity" which I, once only, rubbed under Wagner's nose. In Hitler's eyes, this claim would have disqualified us as complete fools whom he no longer needed to take seriously. As the discussion began to focus more and more on the struggle surrounding half Jews, I worked with the following points, each calculated to influence Nazi thinking:

1. the completely loyal attitude of half Jews up until that point, which would come to an end abruptly;
2. the completely unnecessary creation of a large number of new opponents, each of half Germanic heredity and thus particularly

dangerous because this would predestine them to be leaders in
the struggle on the opposing side;

3. each half Jew had one Aryan parent, thus Aryan relatives and
    friends, all of whom would inevitably turn into enemies of the
    state;
4. the loss of approximately two divisions of soldiers;
5. the comment [the sentence about the laws applying to full Jews
    only] in the German news agency just published at Hitler's com-
    mand;
6. the unfavorable new impression being made abroad;
7. the tearing apart of additional families if the half Jew, male or fe-
    male, is married, especially if children (one-quarter Jews) are in-
    volved;
8. weakening the German economy through the loss of many addi-
    tional hard-working skilled employees;
9. reduced emigration chances;
10. particularly acute emotional burdens because almost all the half
    Jews felt themselves to be German only, thus leading to
11. a jump in the suicide rate;
12. the small number of half Jews, who would otherwise, over the
    course of two generations, be fully and harmlessly absorbed into
    the body of the German people; in other words, the senseless-
    ness of the entire risk.

I still have in my possession the full 15 original pages I prepared at this
time. There is no need to repeat it word for word here. It is preserved in
the form of a position statement to a memorandum along with the
Party's counter proposal. Because these are missing, the document can
no longer be understood by itself. I have merely listed the 12 arguments
contained in it.

On 29 September 1935, Stuckart was ordered to be in Munich where
Hitler wanted to announce and explain his decision on the position of
half Jews to a closed assembly of Party heads, *Reichsleiter* and *Gauleiter,* in
the city hall. Stuckart took me along. The "Deputy of the Führer of Reich
Physicians," Dr. Bartels, met us in the hotel and triumphantly informed
us, "The Führer has pushed the half Jews over to the side of the Jews." I
was very depressed. With some difficulty I was allowed as a civilian to
take a seat at the back of the room. The high and mighty gentlemen in
their impudent uniforms sprawled about the tables in unbelievable pos-

tures, even during the ensuing speech. I was struck by the ostentatious signs of boredom and tedium as they sat through the speech (naturally a two-hour one). One could not call it listening. First Hitler summarized the entire *Mischling* problem, and he did that with a breadth and grasp of knowledge that amazed me. I was gratified to hear that our arguments had, after all, found their way to him and left their mark. I was even more amazed when he ended this part of the speech with the remark that some points still needed clarification, something the Party and the Ministry of the Interior would need to work out in the near future. Nothing then had been decided; either Bartels had lied to us or Hitler had changed his mind shortly before or during the speech, which, given his hysterical manner, was entirely possible. He then went on to other topics and, giving way to the intoxication of his own words, told the assembly things that a statesman should never breathe to another person up until the decisive moment, and unmistakably alluded (in September 1935!) to the fact that one day he would wage war—he needed about 4 years for the right moment. That, at least, is precisely how things happened. My memory of this is exact because Hitler's remark hit me like a bolt of lightening, and I tried to spread word of it as far as possible, despite Hess's imposition of the strictest silence on the assembly.

So the negotiations continued on and on throughout October 1935 in an eternal round of small and sometimes large meetings. Schacht[37] and Gürtner also attended one of them. On several occasions those from the Party tried to bluff us by claiming that they had just come from the Führer and that he had decided this or that in their favor. Once Stuckart had unmasked this swindle by placing a telephone call to Lammers, they abandoned that tactic. It is impossible and probably superfluous to present each phase of this struggle. As I recall, about 30 different drafts to each of the two decrees were proposed and then disputed. Stuckart repeatedly warned me to be more careful in my choice of words, especially with Wagner, who had already deemed me a friend of the Jews. He admonished me not to insist too stubbornly on all of my goals in order not to jeopardize what we had already achieved. He was right. Finally an agreement was reached on the versions of the two "First Decrees," promulgated on 14 November 1935. Their inconsistent and convoluted formulation reflects all the signs of a bad compromise. But even in this form they were a great, though not complete, success. First and foremost, *the large majority of half Jews had been prevented from being equated with the Jews;* this success, anchored in a decree signed by Hitler himself, allowed me to hold onto it until the end. Imagine what the Nuremberg Laws would have looked like, and particularly these decrees, if they had been worked out by obsequious ladder-climbers at the beck and call of the Party. Shortly after the decrees were signed I suffered a complete nervous collapse and was unable to work for three months. The same thing happened to Stuckart one month later.

At that time there was no way of knowing the precise *number* of half Jews who had thus been excluded from the legal definition of [a] Jew. Estimates varied widely between two extremes, something that was irksome to my purposes since a more exact number might have placed new arguments at my disposal. During the preparations for the *May 1939 Census*, at a meeting in the Reich Office of Statistics, I was able to effect the removal of "racial classification" questions from the general census survey. Instead, racial questions were listed in a separate short questionnaire, which everyone, not only those in question, was to return sealed in the envelope provided. The goal was to prevent janitors and others from poking their noses into the matter and to alleviate the embarrassment of those in question from constantly being forced to document their ancestry, thereby improving the reliability of this information. There was also a printed guarantee that the information was to serve statistical purposes only. Soon after the census, of course, two or three *Gauleiter*, including Streicher and Sprenger,[38] demanded that all of the "short questionnaires" from their district be turned over to them, something, however, we were able to prevent. While the outbreak of war soon thereafter precluded the general evaluation of the census, I saw to it that at least the "short questionnaires" were evaluated in the Reich Office of Statistics. I turned over the photocopy of the main overview to the Denazification Commission[39] Berlin-Zehlendorf. I still possess the photocopy of the results from the individual states, districts, and cities.

Of particular interest here is the *number of half Jews in the census area*, that is the Old Reich[40] plus Austria, which was *72,738*. The actual number, however, had it not been for successful camouflaging, was likely to have been higher. In addition to this number there were also the half Jews of the Niemen River [Memelland], the Sudeten, the Protectorate, and the Netherlands, since the Nuremberg legislation had expressly been introduced into all these areas. It is thus no exaggeration to assume that the correct *number totaled more than 100,000*.

In the midst of the struggles during the fall of 1935, Gerhard Wagner, acting on behalf of Rudolf Hess,[41] twice pressed me to accept *the position of a Ministerial Director in the Brown House ("Deputy of the Führer").* Because I was clear in my mind about not wanting to sell my soul to the devil (these were the words I used at the time when talking with my friends), the offer put me in a dangerous dilemma. There was hardly a plausible excuse to explain why one would reject such a career move without arousing suspicion. The position then offered to me was later elevated to the rank of Secretary of State and held by a man named Klopfer. The first time Wagner made me the offer was in September 1935 in the presence of Dr. Bartels, his assistant. We were in the hallway of the Ministry on the way to one of the countless meetings in Stuckart's office. Fortunately the sudden appearance of other gentlemen spared me the necessity of giving an immediate answer. The next time I had already prepared a number of excuses, although Wagner probably never quite believed them. I think I am not off target in seeing this "most honored offer" as one of the not unusual attempts to silence an uncomfortable opponent. This was a way of making an opponent one did not yet want to liquidate serve one's own purposes, a technique that was Himmler's practice. Himmler would use honors to ensnare for the SS every official, economic expert, or artist who began to attract attention, including Stuckart.

It was around this time that Ministerial Director Dr. Gütt, head of the Health Department in the RMdI, started *repeatedly to urge me to join the SS* and painted the great advantages this would have for my future. I managed to get out of this equally dangerous situation by saying that I had also received similar "honored offers" from the SA, whom I could not afford to offend, and therefore would need some time to consider things. I mentioned also how terribly overworked I was at the office, and thus slowly brought the subject to a close.

Throughout my entire period of service in the Hitler regime, I was constantly faced with the offer, or rather pressure, to take on Party offices in my local group. It was easiest to escape this by asking Stuckart or Pfundtner to certify the fact that I was overburdened with official business.

How Some Provisions of the
"First Decrees" Took a Wrong Turn

Early on, Hitler had stopped consulting the Reich Cabinet on matters concerning legislation. Wave after wave of laws kept the German people and the world from catching their breath (which was, in fact, the intent).

The more the pace of legislative production quickened, the simpler became the forms it took, thereby satisfying the impatience of Hitler, who wanted any orders he gave to be implemented immediately. For that reason, the number and importance of "decrees," based on whatever kind of general authorization, soon far outweighed legislation in the more formal sense. Henceforth, the simplest and most convenient means for bringing into being legal measures against the Jews took the form of a "Supplementary Decree" attached to the Reich Citizenship Law. This law's Paragraph 3 provided the basis for ordering a range of directives for its implementation and extension. Had such an authorization not been available in this form, another would have been found, something that was constantly happening in all other possible areas.

Sometimes things proceeded in an even more primitive fashion. The next step after the "First Decrees" had been signed was that Hitler, about two weeks later, gave the verbal order not to implement Paragraph 6 of the First Supplementary Decree to the Reich Citizenship Law which he had just signed and which I had toiled so hard get included. (Paragraph 6 annulled all the Aryan Paragraphs that had so quickly permeated the by-laws and statutes of almost every private club in Germany and thus inflicted so much suffering on "non-Aryans"). At the time he signed the decrees, Hitler had not realized what Paragraph 6 contained. To be sure, this paragraph remained on the books, but its application was secretly forbidden; one was not even allowed to talk about it. Countless personal petitions and inquiries from official agencies regarding the application of Paragraph 6 poured in to the Ministry; demands for the Ministry to decide on these matters became stormier and stormier. In the midst of this "legislative" process, I was called upon to draft the most ridiculous oracular decisions and distribute convoluted information, both of which generated great vexation, some of it directed against my own person.

The immediate effect of the two "First Decrees" was that I was showered with petitions aimed at gaining exemptions from their oppressive provisions. In particular, there was a surge of petitions from female domestic servants seeking exemptions from their forced dismissal as employees in Jewish households. These petitions came in in such a flood that we had to set up a special office in a conference room and add about six employees to work through them all, sift out the hardship cases, and attend to the writing of thousands of letters of refusal.

Procedures concerning the *approval of marriages between first-degree Mischlinge* [those with two Jewish grandparents] and Aryans, as provided for in Paragraph 3 of the First Supplementary Decree to the Blood Protection Law, soon took a particularly ugly turn. From the very beginning it was clear that securing approval for such marriages would encounter the greatest difficulties because the Office of the Deputy of the Führer, i.e., the Brown House in Munich, had to give its consent. On 23 December 1935, the RMdI and the Deputy of the Führer published a joint instruction for implementing Paragraph 3. It ordered investigations into the furthermost corners of the private lives of the two engaged parties and called for position statements from various offices of the Party and State. It also established as the ultimate decision-making body a "Reich Committee for Marriage Approvals," re-baptized three weeks later as the "Reich Committee for the Protection of German Blood." This change in name alone indicated the direction things were taking. Whereas the supplementary decree mentioned above introduced extremely detailed and formal order to the procedure, it did not in itself turn the Reich Committee into a viable functioning body. Stuckart belonged to the Committee (in fact, I believe he was its chairman) and tried to reach agreement on a number of guidelines for decision making within the Committee. His lack of success on this was matched by his inability to push through, against the will of the Party representatives, some particularly difficult cases that had [been] selected for the first meetings. The main opponent was Dr. Blome.[42] According to verbal statements made by Dr. Stuckart, the Committee's few meetings were filled with agitation and fury. The Party used the fact that none of the marriages in question could be performed without its approval to effect lasting success in an area it had long sought to dominate, most recently in the consultations concerning Paragraph 3: that is to exercise a consistent veto upon marriages of half Jews [to those of German blood]. After a few meetings, as I recall 4 or 5, Stuckart realized the futility of continuing this procedure and the Reich Committee came to a standstill, or, to put it in more precise terms, it ceased to exist, although this fact was never made public. In order to "facilitate matters," the petitions were henceforth to be dealt with via the usual administrative channels, which for me meant that I had to check and judge the petitions at my Desk in order to pass them on to the Deputy of the Führer, represented by Herr Blome in Berlin, who then simply rejected them. Because his veto was a given, I was even authorized to pronounce the rejection myself without asking this Party office. All the files bulged with documentation and extensive investigations. For its part, the Health Department of the RMdI under Ministerial Director Dr. Gütt, insisted on drafting a long questionnaire for the Health Authorities and ordered the inclusion of pictures—in a completely naked state if possible. The marriage petitioners had to subject themselves to weeks and weeks of humiliating inquiries by various offices into all aspects of their lives, only to receive the inevitable flat-out no, which an agent of the Deputy of the Führer would pronounce without bothering to look at the case. Nevertheless I did not desist from sending a constant stream of such cases with my endorsement, and to pester and persist in a few particularly hard cases. In a very few instances I was able, with help from the Reich Chancellery, to win an approval; if I recall correctly it was not more than a dozen, a piteous success in the face of the mass of petitions. I cannot name the total number, but I did find notes in my reference files dating from two separate periods. Between 1 January and 22 May 1940 alone, the number of the new petitions for approval of such marriages was 1,630, with another 739 from 1 January to 13 March of the following year. From the end of 1935 to the point when the procedure was discontinued (Circular Ordinance of the RMdI of 3 March 1942), there were several thousand petitions. Throughout this entire period, our side did not cease to present fundamentally differing opinions. They were always shots in the dark as it was impossible to prompt Frick into action. In addition, once he acquired his house in Kampfenhausen on Starnberger See, something that probably happened shortly before the beginning of the war, Frick withdrew from all such tasks for more than half of each year. From spring until fall, even during the war, he was to be reached only by means of written proposals. These were sent to him, as I recall, daily, together with the other files from his ministry, by special airplane. Even before this time, however, attempts to prod him into some kind of action had repeatedly failed, even when the proposals were presented to him as urgent, or pitched in an unusual manner. I will present here the draft of one such proposal I made to Frick on the marriage issue. This was at a time when I still believed I could push through some kind of fundamental improvement. The draft is not dated, but it is from 1936 or 1937. I no longer know what prompted it. Presumably he sent on to me a letter that had been addressed to him personally from an acquaintance who was requesting changes of some sort. This sort of thing happened from time to time.

> The final position of the Deputy of the Führer is clear. Repeated talks with him do not promise any success and are absolutely doomed to failure unless you yourself, Herr Minister, would conduct such talks personally.
>
> At this moment, in my opinion, the only possible route and also the one most urgently necessary is to report to the Führer and Reich Chancellor the

true scope and details of the matter without mincing words, and this must be done by the office most directly responsible. The presentation must not be limited to theoretical arguments, but must instead highlight particularly dramatic cases (cases and decisions to: Pickart, Sondheim, Gumpert, Kohler).

The intention of the Herr Minister not to bother the Führer and Reich Chancellor with these matters has already been thwarted. The Führer has already been bothered, and namely by an *inappropriate* office, with the result, that it is now next to impossible to proceed in the matter.

Additional "Supplementary Decrees to the Reich Citizenship Law" followed over the next several years, most of which were worked out by other departments of the Ministry of the Interior or by other Ministries. Our staff, that is Department I, prepared the "Ninth Decree," which clarified a special case of Austrian marriage law in favor of first-degree *Mischlinge*. The Twelfth and then the Thirteenth Decrees, the most vicious of all (turning the Jews over to the arbitrary control of the police), were enacted after my removal from the Ministry.

The purpose of these pages is not to present the full story of Hitler's Jewish legislation, but rather to record my own noteworthy experiences and observations. I will therefore refrain from listing or mentioning proceedings or legal provisions about which I know little more than what was published in the *Reichsgesetzblatt* [Reich Legal Gazette].

Privileged Mixed Marriages

Before I turn from the topics discussed above, I would like to go into one more matter even though some aspects of it will take us to events that take place quite a bit later.

After succeeding in keeping the vast majority of half Jews from being categorized as Jews, my efforts turned to extracting something for an even more endangered group. The official hatred of Jews had reached the boiling point. It was made clear from the outset that, at best, only partial success was possible. I set to work in the usual way, through remarks in meetings, through written drafts, through talking with colleagues in other departments and ministries, through constant consultations with my closest allies, Dr. Globke in our section and Dr. Killy in the Reich Chancellery. The purpose of all this was to lay the groundwork for providing preferential treatment for full Jews of both sexes who were, or had been, married to those of "German blood." As had been the case with half Jews, my efforts were unrelenting and painstaking. My main argument ran as follows: Because the Führer had decided that half Jews were not to be treated as Jews, and one-quarter Jews were to be treated significantly better than half Jews, it was impossible to treat a family member who was a fully Jewish parent or grandparent, as a complete pariah without jeopardizing the family as a whole. I buttressed this with an array of examples, including the allusion to a "possible" war, the planning of which was fully under way and which I had heard announced by Hitler himself. At this point, my opponents in the Party and the SS were more vicious and dangerous to me personally than my opponents from the time of the Nuremberg Laws. They included above all Dr. Blome and Senior Government Counselor Reischauer from the Party Chancellery, Government Counselor Neifeind, and, as the driving force, the ice-cold fanatic SS *Sturmbannführer* Eichmann,[43] both *[sic]* from the Reich Main Security Office headed by Heydrich. Things for me were complicated by the fact that Stuckart, ensnared by Himmler in the SS, had slowly started to disassociate himself from me. I was no longer a *persona grata*, but he never completely withdrew his support. My tendencies gradually began to get on his nerves, and he probably feared that he would wind up in an awkward position because of my doings. At our last major exchange on 21 December 1941, he made this clear enough (see below). The Party representatives countered my efforts with the argument that if the mixed marriage situation seemed so impossible to me, then the half Jews would simply have to lose their special position and be counted as Jews. A particularly nasty thrust in this direction, perfidiously contrived, actually came to pass in August 1941 (see below).

I had gradually won over my own superiors to the plan for mixed marriages. In addition I had also effected this same kind of exemption in the Reich Ministry of Economics with the unpublished ordinance regarding the "Delivery of jewels and precious metals taken from Jewish property." The main thing however was to embed a provision for the fundamental exemption [of Jewish spouses] in a Jewish Law signed, if at all possible, by Hitler himself. It would then be easier for me to proceed on the basis of such a precedent. The opportunity presented itself in 1939. In his "Four Year Plan"[44] office, Goering had worked out a "Law Regarding Rental Conditions for Jews," the main goal of which was gradually to separate the Jews from the rest of the population and to house them in special Jewish buildings or Jewish quarters. I was able to intervene and, in this special case, I had a relatively easy time of it with my arguments in favor of Jews living in mixed marriages: I pointed out that one could not also stick the Aryan spouse [of a Jew] and the half Jewish children into a ghetto. The Party (which the "Four Year Plan" had naturally asked for its position) finally gave in, but not without negotiating some concessions. Goering then obtained Hitler's fundamental approval. This is how the concept of "privileged mixed marriages" took shape. The only such marriages excluded from this designation were those in which the children were regarded as Jews, as well as those which were childless and in which the husband was the Jewish spouse. At any rate, according to Paragraph 7 of this law of 30 April 1939, the *great majority of all mixed marriages were privileged* and freed from its oppressive provisions.

Once this breach had been opened, I was able to push through the exception for privileged mixed marriages in all subsequent provisions concerning the persecution of the Jews. Since the Ministry of the Interior was no longer "involved" when any given agency or instrumentality produced a "Jewish Law," it was necessary to devote constant attention in order to be on hand at the right moment.

Through my continuous care and intervention, the privileged mixed marriages were freed from the following series of provisions:

1. Ordinance of the Reich Minister of Economics of 1 March 1939, regarding the delivery of jewels and precious metal taken from Jewish property;
2. Law regarding rental conditions for Jews (see above)
3. Tenth Decree to the Reich Citizenship Law of 4 July 1939 (forced creation of the *Reichsvereinigung der Juden* or the Reich Association of Jews);[45]
4. Ordinance of the Reich Minister of Economics from 23 January 1940 (no clothing ration cards for Jews);
5. Ordinance of the Minister of Nutrition of 11 March 1940 (restricted food ration cards for Jews);
6. Decree about war damages by Jews of 20 July 1941 (exclusion of Jews from reparation payments for property damage);
7. Ordinance of the Reich Minister of Finance about the Jewish social welfare payment of 20 September 1941;
8. Implementation decree about the employment of Jews of 31 October 1941 (exclusion of Jews from labor law rights);

9. Police decree about the Jewish star of 1 November 1941 [the date should be 1 September 1941];
10. Order about personal damages suffered by Jews of 22 November 1941 (exclusion of Jews from reparations for bodily and health-related damages).

Most important of all, however, was a success scored outside of "legislation." This was to prevail upon Himmler, via Stuckart, to order the police *to exempt Jewish men and women living in privileged mixed marriages from the deportations to Auschwitz and other sites of murder; that is, to keep them from immediate death.*

The number of Jews in privileged mixed marriages is not certain. I estimate it to be *around 20,000* for the entire area subject to German racial laws, including the Protectorate, Holland, and other occupied areas. This estimate is probably not an exaggeration since the number of half Jews in the entire area under Hitler's laws was definitely more than 100,000 (see above).

The 1938 Pogrom and Spread of Persecution

Starting in 1933, the actual Jewish Question was driven forward by the Party, at first still in "consultation" with the RMdI. By 1936, as Himmler, with his SS, began working his way into the foremost ranks of the powerful, one could begin to sense something that became fully evident shortly thereafter: his usurpation of the "treatment of the Jewish Question," for himself. For their part, the Party and the Propaganda Ministry had to exert themselves to create new measures in the hope of staying in the race with him. My Desk in the RMdI was gradually pushed aside until I was no longer informed or even consulted as a token courtesy. Everything that had to do with terror against the Jews themselves took place without prior knowledge of officials in the RMdI, from the milder to the most satanic degrees. Like every other inhabitant of Berlin, we found out about such things through the press or by word of mouth. Himmler and Heydrich gathered into their own hands more and more powers of every kind, not only in the Jewish Question. In this battle Stuckart lost more and more ground.

Then came the first large pogrom of 8 and 9 November 1938, euphemistically called "*Kristallnacht.*"[46] It not only hinted at the worst to come—the worst actually transpired, especially in Vienna. Here again we had no clue as to what would happen.

Goering issued invitations to a meeting scheduled for the 12th [of November] in his Air Force Ministry.[47] Stuckart took me along. A number of ministers, including Frick, had already arrived, as well as an enormous number of participants who completely filled the places around the horseshoe-shaped table in the large conference hall. There were probably well over 100 people. To Goering's left sat the Reich Minister of Economics Funk, with Frick two or three chairs down from him. Stuckart sat some distance away at the long end of the table, and I was even further away so that with the frequent noisy interruptions in the hall, I did not hear everything that was said. I took notes throughout the several hours of the meeting, which I still have and will cite at points in the following. The essence of Goering's opening speech was outrage over what had happened, but not about the desecration to houses of worship and the theft, mistreatment, and murder of human beings. Essentially he said: "I have had enough of demonstrations. The damages affect me and the insurance companies . . . One might just as well set fire to raw materials . . . The damages do not affect the Jews. But I do not want the insurance companies to have to pay for the damages, except for those that carry reinsurance abroad." With typical National Socialist logic the meeting then turned to consideration of how one could make sure that the entire material damages visited upon the Jews, although the result of excesses organized by the Party, would fall on their shoulders alone, and how one could impose upon them the harshest punishment possible for what had happened. Goering did most of the talking and addressed questions to this or that higher-ranking participant. The most urgent matter in his eyes was the Aryanization of the economy, and he outlined a plan according to the following scheme:

Aryanization of the economy by means of expropriation in return for compensation. The following is to be entered into the Reich account book: "The Jew has to live from the interest."

A.   One must begin with [the Aryanization of] the *smaller shops*, so as to make it a measure "for the German people." The Minister of Economics is to decide to what extent these are to be shut down. The closings are to proceed in the order of their importance. The state will estimate the amount to be paid, meaning that it is to be low. More difficult is the question as to who should acquire the businesses. "I have seen shocking things: chauffeurs and *Gauleiter* have acquired millions in property!" The Aryan purchaser must be from the business branch in question; Party comrades who meet these conditions are to be preferred over other applicants.

B.   As for *factories*, first check if their Aryanization is necessary. If yes, then they must be Aryanized quickly; otherwise they will be scrapped because non-essential factories are already being transformed into essential ones, and this demands space.

C.   From this point on *foreign Jews* are to be treated ruthlessly [*ohne Rücksicht*].

D.   *Jewish export*, Jewish representatives abroad. "No obstacles shall be placed in the way of exports. If the Jew can be of service to us, then no obstacles shall be placed in his way. I want to harness the Jew to our purposes. Replacing the Jew in export businesses shall proceed *only* in accord with economic considerations."

E.   Jews must pay for damages, not the insurance companies. *Only the courts* shall pronounce *expropriations* for Aryanization purposes. "Instructions on this point will come *solely from me*." "Jewelry, jewels, and art have been smuggled out of the country in the most shameless manner." At border crossings, bodily searches are necessary without exception, likewise the total expropriation of items of this sort."

Goering had, in other words, worked out the formula by which Jewish property was in fact to become future Aryan property. The ensuing discussion proceeded in accord with this idea.

He then pursued this line of thinking; the expropriated Jew will become idle. "Once the Jew is idle, there will be nothing but trouble." We are therefore not allowed to keep the Jews among us. They must leave the country. A trust company must be set up abroad in order to convey the Jews from Germany without using hard currency. It is also necessary to continue stripping Jews of their citizenship on the basis of the 1933 law. Until this goal is achieved, we cannot avoid the *ghetto*; it is the only effective means of combating the rumor-mongering of the Jews.

Then followed questions and suggestions from the assembly, which Goering either answered or accepted or rejected. I noted the following:

- There are still 50–60,000 Jewish owners of agricultural property; these properties are to be Aryanized forthwith, but are not to be sold; they will become state domains.
- Schools for retraining Jews in agricultural professions will continue operations because they prepare for and encourage Jewish emigration.

- Individual villas are to be transferred to Aryans, but not to the Party or to state offices.
- Autos are to be taken away from Jews.
- Titles [e.g., Dr.] are to be rescinded whenever possible.
- The question of how to treat Jews who are not independent businessmen, but rather salaried employees or workers, is a dilemma because they are indispensable. One could perhaps turn others, the superfluous ones, over to work crews.

Once again Heydrich pleaded for a special Jewish badge.

Despite everything that had been said, the proceedings took a surprising turn when Goering declared in a particularly shrill and strident voice: *"As penalty for the crime"* German Jewry would have to pay a "contribution" [he meant a fine] of RM 1 billion. He pointed out that the remaining population would be making the "Thank-Offering for Greater Germany," in which the Jews would not participate.

Goebbels then addressed the assembly and outlined his plans.

1. The Berlin Synagogue Community will cover the damages in Berlin.
2. All synagogues in Germany, of which 191 had burned down, must be torn down by the Jews themselves.
3. Jews are prohibited from going to the theater, movies, variety shows, and circuses. One could perhaps set up special Jewish movie theaters.
4. Jews must be kept out of public view. For railway travel, one should set up special passenger cars and sleeping compartments for them. They are to be prohibited from going to German spas and recreational areas, except perhaps for those to be set aside for them, and kept from "setting foot in the German forest" and on public grounds.
5. Jewish children must leave German schools.

As for the amount of damages, a question of the liveliest interest to Goering, he turned the floor over to an insurance specialist named Hilgert[48] or something like that. Hilgert informed us that the glass damages alone, especially plate glass, amounted to 6 million marks. Three million of that had to be paid abroad, particularly to Belgium, to purchase new panes. It would take half a year, he said, for Belgium to produce the amount of plate glass necessary for replacement. The trickiest question would be how to calculate the damages to Aryan property owners who had rented their stores to Jews. The largest case of damages involved the Jeweler Markgraf on Unter den Linden,[49] from whom jewels valued at 1.7 million marks had been stolen and whose damages were fully covered by insurance.

At this point Goering, turning to the two men he was addressing, flared up and shouted in his sharpest commanding tone: "Daluege! Heydrich! You two have to get those jewels back to me! Search the Hitler Youth!" (Literally word for word. At that time Daluege was "Chief of the Order Police," Heydrich "Chief of the Security Police.") This demand was reiterated when someone mentioned how many furs had been stolen.

The speaker for the insurance companies went on to say how important it was to them not to be prevented from fulfilling their legal obligations to pay the policy-holders. Heydrich interjected: They should pay, but the payments should be confiscated. Goering made clear that any confiscations must benefit the Finance Ministry, not the insurance companies.

The insurance representative then informed the assembly that the damages from the two days were more than double their average annual damage. Any calculation would be chaff in the wind since it involved damages of 25 million. Heydrich interjected that he estimated the damages at 100 million. Daluege then asked who was to pay for the missing goods that Aryans and foreigners had given to Jewish businesses on commission.

In conclusion Goering said that the small insurance companies should be allowed to go bankrupt if they could not cover such damages. "I will ask the Führer to order that the destruction of businesses be met with draconian punishment, regardless of who was the perpetrator or instigator."

As the assembly was getting ready to break up and we were all already standing, Stuckart called me over and dictated the following radio message to the Reich Governors and Regional Presidents:

Herewith I prohibit any independent action against the Jews, particularly in the economic sector. Should any future damages result from measures initiated by the offices under your jurisdiction, I will hold you, Herr Reich Governor, Herr Regional President, personally responsible. General Field Marshal Goering will determine all necessary measures centrally.

Signed *Frick.*

Because Stuckart did not have time to drive me to our Ministry at the Königsplatz, he ordered that I relay the message to the Ministry's teleprint office via telephone from Post Office 9 at Potsdamer Station, using an imaginary file number, something that later became the source of some confusion. The place from which I called was only 2 km from the Ministry where everything could have been taken care of properly in a few minutes.

About one week later a meeting was held in the RMdI, chaired by Frick and attended by Reich Minister Funk, Berlin Police Superintendent Count Helldorf,[50] all the Regional Presidents, and others. Frick read a speech that had been prepared for him, which again emphasized that occurrences similar to *Kristallnacht* needed to be prevented. It was and remained an empty gesture since neither Frick nor the Reich Governors had any real power: under Himmler, the police had long since become independent. Count Helldorf, however, was already a member of the "Resistance" (Goerdeler Circle).

One of my lasting impressions of this meeting is how Funk, bloated and pale, with a blasé expression and resigned tone, leaned far back in his armchair and uttered a few insolent, gruff words in his Berlin dialect about the "bankrupt mess" he had to administrate. And that was only 1938.

Immediately following the meeting in the Air Force Ministry, indeed some of it that same day, "legislation" started to roll out of offices of the Four Year Plan and Reich Ministry of Economics. Its aim was the utter exclusion of Jews from economic life and the seizure of whatever remaining property they might have had.

The legislation began on 12 November 1938 with three decrees by Goering, starting with the "Decree Regarding Penalty Payment by Jews who are German Subjects," which ordered them to pay a "contribution" of 1 billion Reichsmarks to the German Reich. Its preamble read: "Jewry's hostile attitude towards the German people and Reich, which does not shy from cowardly deeds of murder, demands resolute defense and harsh penalty. I thus decree . . . ." There was also the "Decree Regarding the Restoration of the Streets in Front of Jewish-owned Shops and Businesses," which imposed the repair costs on Jews who owned the businesses and buildings in question; and the "Decree to Remove the Jews from German Economic Life," which prohibited Jews from all economic activity as of 1 January the following year.

The legal measures in the economic sector, which had already gotten under way that summer with the "Third Supplementary Decree to the Reich Citizenship Law" of 14 June 1938, became ever stricter, a process that continued far into the war years, until the Jews were stripped of every last right in all areas of life.

The Beginning of Forced Emigration

That same year, 1938, forced emigration in closed transports was organized by the Reich Security Main Office (Heydrich). We were informed of the plans (in excerpts) only after everything was already underway. In March 1939 Stuckart sent me to Vienna for a few days in order to gather more information. There things had gotten underway on a large scale, directed by one of the most sinister men of the SD, *Sturmbannführer Eichmann*. He led me through all the offices he had established for emigration. The main office was in the Rothschildpalais, once the Belvedere Palace of Prinz Eugen.[51] The splendid old rooms and the corridors of the various offices through which the emigrants had to pass were crowded with Jewish people who had left, or wanted, to leave. I did not have the courage to approach any of them because I too felt myself to be under Eichmann's surveillance. Eichmann himself was polite, even studiously attentive, but one constantly sensed his icy resolution. In the overfilled corridors, women pulled their children aside in horror as soon as they saw Eichmann, who casually passed by as though along an empty street, shoving aside all the waiting human unfortunates. I followed in his wake, receiving the same looks as he did, and felt miserable enough. Eichmann also took me to the office of the synagogue community in Leopoldstadt,[52] where he had announced my visit in my official capacity from the Ministry of the Interior. Upon my arrival I saw a number of Jews seated on several chairs where they had clearly been waiting for me for hours on end. As we entered, they immediately jumped up; they were the persons charged with various matters of the Vienna synagogue community. Eichmann rapidly pointed out each by name, told me with equal rapidity which area they would report on; they then immediately droned through their information like trained animals. The expression of a justifiable mortal fear could be read in each face. I asked some of them about their profession and private circumstances, whereby I felt foolish beyond words because I too felt under Eichmann's surveillance. He could not, however, prevent me from looking at the register of the Vienna synagogue community. I was particularly interested in the death register for 1938. I leafed through the pages slowly, feigning indifference. Each day contained a few entries. On 8, 9, and 10 November 1938, however, the deaths covered many pages. Although no mention was given to murder, "suicide by jumping out of the window" was the cause of death listed for a frightfully large number of people during these days; other kinds of suicide were also mentioned. Eichmann stood behind me the entire time I was turning the pages. I knew as little then as I do now about whether he was involved in this murderous work. To judge by his behavior and person, though, I have very little reason to doubt it. He had in any event approved of everything that happened. Next to Heydrich, his boss, Eichmann was the most powerful embodiment of the satanic principle I could directly observe from my level. Like everyone else who lived at that time, I could view Hitler, the highest of them all, only from a distance, and Himmler was a scoundrel but no demon. Someone once told me from what he said was first-hand experience that even as a schoolboy Himmler was known as a tattletale and informer, feared and avoided.

The War Years

As had been the case since 1933, Department I of the RMdI, with its narrowly defined jurisdiction in matters related to the "Jewish Question," turned out to be fully inadequate in achieving anything whatsoever against the efforts of the Party. The Ministry was simply "passed over," as the Party called it. Only in the *"Mischling* Question" and in the matter of the "privileged mixed marriages" did we in Dept. I go beyond our formal jurisdiction in the area of "Racial Law." It took painstaking effort to conquer and hold onto these bastions of resistance against the loudly proclaimed goals of the Party. With the outbreak of war, believing in some prospect of success, I thought the moment had come to attempt to classify not only one-quarter Jews, but also half Jews in the *same category* as Aryans.

Stuckart agreed to a verbal suggestion I made but felt that we would jeopardize the entire plan from the outset by suggesting the suspension of all restrictions on half Jews. We should, he said, limit ourselves to half Jews who were serving as front-line soldiers in the current war or had done so in the War of 1914–18.

For similar reasons, a sentence about easing restrictions on the so-called *"Geltungsjuden"*[53] had to be deleted. I still have the memorandum I prepared for the meeting, according to which I made the following points: since the Nuremberg Laws, everyday practice had shown that the stipulation that automatically stamped a half Jew as a Jew because of membership to the Jewish religious community was mistaken. Formal religious affiliation did not always point to inner conviction. The sources of such an error, as I listed them, were: "1. Indifference toward the registered religion; 2. Moral reservations in memory of deceased ancestors; 3. Lack of knowledge about the legal provisions for leaving the Jewish religious community (very different across the states of the Old Reich and prohibited by an 1858 law in the *Ostmark* and Sudeten district for anyone between the ages 7 and 14)." My suggestion was to reclassify as first-degree *Mischlinge* the "*Geltungsjuden*" who had left the Jewish religious community by 30 April 1939.

I sketched in pencil a draft for a "Decree by the Führer and Reich Chancellor" and read it aloud to Stuckart. He felt it was advisable to add another restriction, i.e., to continue the marriage provisions even for front-line soldiers. Concurrently, Department II (civil service law and personal data) prepared the draft for a Führer Decree to grant political amnesty to former members of the disbanded political parties and to former Free Masons. I prevailed upon the official responsible for the draft to include a provision on "Jewish *Mischlinge*." When the draft from Department II was discussed in our offices, I had to work out, as a counter proposal, the draft from Department I, which was already more watered down. These proceedings played themselves out beginning on 6 September and continuing through the following days. The drafts ran into immediate Party opposition and had to be set aside, after which they took a permanent back seat to the welter of legislation prompted by the war. My repeated urgings were unsuccessful. The stormy triumph in Poland tipped the scales in favor of the plan's opponents, who maintained that "we do not need it."

In the meetings held during the first days of the war, the Party and "Security Police" (*Sicherheitspolizei*) again suggested other measures, but for the time being these stayed within relatively narrow boundaries. Former Jewish doctors, who had been banned from practicing medicine by the Fourth Supplementary Decree to the Reich Citizenship Law of 25 July 1938, and former Jewish orthodontists, dentists, and pharmacists (banned from practice by the Eighth Supplementary Decree of 17 January 1939), were to be assigned to practice in prisoner of war camps and concentration camps. The idea was to free up persons of "German blood" in these professions to take care of the German population, which, once the Jewish doctors had been banned, was starting to suffer from the critical shortage of doctors.

Furthermore, a radio decree was supposed to order measures to make it impossible for Jews to receive foreign broadcasts. Ministerial Director Schmidt-Leonhard of the Propaganda Ministry attacked this issue with great zeal and held one meeting after the other. The notes I presented to Stuckart from 14 September 1939 read as follows:

Yesterday afternoon the Propaganda Ministry ([Min.Dir.] Schmidt-Leonhard) issued an invitation per telephone to a meeting at 5 P.M. in order to discuss a draft proposal for the Council of Ministers. I am enclosing the draft of the decree about the seizure of radios from Jews as it emerged at the end of the discussion. The Propaganda Ministry will be sending over a new version.

As explanation we were told that the troops, military hospitals, other hospitals, NSV [the Nazi Party's Welfare Agency] etc., needed more radios than could be produced by industry. One therefore wants to confiscate the radios from the Jews, a measure that also has the advantage of cheapness. It was also said that this was the most effective way of preventing Jews from listening to foreign broadcasts. The number of such radios is estimated to be 50,000 at most. In my opinion, this estimate is about three times too high.

I made the following reservations from the standpoint of Dept. I:

1. Extending the decree to the Protectorate [of Bohemia and Moravia][54] means that the position of the Reich Protector must be heard. I informed Senior Govt. Counselor Volkhardt in Prague about this over the telephone; he will relay his position as soon as possible.
2. In my opinion, the decree needs to add an exception for the privileged mixed marriages for it to be consistent with the new practice. It is not clear why a wife of German blood who is married to a Jew who, for example, has been drafted into a work crew, should not listen to news and announcements on German radio with her children (first-degree *Mischlinge*). The same holds for the Jewish wife and the children of a man of German blood who has been drafted into military service. The additional instruction would read as follows:

Paragraph

The instructions of Paragraph 1 apply to Jews living in mixed marriages with spouses of German blood only if:
a. the Jewish partner is a man and there are no offspring from the marriage, or
b. the offspring are regarded as Jews.

The head of the negotiations, Schmidt-Leonhard, as well as the *Parteigenosse* [Party Comrade] Schmidt expressed their adamant opposition to

such a provision. The decree's brevity, ran their basic argument, should not be
interfered with. They also argued that the exception might enable a Jewish
person to listen not only to the German, but also to the foreign news service. I
stuck to my position. The representatives of the *Reichsführer* SS and the
Gestapo Headquarters left their position open and agreed to send it over soon
in writing. Schmidt-Leonhard insisted that the matter was extremely pressing.
Please send instructions with regard to the privileged mixed marriages.

By this point Heydrich had pushed himself to the forefront to head the
persecution of the Jews. Because he had the police in hand, he could carry
out his notions with lightning speed. Officially, by this point, the RMdI had
little more than a ridiculous role to play since it was constantly chasing after the Reich Main Security Office with a "please inform us" every time
something terrible occurred. Naturally I was the one who received such as-
signments and I had to be content if Eichmann, to whom I was henceforth
to turn in all such questions, subsequently gave me at least somewhat detailed information. This I then wrote up and presented to Pfundtner via
Stuckart; Pfundter passed it on to Frick. Once each of them had made a
marginal note, perhaps an exclamation point, that he had read it, the matter was closed as far as the RMdI was concerned. Hardly any of the gentlemen still dared to turn directly to Heydrich, or even Himmler, with the request for information, even though the police were technically subordinate
to the RMdI. Himmler's official designation was "*Reichsführer* SS and Head
of the German Police in the Reich Ministry of the Interior."

This is how things stood in November 1940 when the first forced deportation of Jews from Baden and the Palatinate was directed into the unoccupied territory of southern France.

Pfundter, the "Leading Secretary of State,"[55] got wind of this and gave
me the assignment of investigating the matter. I presented the results to
him in the following note:

> In response to the information that Jews are being deported from Baden
> and the Saar Palatinate, I contacted the *Sonderdienststelle* [Special Action
> Chief] of the Gestapo, *Obersturmbannführer*[56] Eichmann. On 4 November,
> Eichmann dispatched his colleague *Sturmführer* Günther, who provided me
> with the following information from his files:
> The deportation proceeds from a command by the Führer, contained in an
> order of the RFSS [Himmler] of 30 September 1940. A copy of this order has
> been promised to Dept. I.

The order was carried out on 22 and 23 October. A total of 6504 Jews in 9 trains were removed from the two districts from the train stations Constance, Heidelberg, Pforzheim, Mannheim, and Ludwigshafen via Chalons s.M. to the demarcation line. There the French, who apparently assumed they were in transit to Portugal, allowed their entry into unoccupied territory.[57] Nothing else is known about their further whereabouts.

The Jews were allowed to take 50 kg of baggage and 100 RM. The Regional Presidents have been charged to act as trustees for the administration and disposal of the property left behind. The Jews living in *mixed marriages* were left unmolested. There are no plans for further such deportations from other areas.

The case was thus over and done with for the RMdI.

The same thing happened during the first winter of the Russian war with the first forced deportations of German Jews to the East, beginning with those from Schneidemühl, then Stettin. According to rumors, many of them froze to death.

For a time, however, we did not receive any official word whatsoever, and so we ceased our questioning. The humiliation of the Ministry was complete. From this point on all that I learned was from private information and the London radio broadcasts.

The So-Called Final
Solution of the Jewish Question

In August 1941, the *"Mischlinge"* and "mixed marriages" faced the gravest danger since 1935. By some dark and forever secretive means, Heydrich had obtained for himself from Goering (not Hitler!) a "Commission for the Final Solution of the Jewish Question."[58] Despite all my efforts, I never succeeded in actually getting a look at this commission. At one point Eichmann read it aloud to my assistant, Govt. Counselor Feldscher, but he never actually turned it over to him. It is an open question as to whether this was the actual commission. On about three different occasions Eichmann agreed to send me a photocopy, but never did. From this point on, however, Heydrich, Eichmann, Neifeind, etc., all referred to this "Commission for the Final Solution to the Jewish Question." We were never told what in fact the Final Solution was. On one occasion, 3 December 1940, Eichmann informed me verbally about a short-term and long-term plan for a "Final Solution," which was to culminate in the expulsion to Madagascar of the Jews "from the entire European space dominated by Germany." I presented the following note to the Ministry:

Note

regarding the plans of the Reich Security Main Office for the final solution of the Jewish Question in the German Empire.

On 3 December 1940 *Sturmbannführer* Eichmann, who is preparing and carrying out the deportation of the Jews, gave me the following verbal explanation:

The deportation of the Jews is being carried out according to several short-term plans and one long-term plan. He told me that all the material he has prepared on this matter has been turned over to *Gruppenführer* Heydrich for his signature. He assumes that Heydrich will send the plans to Dept. I and the other parties involved after he has finished examining them.

The *short-term plans* involve only the displacement of Jews where it is necessary to make living space available for Germans returning to the Reich.[59] For this reason, by the end of December, about 3000 Jews will be deported from cities in East Prussia into the General Gouvernement[60] in order to make room for Germans from Lithuania. The General Gouveneur [Hans Frank] has agreed to this. Another 1700 Jews will follow later. The short-term plans should, however, be confined to only what is strictly necessary because the long-term plan will, in the foreseeable future, make everything else superfluous.

In the *long-term plan*, Jews from the entire European space dominated by Germany will be deported after the end of the war to *Madagascar* within the framework of a four- to five-year plan. This will involve around 6 million persons (including Gen. Gouv.). The island location will make it easier to control this large number of persons. Only non-German ships will be used for relocation purposes. The Jews should be productively employed once they arrive. The assets left behind here are to serve as their means to purchase the necessary machines and tools for agriculture and trade, which will be delivered to them in M. There production and trade will be directed by organizations under German supervision. Purely German and purely Jewish enterprises will be created. The *central foreign trading post* and *the bank of issue and transfer* will be German. All foreign trade will pass through the hands of the former; the Jews are not to maintain any direct business relations with the rest of the world. The bank [of issue and transfer] will regulate the monetary system and subtract payments for the delivered goods from the Jewish assets remaining in the Reich. The *working bank* and the *production organizations* (similar to cooperatives) will be Jewish. The Jewish institutions regulate only the island's internal commerce.

The "Final Solution" of 1941, however, was to be of a different sort—after all, Hitler did not yet have Madagascar—but Eichmann said only that the plans were not yet ready, but would "of course" be sent to us. Of course that never happened. From that moment on I myself never again doubted what sort of new final solution this involved. For his part, Stuckart found out more details at the notorious "Wannsee Conference"[61] in January 1942 at the latest, about which I did not hear anything specific until two years after the war during the Nuremberg Trials. But now the Party, represented by Senior Govt. Counselor Reischauer, and the SS-SD, represented by Eichmann, made an underhanded attempt to include the half Jews and Jews living in mixed marriages in this "Final Solution," and to use my name in support. Reischauer and Eichmann passed the balls back and forth into each other's hands. Someone on Eichmann's staff called at the last minute to tell me about a meeting scheduled for 13 August 1941 in Eichmann's office to discuss a plan by Seiss-Inquart[62] to introduce the blood protection measures into the Netherlands. I was asked to send over "one of my own men." I thus asked my sole assistant, Govt. Counselor Feldscher, to attend. He returned in outrage from the meeting, which had been a gross attempt to take us unawares. It had included the attempt to introduce a *"new definition of the Jew"* into *all* the occupied territories, to keep me personally away from the meeting, to intimidate Feldscher, and to prevail upon him to declare his assent. Feldscher's presence of mind had frustrated the matter. A new meeting was called, which I attended myself. Eichmann had invited "his men," about 10 strong in SD uniform, some criminal faces among them, who sat in a circle around me, with Eichmann, and Reischauer, fixing me with their hostile glances. It was not a very pleasant situation for me, as was its calculated effect. I was supposed to be "softened up" or nailed down for holding to a faulty ideology. I was able to avoid the one as well as the other by posing a stream of questions to Eichmann and Reischauer, both of whom liked to hear themselves talk. In this way the meeting lasted an acceptable length without it seeming as if I were guilty of breaking it off too soon. I myself used a great many words to say very little of substance. I first needed, I said, to process the abundance of impressive new material and then present the results in my Ministry. I could not as yet formulate a precise position, but would "of course" submit it to them as quickly as possible. Eichmann's office was the former Jewish Lodge on Kurfürstenstrasse. He loved the ghostly impression the rooms made in light of their present use. I was happy when I left the building that day a free man. To my recollection, I returned only once to a meeting on the same subject, that being after Stuckart had signed a counter draft from my pen to Heydrich. The document contained my oft mentioned arguments. Copies were sent to the Party Chancellery and to Lammers.[63] Eichmann did not attempt to stage the new meeting as he had the earlier one. The discussion was tough but unsensational, and both Eichmann and Reischauer started to get bored. The failure to reach a conclusion became palpable. In order to save face, Eichmann called another meeting, to which I again sent Feldscher. He reported to me that it had merely rehashed the same old worked over matters. Eichmann and Reischauer's action thus came to naught.

A renewed attack in the same direction followed in September 1942. I went to Stuckart and declared that I had no intention of facing the music alone again in this matter, especially because there was little chance it would have any effect. The two of us were already in the midst of an open breach of trust because I had applied for a transfer from the Ministry, of which I will speak below. Finally Stuckart declared himself ready to take what was for him no easy step, i.e., sending a so-called "private correspondence" to Himmler personally. I wrote up the draft he had sketched out in a few words. The letter fulfilled its purpose. I handed over the first carbon copy of the draft to the *Military Tribunal in Nuremberg*, which allowed me to make a copy. At Stuckart's Nuremberg Trial, the details of his proposals for the sterilization of half Jews at first weighed heavily against him.[64] He was said to have already made them at the beginning of the year in the secret meeting at Wannsee called by Heydrich and mentioned above. When Stuckart gave me the instructions for this draft, he told me that [against hard-line opponents] one could only succeed on the main point by offering the opponents a compromise; carrying out this compromise [sterilization of half Jews] was, however, illusory since technical reasons would necessarily forestall sterilization until after the end of the war. One could then wait and see; he then hoped for a noble gesture. In the judgment of the Military Tribunal IV, this letter weighed heavily in Stuckart's favor (p. 28062 and /63 of the judgment).

The letter [from Stuckart to Himmler] read:

Most honorable *Reichsführer*!

Once again there are rumors circulating among the population about an imminent discriminatory step to be taken against the first-degree Jewish *Mischlinge*. They claim that first-degree *Mischlinge* will soon wear the Jewish star and likewise be classified as Jews in all other matters, particularly as far as evacuation goes. As I can tell from countless inquiries, great anxiety is sweeping through not only the *Mischlinge* themselves, but also through wider circles of the population. Again and again questions are raised about whether at the present time there are not more important problems to solve, and about why this particular group of persons is being made the object of persecution at all.

Ever since my duties have come to encompass the solution of the *Mischling* question, it has always been my aim to find a reasonable balance between the extent of the actual danger and the severity of measures that situation requires. Several times over the last few months, I have detailed my position, both verbally and in writing, in response to the discussion prompted by *Gruppenführer* Heydrich about the Final Solution of the Jewish Question. Since his death has for the time being interrupted the discussion, and since these new rumors have now unleashed another wave of tension, I believe that the time has come to present a summary of my views on the future treatment of first-degree *Mischlinge*. My goal is to bring about a solution that does full justice to the interests of the German people, but that also settles this issue as conclusively and quickly as possible, without causing what would, at the present time, be a superfluous and damaging animosity and agitated discussion. I believe it is imperative for German interests to avoid the latter. These constitute, as I hardly need to emphasize, my sole overriding purpose for considering the entire problem and my suggestions for solving it.

It is absolutely clear that Jewish blood, including that carried by half Jews, is to be removed first from the German and, thereafter, from the European blood stream. *Gruppenführer* Heydrich wanted to achieve this goal by treating the first-degree *Mischlinge* like Jews in every way, first and foremost by evacuating them. The only exceptions were to be those married to persons of German blood if the marriage involved children (second-degree *Mischlinge*); in addition, those "for whom the highest authorities of the Party and the State have granted exemptions for special reasons." The *Mischlinge* exempted from evacuation should, however, be sterilized.

This deportation plan is deceptive in that it seems to solve the problem easily, quickly, and effectively. It would however entail a series of consequences that would be disadvantageous to the German people and thus demand serious deliberation.

1. I will start with the most important and, in my opinion, decisive counter argument: with the deportation of the half Jews, we would not only relinquish their half Germanic genetic make-up—we would for all practical purposes be turning it over to Germany's opponents. Experience shows this genetic make-up, when combined with the intelligence and the good education most half Jews have, would make them born leaders in the camp of our opponents. Anyone who studies the leading classes of the European Nations and States, including those not determined by the Nordic element, finds again and again that a part of them is half German. Here, in support of this observation, I point only to the disproportionately large number of French military leaders and statesmen. The present should draw the necessary conclusions from the dangerous mistakes of the past.

2. Most half Jews as defined by blood have already been sorted out by the definition of Jew in the Nuremberg legislation. To the extent that certain features demonstrate their tendency to Jewry, they are, even today, regarded as full Jews. So seen, a considerable portion of the half Jews has already been cast off.

3. Even the deportation plan deems it unavoidable that some groups of half Jews should be spared. This leads, then, to a further sorting above and beyond that listed under 2, and would result in a situation wherein some members of the same family, with the same genetic make-up, for no intrinsic or, in any event, for no biological reason, would be left behind while others would be deported (for example siblings, where one is married to a person of German blood and has children from the marriage, while the others are not married or are married but have no children).

4. Given what they have experienced over the last years, first-degree *Mischlinge* have, to a not inconsiderable extent, made great efforts to advance German interests. Apart from their contribution to the war economy, I may be allowed to point out that the Führer, outside the regular reprieves, has re-classified a large number of active officers and officer wives who were first-degree *Mischlinge* so as to make them equal to persons of German blood. The Führer has also held out this same prospect after the war for the large number of first-degree *Mischlinge* who remained in the army, should they continue to prove themselves. (The number of the latter decisions today amounts to around 260, including,

however, some second-degree *Mischlinge*.) These selective measures, confined to relatively few numbers, show that the half Jew, to the extent that he is productive in the German Reich, does not necessarily and always need to have only negative value for the German people.

5.   In this connection the fact cannot be overlooked that the Führer has, to date, classified around 340 *Geltungsjuden* as first-degree *Mischlinge*. It would not be in accord with the intent of a decision by the Führer to once again, through a general regulation, stamp these persons as Jews. It would, on the other hand, contradict the most elementary precepts of racial policy to exempt in the future these persons from the new measures, while at the same time assigning to Jewry *other* half Jews who have never been regarded as Jews.

6.   Also, one should not underestimate the importance of psychological-political repercussions. Every half Jew has a full Aryan ancestral clan with branches of relatives and friends. For the Aryan clan of ancestors and relatives, the treatment of relatives of first-degree *Mischlinge* as Jews would create a very great emotional burden.

7.   Given the situation on the job market, the removal [of half Jews] from [their] existing employment would have to be seen as very difficult for the foreseeable future.

For these reasons, I cannot view the deportation plan as fitting German interest in its rightly understood sense. Because this primarily involves a racial biological problem, I would like to have preference given to the *sterilization* of half Jews and, consequently, their natural extinction. Neither deportation nor sterilization could, of course, be undertaken until the current conditions have changed, presumably after the end of the war. With sterilization, the *Mischling* problem will resolve itself within a generation. I should like to point out that the deportation plan does not solve the problem with one blow, because this suggestion also foresees certain categories of half Jews remaining in the Reich. The reason why there is no single satisfactory solution is due to the fact that one cannot purge the mistakes and sins of the last 200 years overnight if one wants to avoid compounding old mistakes with new ones.

One should not overestimate the amount of administrative work involved in letting time take care of the problem, since the position of first-degree *Mischlinge* has already been regulated in all the important areas. Once sterilization is implemented, there would no longer be any real need to reexamine this question. The implementation of sterilization involves a *single* round of administrative work and is thus simpler than the implementation of deportation which would have to be preceded by a process of selection. Sterilization cannot, of course, be linked to any extensive investigative procedures. The only essential requisite is the fact of half Jewishness by blood. According to the population census of 1939, the Reich area at that time contained around 64,000 persons in the legal classification of first-degree *Mischlinge*. This number is calculated by subtracting the half Jews who are regarded as Jews *(Geltungsjuden)* from the total number of half Jews (72,000). In my opinion, there is no need for sterilization of women over 45 and men over 60, or of persons who are infertile for other reasons. This would reduce the number of persons by about 25,000 *Mischlinge*, leaving 39,000 persons for sterilization.

Another possible addition to the plan would be to allow the *Mischling* who had been suggested for sterilization to elect deportation instead.

Because the problem of German-Jewish mixed marriages is so closely linked to the *Mischling* problem, these two problems should, where possible, be given a uniform and conclusive regulation. Instead of the compulsory dissolution of mixed marriages by law, which is one of the solutions suggested, I believe it would be sufficient and more practical to permit divorce if proceedings were initiated by the spouse of German blood or by the state attorney.

In summary, I would like to note that I do not concede the same degree of significance to the *Mischling* problem that others are currently attributing to it (and the related problem of mixed marriages). If this question were not repeatedly pushed to the forefront, more or less artificially, it would be long forgotten simply because of its intrinsic insignificance for the German people and Reich. Nor has anyone been able to convince me of an actual serious danger posed by a part of the population that in the summer of 1939 comprised less than one thousandth of the total Reich population and whose conduct is completely unobtrusive and loyal. This is a population which legally and otherwise stays within the confines of its extraordinarily limited situation, a situation, moreover, which precludes any influence whatsoever on public life. To my mind, given the abundance of constantly new and real problems brought on by the war, one does our cause a great disservice by stirring up problems solved long ago. This creates not only superfluous work, but also generates additional anxiety in broad circles of the population, and all this without a single, sound reason.

In any event, this anxiety must be dispelled. Its effects run particularly deep precisely because once racial politics have started to encroach upon the area of the *Mischling* question, there is no recognizable limit, natural or logical, to its continued spread to ever remoter *Mischling* degrees. This is also the reason why these limits should be drawn as clearly, quickly, and conclusively as possible—and those should end where the racial mixture ceases to pose a serious danger to the German people and Reich.

Although I do not ascribe any vital significance to the *Mischling* question itself as far as the war is concerned, the constant rekindling of action surrounding it is another matter. It is necessary, as I see it, to put a stop to this completely, and the sooner the better. At the first available opportunity, I would thus like to present the matter to the Führer in order to bring about a conclusive decision, or a decision that will allow the problem to settle down at least until the war is over. I would value it most highly if you, Herr *Reichsführer*, would inform me as to your views in this matter.

These arguments made an impression on Himmler who was, after all, somewhat more tolerant on precisely this issue. He intervened and, among other things, directed the police to exempt from deportation the Jewish men and women living in mixed marriages.

Soon thereafter I finally received the transfer I had requested, so I cannot report anything else about the final developments from first-hand knowledge. But one thing remains clear, that until the very end, the first-degree *Mischlinge* and Jews in mixed marriages were essentially spared from the fate of the Jews.

The Jewish Star

The notion of identifying Jews with some sort of outward marking also has a longer prehistory. The demand had repeatedly been made long before [it actually happened], including the one by Heydrich in the meeting of 12 November 1938 following the first large pogrom (p. [000] above). At a *Gauleiter* meeting on 6 December 1938, Hitler had spoken about this matter and decided against moving ahead with the identifying marker. In a letter to Frick in February 1940, *Gauleiter* Mutschmann (Saxony) again demanded the introduction of a Jewish badge. In my position statement regarding this demand, a copy of which I have before me, I wrote in conclusion: "The justification for the planned measure is extremely inadequate. If affairs were really in such a deplorable state that a legal remedy was unavoidable, it would have seemed more than reasonable to emphasize several actual examples in justification. I cannot avoid the impression that the suggestion is more truly the result of an effort to avoid being ignored in the handling of the Jewish Question."

In the end, the promoters of this plan pursued another path in order to present the Ministry of the Interior with a *fait accompli*. With one day's advance notice, the *Propaganda Ministry* invited us to a *meeting on 15 August 1941 about the identification question*. Stuckart sent me as representative and charged me with claiming jurisdiction in this matter for the Ministry of the Interior. As I entered the meeting hall, it was already filled with people, almost all of them in brown uniforms and, with few exceptions, unknown to me. One saw at once that this was no ministerial meeting in the usual style. Rather, Goebbels's Ministry had brought in a full force of Berlin Party officials and office-holders in order to ensure that the discussion would take the desired turn. Apparently these people had been told to arrive somewhat earlier, and so the only seat I could find was at the far end of a very long table. The entire swarm of uniformed and very nonchalant Nazis filled the table between me and the *Chairman, Secretary of State Gutterer*, something that made it almost completely impossible for me, the only opposing player at this meeting, to speak up. I am convinced, then as now, that this was the intention behind the whole arrangement. The atmosphere was that of a Party rally, and the meeting proceeded along those lines. In the following I quote from the memorandum which I presented to Minister Frick (via Stuckart and Pfundtner):

> There were about 40 participants, most of whom were unknown to me; nor were their official positions usually stated when they spoke.
>
> The chairman explained that a constant stream of military personnel on leave or being transferred from duty on the Eastern Front, officers and enlisted men alike, was coming to Reich Minister Dr. Goebbels and declaring that they could not understand how, given the monstrous impressions of the war experience in the East, one could still allow the Jews here at home so many liberties and be tolerant of their impudent behavior. The Propaganda Ministry was of the opinion that the Jews had not yet been set upon with real severity, and that immediate measures were necessary to dispel the ill humor among the front-line soldiers. Berlin's Jews are creating an inflammatory situation; those [Jewish landlords] who had taken in foreigners as subtenants are removing them from their apartments and replacing them with reliable Aryans as main tenants, but these in turn are keeping the foreigners as subtenants. Given the housing shortage, one should consider the idea of removing Jews from their apartments and placing them in barrack camps.
>
> As for shopping, he went on, the Jews, despite the shopping hours [set aside for them], are continuing to come into too much contact with the shop-

ping of the working population. Therefore one needs to create special Jewish shops. At the early fruit market in Werder, it has become evident that 40% of the worst hoarders were Jews. These, then, are responsible for the strawberry shortage in Berlin.

There are still 70,000 Jews in Berlin, stated Gutterer, with only 19,000 involved in producing something. One should comb through the others looking for those able to work and "cart off" the rest "to Russia." It is also necessary to assign Jews to special compartments in public transportation. The meat ration for non-workers should be reduced to 200 g; best would be to knock this ration off completely.

The basic precondition for carrying through all measures, however, is the outward *identification of the Jews.*

As to the question of identification, *Sturmbannführer* Eichmann, the Jewish expert from the Reich Security Main Office, stated that another petition to this effect had recently been directed to the Reich Marshal [Goering]. The latter had responded with the observation that this was for the Führer to decide. The Reich Security Main Office had therefore revised the petition; this will be sent to *Reichsleiter* Bormann so that he can present it to the Führer.

Still other suggestions were made by the assembly: Jews should be prohibited from entering air-raid shelters. Jewish consumer cooperatives should set up places for Jews to shop, or the goods should simply be given to the Reich Association of Jews *(Reichsvereinigung der Juden),* which should then see to the distribution of goods to individual households.

As to the housing question, the representative of *Generalbauinspektor* [Inspector General of Construction] Speer[65] stated: the Führer has designated the Jewish apartments to be held in reserve for the damaged apartments that are to be torn down after the war. It is therefore not feasible at this point to put new occupants into the apartments made available. At the moment Berlin needs another 160,000 apartments. There are only 19,000 Jewish apartments. In the first year after the war, moreover, 10,000 apartments in Berlin will be torn down, with the number to increase rapidly after that.

As to the question of evacuating the Jews from the Old Reich, *Sturmbannführer* Eichmann also announced that the Führer had rejected a petition by *Obergruppenführer* Heydrich for evacuations during the war; Heydrich had subsequently worked out a proposal aimed at the partial evacuation of larger cities.

Before the conclusion of the meeting, both the representative of the Four Year Plan, Senior Government Counselor Schmidt, and the undersigned pointed out that all measures related to the Jewish Question are to be presented to the Reich Marshal, and that Department I of the Reich Ministry of the Interior is in charge of all matters related to the Jewish Question; the Propaganda Ministry is responsible only for the propaganda aspect of this question. In his response, the chairman gave the assembly to understand that he fully recognizes this, but that it is the task of the Propaganda Ministry to become active when the popular mood—in this case, the mood of front-line soldiers—is aroused by certain events or a deplorable state of affairs; precisely because help is urgently necessary in this case, his Minister had decided to present the matter to the Führer, and therefore called this meeting at such short notice.

The intention here is clear: to use the above justification to give the Propaganda Ministry the most important leadership role in the Jewish Question; namely, to lead the discussion and examination of the necessity and practicality of anti-Jewish measures, and to use Reich Minister Dr. Goebbels' impending exclusive presentation to the Führer to push through the views of the Propaganda Ministry and, in this manner, to effect a *fait accompli.*

In the question of identifying Jews in the Old Reich, the same objective holds true for the Reich Security Main Office. This agency's earlier attempt to push through a similar petition by using the Reich Marshal, thereby circumventing the General Plenipotentiary of Administration, failed because the Reich Chancellery requested our position statement on the matter and subsequently refused to pass the petition on to the Reich Marshal. Now they have elected to approach the Führer via *Reichsleiter* Bormann, a path which, they believe, guarantees to exclude us and the Reich Chancellery. Without the offhand statements by *Sturmbannführer* Eichmann at this meeting, we would never have heard about the new plan.

Regarding the matter itself I would like to note the following: Should new general measures be ordered against the Jews, it is absolutely essential that Jews living in mixed marriages be exempted from them, first and foremost from the one requiring their outward identification. Otherwise the arrangements, constructed and maintained with such pains against the constant counter efforts of the Party, would be rendered practically worthless. During the war, the Führer has classified a number of half Jewish officers (and wives of officers) as being among those of German blood, and left them in active service; as of today he has allowed around 125 *Mischlinge* to hold senior positions in the *Wehrmacht*,[66] in part by classifying them to be among those of German blood, in part by holding out this prospect to them for after the war. Most recently, according to information by Ministerial Director Kritzinger, he has reactivated two former active officers who had been discharged as half Jews and declared them to be equal to those of German blood. Moreover, as Min. Dir. Kritzinger informed me verbally on the 16th of this month, he [still the *Führer*] does not approve the Party's plans to classify half Jews as Jews. He commissioned Reich Minister Dr. Lammers to write a letter to this effect to Prof. Dr. Gross because of the latter's lecture at the Frankfurt Conference (we are supposed to receive a copy of this letter). As matters stand, there should be no question of subjecting the fathers or mothers of such persons to the worst injuries and forcing them to appear with the Jewish Star in public, thus making it impossible for them to associate with their sons, particularly when in uniform or especially in officer uniform.

In response to my inquiry, the representative of the Four Year Plan informed me on 18 August that he presented the matter to Min. Dir. Gramsch, but has yet to receive any further instructions; he wants, he says, to keep me abreast of views in that quarter and any possible steps.

As far as the identification itself goes, I have refrained from contacting the Reich Security Main Office. On several occasions this office has been instructed or made aware, once even with the signature of the Herr Minister [Frick], that it is to involve us in all fundamental matters pertaining to the Jews. It can be assumed that once again this has not happened, that in fact a round-about path has been selected intentionally in order to make sure we are excluded. It would, I believe, be humiliating for me to request our involvement this time around. Because of the mixed marriages it would naturally be desirable for the petition itself to suggest an exception for them, and thus be mentioned in the decision by the Führer. However, this would mean that Department I had from the outset declared its agreement both with identifying the other Jews and likewise with the procedure that required seeking the path to a Führer decision by way of *Reichsleiter* Bormann.

Berlin, 18 August 1941

Signed *Loesener.*

On 20 August I submitted the following draft to the Minister:

Regarding the matter from the Propaganda Ministry, I just received a telephone call from the Desk of the personal assistant to Secretary of State Gutterer, informing me that Reich Minister Dr. Goebbels has already made his presentation to the *Führer,* and he has expressed his fundamental *agreement with identifying the Jews in the Old Reich* as preparation for all further measures. To begin with I have requested written confirmation of this information. This was promised to me, along with our involvement in carrying out both this and all other measures. Given these circumstances, it is at the present moment probably no longer appropriate for you, Herr Minister, to write to Reich Minister Dr. Goebbels with an explanation of how we understand our control in the Jewish Question. This would have been expedient only *before* the presentation to the Führer. Because Reich Minister Dr. Goebbels has brought about the decision with such speed, however, the appropriate moment for such a letter will probably not arise until the Propaganda Ministry approaches us about further measures.

Berlin, 20 August 1941
Signed Loesener.

Herr Secretary of State Pfundtner added the following note:

In my opinion, we must contact Minister Lammers and Reich Marshal Goering *as soon as possible* in order to determine the authenticity of the Führer's decision and to make sure of our control over the identification question etc.!

Signed Pfundtner 20 August

The Herr Minister agreed to this note.

I immediately drafted a letter from Minister Frick to Minister Lammers, which was then sent in this form. Goering received a copy with the request to inform us of his view. The letter read;

Dear *Parteigenosse* Lammers!

As my Desk for the Jewish Question was informed on 20 August per telephone from the Reich Ministry for Public Enlightenment and Propaganda [*Volksaufklärung und Propaganda*], the Führer has recently given his approval to the proposal by Reich Minister Dr. Goebbels that *Jews* throughout the entire Reich be identified by wearing an *external badge*. The necessary steps for carrying out this measure are to be undertaken forthwith. I have not yet received written notice. Because control over questions of racial law is handled by me, I request notice as soon as possible if a decision by the Führer has in fact been made to this effect.

At the same time I would like to point out the following:

Should a decision have been made regarding the identification of the Jews, it must not, under any circumstances, be applied to those who are living in a privileged mixed marriage. The precise provision of this definition is set forth in the enclosure appended to this letter. This privileging dates back to the preparations for the law about rental stipulations for Jews,[67] and came into being at the express decision of the Führer in response to the presentation of Herr Reich Marshal. In all measures directed against the Jews, those living in such mixed marriages have since been exempted from such measures. I include a list of these here. As justification, little more needs to be said than that identifying these Jews would invalidate the entire privilege granted in consideration of the spouse of German blood and the non-Jewish children. I do not think it amiss to assume that this does not correspond to the Führer's will. Here I am also thinking of the decisions of the Führer in a vast number of cases regarding petitions for clemency by first-degree *Mischlinge*, that is, sons from privileged mixed marriages. These decisions also affected Wehrmacht members with a wide range of rankings.

If the Jews living in privileged mixed marriages are not spared from identification, then the fathers or mothers of the soldiers and officers mentioned here would not only be subjected to every kind of injury, but it would also be virtually impossible for their sons to appear with their parents in public, or to associate with them in any other way.

Given these circumstances I request that you, as soon as at all possible, effect a decision by the Führer so that any identification order will not be extended to Jews living in privileged mixed marriages.

In addition, some passages in your letter to me dated 2 August 1940 Rk 10675 B give rise to the assumption that it would not be the intention of the Führer to subject another circle of Jewish persons to the most severe measures possible. I refer to the former Jewish civil servants who, because of their professional, political, and personal behavior, had been left in office until December 1935, because it had been determined that there was no reason to carry through the measures based on the Law for the Restoration of the Professional Civil Service. Whether this assumption of mine is still valid today, I leave to your examination and judgment.

In this connection I would like to direct your attention to one more point. On 21 August [1941] a representative from my Desk participated in a meeting held in the office of the Secret State Police [Gestapo], the subject of which was *the final solution of the Jewish Question*. Here the representative of the Party Chancellery, Senior Govt. Counselor Reischauer, mentioned a letter of *Reichsleiter* Bormann to *Gruppenführer* Heydrich, according to which the Führer is said to have announced that in the final solution of the Jewish Question the half Jews should, in principle, be classified with the Jews. This would, in other words, result in their deportation with all the attendant consequences such as the ripping apart of families, loss of property, and the like. Senior Govt. Counselor Reischauer did not allow the person from my Desk either to see the letter or agree to have a copy sent to us. If, on the other hand, I correctly understand your letter from 16 August 1941 Rk J 11 [secret] to Prof. Dr. Gross, a copy of which you sent to me, then the Führer does not in any way hold the viewpoint related by *Reichsleiter* Bormann. Given the current vehement pressure by the Party Chancellery and Reich Security Main Office to "sharpen" the definition of Jew as stated in the Nuremberg Laws by including the half Jews, it would be of utmost importance to me to know the actual standpoint of the Führer. In case you are unable to provide such information based on your own knowledge, I request that you consider the advisability and practicality of bringing about a rearticulation of the Führer's will.

The draft of this letter was hardly out the door on its way to the Minister [Lammers] when, on 24 August, I received a phone call from the Propaganda Ministry and was told that written information about the Führer's decision on the identification question would be sent to us, and that Gutterer wanted to convene another meeting in order to discuss preparations for the identification.

Shortly thereafter Govt. Counselor Neifeind from the Reich Security Main Office called to say that *he* had been commissioned to draft a police decree that, along with instructions about the identification itself, was also to contain provisions about districts from which Jews were banned and a prohibition upon their wearing of medals or decorations. I presented Stuckart with the following response, which he then signed:

Until now, the only news made available to the Reich Ministry of the Interior about a decision by the Führer that Jews throughout the Reich had to wear a badge on their clothing, was the information relayed by telephone from the office of Secretary of State Gutterer of the Propaganda Ministry to the Desk for Racial Affairs. In the meantime I have taken steps to acquire official knowledge of the Führer's decision via the regular channels. In response to my presentation, Herr Minister [Frick] has decided that, should this information prove correct, Dept. I of the RMdI will exercise control over the identification. This would primarily involve determining the circle of persons who would have to wear the badge, while your jurisdiction over all implementation measures would remain untouched. Our mutual close cooperation is a matter of course.

Throughout this whole business, one has to keep in mind that the "Main Office Security Police" [Gestapo], where this matter played itself out, was a department of the RMdI and thus formally subject to Frick's jurisdiction. In practice, of course, Heydrich did not pay the least regard to this circumstance, to say nothing of Himmler. Their success was programmed from the very beginning. The letters and steps of the RMdI remained without effect. Before our delaying tactics or counter measures described here could succeed, the "Department Heydrich" completed the "Police Decree on the Identification of Jews" with utmost dispatch, and published the decree in the 1 September edition of the *Reichsgesetzblatt*. By constantly myself working on Govt. Counselor Neifeind at his Desk, I was at least able to secure Paragraph 3 with its exception for the privileged mixed marriages.

Fortunately, because I did not lose the records, outlines, or carbon copies related to this sad chapter, it is possible to describe, at least for this one prominent case, the details of how "the Party dictates to the State"; how one worked when the "State" did not parry with the "Party"; and how lamentable was the role played by the Reich Ministry of the Interior because of the utter indolence of its Minister.

The Treatment of Individual Cases

Thus far, I have described the efforts and battles over a period of almost 10 years. Their goal was to influence legislation so that the largest possible number of people would, from the outset, be spared from the clutches of anti-Semitic legislation. Running parallel to this over the same period was the constant advice I dispensed to individuals who turned to me seeking help, both in and outside of my official capacity. I could help many of them, for example, by either pointing out hidden legal possibilities they had overlooked, or by providing information and assistance of a different kind. The latter presumed absolute mutual trust and secrecy. My assistance included warnings of planned or imminent legal or police measures, as well as about impending rulings and decisions. These warnings were often able to provide effective protection to the persecuted, but would not, to be sure, have withstood close scrutiny.

The number of those seeking advice shifted according to the severity of the waves of persecution, but it was always considerable. This was of course one of the reasons why I myself fell under suspicion since, to Party comrades, nothing would have been better than for me to have received absolutely no one of Jewish blood. "What do all those Jews always want with Loesener, when they come and sit for hours in his office?!" Remarks of this sort often came to my ears, and more than once the attempt was made to instruct the concierge to deny such visitors entry to the Ministry. Frequently I was sought out at home, later even at the Reich Administrative Court, by the persecuted or their friends and agents, not to mention my own Jewish or half Jewish friends and acquaintances with whom I never broke off personal relations. Even if I assume an average of only one visitor per day, this amounts to a quite imposing number over the course of years. In most cases, these warnings and counsels helped more than just the individual visitor, as he in turn promptly spread the word through a larger circle of persons affected. Some visitors, especially the pastors from both Churches [Protestant and Catholic], did not come on their own account but rather out of concern for a larger circle of community members and acquaintances. Likewise, the things attorneys learned from me benefited more than just one of their clients. Often the visitors came from great distance, many for example from Vienna. The trust, on my part as well, proved itself to be well placed. Not one of them ever betrayed me, some even informed me that they had been interrogated by the police as to what we had discussed and told me what they had said. The first of these was the Berlin attorney Plaut in the summer of 1935. Nor did I ever, as did so many other Desk-holders, receive a threatening letter or the like from the circles of those affected; the danger came from a different corner.

Because of the nature of the matter, I could not help many people seeking help. My *official* task in the Hitler State should have been to see to the strictest implementation of anti-Semitic legislation—in other words, to refuse help of any kind. With every act of assistance I was doing exactly the opposite of what was demanded by "Party and State." And given the overwhelming pitilessness of the persecution of the Jews, I soon ran into obstacles from every corner, obstacles not even the strongest human will could overcome.

Some of the ways in which I could shield the persecuted by means of written rulings and decisions were recorded in a sworn affidavit on my behalf by my most trusted colleague at that time, Counselor Culmsee, today an Administrative Official in the Federal Ministry of the Interior. Here is an excerpt from what he wrote:

I now come to a detailed description of Loesener's activities and how they were related to my particular area of work. My main responsibility with his

Desk was in handling cases of doubtful ancestry. The Ministry of the Interior was the final decision-making body for petitions requesting review of ancestry cases; in other words, it made the final determination about whether someone was to be regarded as Jew, *Mischling*, or of German blood. I was to prepare these decisions according to Loesener's instructions. In this area of work, Loesener also attempted to help victims of the Nuremberg Laws, about which I will relate the following.

All objections of the petitioner were investigated, even if they appeared to be threadbare. When they sought us out, we often gave the examinee or his legal representative the correct tip by asking if they perhaps had reason to believe that their documented Jewish ancestry did not accord with their biological ancestry; if they could, for example, prove that the critical Jewish ancestor was conceived by a person of German blood in an adulterous relationship, etc.

As a rule, this gave rise to lengthy petitions, genealogical examinations, and other complicated investigations. The goal of these was always to help the person in question as much as possible since, in the intervening period until the final decision, the general rule was not to apply the directives of the Nuremberg Laws to them. When at last it came time for a decision, we always made use of the principle *"in dubio pro reo"*[68] in the most generous sense and extracted the most favorable possible result for the examinee, often justified with much long-winded reasoning. Unfortunately, however, word of this practice soon got around. As a result, the Party Chancellery and Reich Security Main Office presented the Ministry of the Interior with entire lists of cases in which we were accused of doctoring decisions in favor of the examinee. It was often difficult to elude these dangerous attacks. What particularly infuriated these circles was, for example, the fact that despite their repeated nasty letters, we consistently continued to classify the illegitimate children of Jewish women, whenever there was any doubt as to the identity of the father, not as Jews, but as *Mischlinge*. We were also subject to repeated attacks because we frequently denied that membership in the Jewish religious community would, despite existing indications to the contrary, be the determining factor in assigning racial designations. In all these attacks, Loesener remained firm and did not change his practice. During our consultations, I frequently noticed his great inner satisfaction when given the opportunity to help a person in distress. Such cases, of course, involved the very existence of those in question; often it was a matter of life and death. Loesener's instructions were unequivocal: when judging the individual cases, it was assumed that my primary assumption was to help the person affected;

as far as he was concerned, it was not important to make an absolutely correct decision on the basis of the actual facts. Once the deportations of Jews to the East began, many of these victims turned to us for help. For these cases, Dr. Loesener came up with the following way out:

Whenever the question of full Jewish ancestry was in dispute, instructions were given to the appropriate authorities that the Reich Ministry of the Interior was investigating the ancestry of the person in question and that the examinee was not to be treated as Jew until the proceedings had been concluded. These certificates saved the lives of many people at the last second because the Gestapo then frequently refrained from deporting them.

In one area, however, I had been given at least one task that allowed me to intervene on behalf of the persecuted in a *legal* way. It was my responsibility to prepare the petitions for clemency directed to Hitler whenever they involved hardship cases falling under Paragraph 7 of the First Supplementary Decree to the Reich Citizenship Law: in other words, to the extent that a person sought, with valid reason, to be assigned to a more favorable racial classification than that allowed by the letter of the provisions—for example, to be classified not as [a] *Geltungsjude*, but as a first-degree *Mischling*. In many cases this involved first- or second-degree *Mischlinge* who sought to be classified with those of German blood—the so-called *"Gleichstellung." Until the very end, Hitler reserved such decisions for himself personally.* Countless petitions were condemned to failure from the outset. But where there was the least prospect of success, I attempted to obtain the necessary approval of the "Office of the Deputy of the Führer," later [after May 1941] called the "Party Chancellery," so that the request could proceed via Stuckart to the Reich Chancellery and be presented by Lammers to the "Führer." Some cases involved weeks and months of fighting with the Party.

According to a note from 10 September 1942 still in my possession, Hitler to that date had approved the requests for clemency to the following extent:

- 339 cases wherein the *Geltungsjuden* had been classified as first-degree *Mischlinge,*
- 258 cases wherein first-degree *Mischlinge* were admitted to military service and qualified as superior officers;
- 394 cases wherein the persons were classified as being of German blood
- 991 persons total

The End of My Work in the Ministry

Essentially, the preceding sections bring the purpose for this record to a close. In early 1943 I went on a long vacation and that spring moved to another position as judge in the Senate for Material War Damages of the Reich Administrative Court. What happened after 1942, in other words, no longer falls in the framework of this record.

However, because my personal life throughout these 10 years was closely tied to all the things described here, a short report about the end of my activity and subsequent personal fate seems to be relevant here.

Despite the tremendous strain on my physical and emotional strength, I maintained a tenacious hold on this area of work, because I was aware of the fact that without my efforts many highly endangered persons would, from the very beginning, have fallen victim to the general Jewish fate, and that they might still do so should I ever be removed from my office. It probably would have been better for me, then and still today, if I had sought a different position in the Ministry or one outside of it in some other area of administration. At times the ambiguity of my position, the condemnation to constant hypocrisy and webs of intrigue, the consciousness of being powerless to effect any real change, as well as the ever increasing threats of danger to my person turned life into true hell for me. Therefore, I must explain here why I held on to this vulnerable position: I arrived at this strange situation—one I had never aspired to—through circumstances which presented themselves to me, so to speak, by way of a series of most unlikely accidents that all happened on the one single day when I was supposed to receive the position as personal assistant to Secretary of State Reinhardt in the Ministry of Finance. I regarded this as providential, a commission from a higher authority to do that which I then proceeded to do.

But even here there was a point beyond which I could not remain in my position. Shortly before Christmas 1941, Govt. Counselor Feldscher came to my office and told me what a reliable acquaintance of his had related the day before: about being an eyewitness to the mass murder of German Jews near Riga, especially Jews from Berlin. It was so gruesome that I will refrain here from relating details. For the first time I learned that my worst fears for the fate of the deportees had come to pass—or better put, had been far exceeded. I sought an immediate and urgent conference with Stuckart. Although in the last several years, ever since my personal relations to him had become increasingly cooler, it had often taken weeks until I could attain an appointment with him, this time the determination in my voice secured the appointment for the following day. It was 21 December 1941. I reported to Stuckart what had come to my ears, and told him in no uncertain terms that although none of us had anything to do with these horrors, nonetheless, as a result of my official duties, my name was connected with the Jewish Question and because of my comments was known to broader circles. For this reason, the time had come when I could under no circumstances continue in this position, even though it was very painful to me thus to jeopardize what had been achieved. I asked Stuckart for immediate release from my Desk, but not to give me a different one either in his department or in the Ministry. It was very important to me, I said to him, that my change in position be made known as widely as possible, also to the outside world, and therefore requested that I be transferred out of the Ministry altogether because such changes were usually announced in the *Ministerialblatt* [Ministerial Newsletter]. At first Stuckart countered: "Don't you know that these things are happening on the highest orders?" I pointed to my breast and replied that there was a judge here who told me what I had to do. Stuckart, now likewise agitated, began to remonstrate with me. I was, he said, completely "cramped up" [*verkrampft*] because of my years of rejection of the Party's position and that I was "not dynamic enough" and had "held too rigidly to the Nuremberg Laws." This was why "the leadership in the Jewish Question" had "slipped further and further away from us." I had not understood, he continued, the need to maintain contact with the Party and the Reich Security Main Office, and thus had brought about the entire and constant friction and difficulties. This was, he added, the reason why I had not been promoted. The conference lasted about 50 minutes, but for all the tension the tone remained decent. At the end Stuckart stood up, shook my hand and said that if I could no longer live with my conscience, then he would immediately release me from my Desk and for the time being transfer it to my assistant Feldscher; the question as to where I would be transferred could not be decided overnight.

However, incessant pressing on my part was necessary before the promised discharge from my Desk and transfer became reality. Much against my will, I continued to conduct the most pressing official business and finally took an unusually long vacation. Afterwards I was finally detailed to the Office for War Damages of the Reich Administrative Court, namely as judge in the Senate for War Damages (March 1943).

During cross-examination as witness in the trial against Stuckart before the Military Tribunal in Nuremberg, the so-called "Wilhelmstrasse Trial," I repeated the above exchange with Dr. Stuckart in great detail.

My Arrest by the Gestapo

After everything I have recorded here, there is probably no need to explain in detail to anyone who is able to step back into this period just how much danger this put me in. At several points during discussions with Party representatives, I was labeled "friend of the Jews" and the like, always with the undertone of an already palpable threat. More than once I burned letters and other correspondence in my apartment because of the constantly growing mistrust of the Party and the possibility they would search my home.

February 1938 was a time of great anxiety for me. I received telephone calls from several persons unknown to me, who said they were from the "Security Service." They accused me of making statements hostile to the State, something I really had done, and demanded that I submit my letter of resignation and leave the Party by 28 February at twelve noon. Otherwise they would "do me in." Because it was in no way clear if the phone calls were "real" or not, I finally turned to Stuckart with the request that he make inquiries of Heydrich in the matter. This he willingly did and several hours later received the information that the SD had nothing whatsoever to do with it, and would in fact attempt to track down the persons behind it in order to put them into a concentration camp. I was happy that the investigation was not successful. Some time later I was able to establish on my own that the whole thing had been an act of revenge on the part of a married couple, relatives of mine, whom I had tried to convert from their fanaticism.

On 13 August 1944, I took Captain Gehre[69] from the OKW [High Command of the Armed Forces] and his wife, née Herpich, into my apartment for several days. He was a close friend of Count Stauffenberg[70] of the July assassination attempt and was himself deeply involved in the conspiracy and sought by the Gestapo, as was his wife. He had to leave his previous hiding place—with my personal and political friend Ministerial Counselor Münz—because of the threat of imminent discovery. Although I was not in on the secret preparations behind the assassination attempt, I was known as being trustworthy to those involved. On the third day the

Gehres left my house in order to move closer into the city where they thought themselves more secure.

During the night of 11 November, around 1:30 A.M., I was dragged out of bed and arrested by the Gestapo, led away in handcuffs and taken under guard to Berlin in the Albrechtstrasse.[71] The arrest took place in Torgau, where the Office for War Damages had been moved some time previously. During the fierce interrogation by the "Sonderkommission 20. Juli," Detective Superintendent Stawitzky confronted me with exact details. I realized that everything had come out and that it was senseless to deny it. The Gehres had been careless enough to show themselves on the street, had been recognized and were arrested. Frau Gehre had shot herself when the officials seized them, but her husband could only inflict a severe head wound upon himself. Interrogated while feverish from his wound, he bungled a statement and the police were thus able to find out the name of one of the persons who had hidden them. Given their interrogation methods, it was then no longer difficult to determine the rest.

Until the end of the war I was imprisoned in solitary confinement, in the B wing reserved for the "criminals of 20 July" in the Lehrter Strasse 5 prison [in Berlin], and awaited my trial before the *Volksgerichthof* [Peoples' Court].[72]

There I sat together with all the men who were known for their greater or lesser involvement in the events of 20 July. Most of them lost their lives by hanging or in the "wild" nighttime shootings while fleeing from the Gestapo. None of the remaining 36, with Reich Minister [retired] Andreas Hermes at the top, who on 25 April 1945 were released into the street fighting,[73] or "freedom," so to speak, knows why he too was not hauled out around 2 A.M. on that murderous night. For the next week I had to see myself through the last pocket of street fighting in Charlottenburg before I could start home to my family on 2 May, during which I was mugged three times.

During my imprisonment I had also received a letter dated 3 January 1945 and signed by Martin Bormann,[74] according to which he threw me out of the Party "for treason to the Führer and German people." This says very clearly what kind of judgment I would have had to expect.

As to my fate after the end of the war, which is still related to the fact that I had held the ranking of Ministerial Counselor in Berlin, I need to mention the following:

Two days after returning home to my family, a political friend of mine, Min. Counselor Dr. Conrad, today Municipal Counselor in West Berlin, took me to a high-level Russian Commando whom he had already contacted in the mistaken, but at that time excusable, opinion that the Russians were interested in finding German administrative officials in order to restore some kind of immediate order. I went through a very long interrogation, according to Russian methods, where no headway was made at all. Afterwards they kept me in prison for a time. Two of us they had released immediately, the others they kept until their wretched death, including my friend Münz and his friend Min. Counselor Grünewald whom he had also brought along. Me they turned over to a search commando. One morning, about eight days later, it suddenly pulled out and I was left behind unnoticed.

When the Americans, whom we had longingly awaited, occupied Zehlendorf, they brought me my third and longest imprisonment. On 14 August 1945 they took me, half-starved, into "Automatic Arrest" because of the civil service rank I had held. I essentially served my sentence in the camp Berlin-Lichterfelde-Süd. It lasted 14 months. I prefer to remain silent on the details.

After my release on 19 October 1946 I immediately applied for my denazification with the Denazification Commission Berlin-Zehlendorf (November 1946). A large number of exonerating documents that I had saved and presented to the Americans, first and foremost from my personal reference files, disappeared without a trace from the camp office. The proceeding was as exhaustive as it possibly could be. The commentator in charge of my case, Herr Erich Alenfeld, Berlin-Zehlendorf, was himself a Jew, according to the Nuremberg Laws, who had lived in a so-called privileged mixed marriage. Beyond this he was (and still is) very involved in church activities in Zehlendorf. For these two reasons I was already a "name" to him when my proceeding began, although he did not know me personally. The Commission proposed my full denazification to the Military Government. Thereafter, I was again questioned about various points by the American Special Branch. Afterwards I received my Denazification in August 1947 from the American Military Government in Berlin, along with the embossed seal "Rehabilitated" in my personal identification papers.

Despite all this, I have never again been able to gain an appointment in the civil service, neither in Berlin nor in West Germany. My attempts, before a Hessian Trial Tribunal, to be counted among the group of the exonerated have come to nothing. Although the appeal I submitted to contest my being counted among the "fellow travelers" *[Mitläufer]* had every prospect of success, it remained without effect because the Federal State of Hesse passed a law that the proceedings, regardless of their status, are to be suspended on 31 December 1949.

26 June 1950

Notes

1. At Nuremberg, Germany, between November 1945 and October 1946, the International Military Tribunal, composed of American, British, French, and Soviet judges, tried twenty-two high-ranking Nazi defendants, the most senior of whom was Hermann Goering.

2. Wilhelm Stuckart (1902–1945) joined the Reich Interior Ministry in March 1935. Although he held the rank of secretary of state (the highest civil service ranking), he remained technically subordinate to the sitting secretary of state, Hans Pfundtner.

3. The German initials for the National Socialist German Workers' Party, also called the Nazis.

4. Fritz Reinhardt (1895–1969), instrumental in helping the Nazis solve Germany's unemployment problem by way of work-creation projects.

5. The German initials for the Reich Interior Ministry and a common abbreviation.

6. Hans Pfundtner (1881–) became secretary of state in the Reich Interior Ministry in February 1933. A member of the conservative German National People's Party (DNVP), he joined the Nazi Party in March 1933.

7. The official designation for a Nazi Party member, meaning "Party Comrade."

8. On April 11, 1933, the Nazi government added a supplementary paragraph to its Law for the Restoration of the Professional Civil Service of April 7. This "Aryan Paragraph" defined as "non-Aryan" anyone with "one grandparent who adhered to the Jewish religion." The provision led to the dismissal of over 10,000 Jews in the civil service, including judges, prosecuting attorneys, medical doctors, patent attorneys, professors, and the like.

9. Members of the German National People's Party, the most conservative of the German political parties of the 1920s and early 1930s, were informally called "German Nationals."

10. Point 24 of the Nazi Party program promised vaguely that the party "stands for positive Christianity." The "Church Question" refers to conflicting views within the established German Protestant Church about how to respond to Nazism. A large group calling itself the "German Christians" eagerly supported the Nazis. A rival group, calling itself the "Confessing Church" rose up in protest against the German Christians and Nazism.

11. The color brown came to be associated with the Nazis because of the brown uniforms worn by the party's Storm Troopers (SA).

12. Wilhelm Frick (1887–1946) was from 1933 to 1943 the Nazi's Reich minister of the interior. A lawyer, he had been one of Hitler's earliest supporters. He was sentenced to death at Nuremberg in 1946.

13. Arthur Gütt (1891–). A racist medical doctor and closely connected to Hitler, who served as godfather to Gütt's son. In 1933, Gütt joined the Medical Affairs Department of the RMdI.

14. Leonardo Conti (1900–1945) was an ardent Nazi and anti-Semite who in 1929 was one of the cofounders of the League of National Socialist Medical Doctors. Upon Dr. Gerhard Wagner's death in 1939, he succeeded to the headship of the Nazi Association of Medical Doctors.

15. The informal name of Nazi Party headquarters in Munich and the stronghold of the party radicals Loesener identifies as his opponents.

16. Carl Goerdeler (1884–1945), the former mayor of Leipzig, became the center of a prominent group of conservatives who conspired to overthrow Hitler. He was captured by the Nazis after the spectacular failure of the conspirators to assassinate Hitler on July 20, 1944. He was hanged by the Nazis a few months before the war ended.

17. Literally, a "people's (race) community"—the Nazi vision of an ideal society from which racially impure elements had been removed and in which racially pure Aryans would exist in a setting of social fairness, prosperity, and contentment.

18. Loesener's reference is to the farcical elections of November 12, 1933, which produced a new *Reichstag* and included a plebiscite asking the German people whether they approved the government's recent decision to withdraw from the League of Nations and from the Geneva Disarmament Conference. The Nazis "won" all of the parliamentary seats, and 96 percent of the voters approved their decisions on the League and the Disarmament Conference.

19. After the dissolution of the unions on May 2, 1933, the Nazis created a German Labor Front (*Deutsche Arbeiterfront,* or *DAF*) to take their place. Its purpose was supposedly to help workers transcend their notions of class conflicts associated with communism and socialism.

20. The Enabling Act, passed by the *Reichstag* on March 23, 1933, authorized the Reich cabinet (Hitler) to enact legislation by decree. It established the "legal" basis for Hitler's dictatorship.

21. Leo Killy (1885–), since 1933 a ministerial counselor in the Reich Chancellery, was responsible for matters related to Jews and to Jewish *Mischlinge.* His wife was half Jewish. The Reich Chancellery was the official government executive office for affairs of state and government. It is to be distinguished from the Party Chancellery.

22. Hans Globke (1898–1973), although never a Nazi Party member, helped Hitler formulate the emergency legislation that gave him dictatorial powers. Together with Stuckart, he coauthored a commentary on the 1935 Nuremberg laws. After the war, in the 1950s, he became a controversial adviser to the West German chancellor, Konrad Adenauer.

23. Helmut Nicolai (1875–1955) was briefly (1945–1935) the director of Loesener's section in the RMdI. Nicolai had joined the Nazi Party in 1928 and served on its planning staff at party headquarters in Munich.

24. A law of September 15, 1935, by which the Nazi Party colors and its swastika became the official flag of the German Reich. It was one of the three so-called Nuremberg Laws of that date.

25. Franz Albrecht Medicus (1890–) was a career civil servant in the RMdI and a colleague of Loesener who served at the same rank as ministerial counselor.

26. Walter Sommer (1893–) was a party official, trained in law, at the party headquarters in Munich. He was known for his radical racist views.

27. The rabidly anti-Semitic Dr. Gerhard Wagner (1888–1939) joined the Nazi Party in 1924 and in 1929 was a cofounder (with Dr. Leonardo Conti) of the Association of National Socialist Physicians. He headed the Public Health Section at party headquarters and remained head until his death in 1939.

28. Frick had been the leader of the Nazi Party's Reichstag delegation since 1924. He remained in that position after the dissolution of all other parties in 1933.

29. Kurt Daluege (1897–1946) was a swashbuckling rowdy who joined the Nazis in 1926. In 1933, he was instrumental in transforming the old Prussian Political Police into the *Gestapo.*

30. Konstantin von Neurath (1873–1956) was the Reich foreign minister from 1932 until 1938, when he was replaced by Hitler's lackey Joachim von Ribbentrop. He was not a member of the Nazi Party.

31. Franz Gürtner (1881–1941), the Reich minister of justice from 1932 until his death in 1941. Although not a Nazi Party member, he sympathized with right-wing extremists and in 1923, as the Bavarian justice minister, had helped shield Hitler during his trial following the abortive Beer Hall Putsch.

32. Translatable as the "Racial People's Observer," the official newspaper of the Nazi Party.

33. Julius Streicher (1885–1946), a notorious Jew-baiter and since 1923 the publisher of *Der Stürmer,* a weekly paper devoted to vicious and pornographic anti-Semitism.

34. The civil registry offices (*Standesämter* in German) existed in each local governing district and registered births, deaths, and marriages. Marriage licenses were issued by this office, and civil marriages were performed there.

35. The Nazi Party divided the country into party districts (*Gaue*) which corresponded roughly to electoral districts. The district leader was called a *Gauleiter.* The *Gau* itself was divided into subdistricts (*Kreise*), each headed by a *Kreisleiter.*

36. Walter Gross (1904–1945), a Nazi physician and ardent racist who in 1934 became head of the Racial Policy Department at party headquarters. He was among the most fanatical advocates of racial purity.

37. Hjalmar H.G. Schacht (1877–1970) had the reputation of being a financial wizard. He was president of the *Reichsbank* from 1933 to 1939 and the Reich minister of economics from 1934 to 1937. He was fearful that Jewish persecutions could undermine the German economic recovery and so was eager to insure a continued Jewish presence in economic activity. His objections to persecution seem to have been based on economic concerns rather than humane ones.

38. Jakob Sprenger (1891–) was the Party district leader (*Gauleiter*) in the *Gau* of Hesse-Nassau, which had its administrative center in Wiesbaden.

39. Early in their occupation of Germany, the British and Americans established Denazification Commissions in their occupation zones in order to remove

Nazis from positions of influence in public affairs, politics, culture, the press, schools and universities, and so on.

40. After the Nazi annexation of Austria in March 1938, the term *Altreich,* or "Old Reich," was used to designate pre-annexation Germany.

41. Rudolf Hess (1894–1987) was, until his flight to England in May 1940, the deputy of the *Führer,* the official head of the party apparatus in Munich, and the presumed successor to Hitler.

42. Kurt Blome, a medical doctor in Gerhard Wagner's Reich medical office.

43. Adolf Eichmann (1906–1962) was the "Jewish Expert" in the SD, the Security Service of the SS. Eichmann emerged after 1938 as a major figure among Nazi perpetrators for his success in forcing Jewish emigration from Austria. During the war, he was in charge of transporting Jews from across Europe to the death camps in Poland.

44. In 1936, Hitler placed Hermann Goering in charge of preparing the German economy for war within four years. Goering's agency came to be known as the "Four-Year Plan Office."

45. The *Reichsvereinigung* was established in July 1939 as the umbrella organization to which all Jews in Germany were forced to belong. Its purpose was to facilitate control over all Jewish activities and movement, especially to oversee Jewish emigration.

46. The *Kristallnacht,* or "Night of Broken Glass," was a nationwide pogrom directed by the Nazis against the Jews. Hundreds of synagogues were burned down, countless Jewish-owned shops and stores ransacked, and some 30,000 Jewish males arrested and sent to concentration camps. The name came from the shattered glass of store windows. Loesener gets the date wrong; it was actually November 9 and 10.

47. The meeting was chaired by Air Force Minister Hermann Goering who opened the meeting by announcing that Hitler had given him the task of coordinating Jewish policy.

48. Loesener has misspelled the name; it should be "Hilgard."

49. The broad and elegant shopping street running through central Berlin.

50. Wolf Heinrich Count von Helldorf (1896–1944), a Nazi since 1926, had become Berlin's police chief in 1935. He engaged in various rackets, including trafficking in passports for wealthy Jews. He eventually became involved in the July 1944 plot to kill Hitler, for which he was hanged in August 1944.

51. Prince Eugen of Savoy (1663–1736), a brilliant commander of imperial Austrian cavalry troops who was rewarded with a palace on Vienna's outskirts. In the nineteenth century, the palace became the property of the Rothschild family, who were Jewish. In 1938, the palace was confiscated by the Nazis and used by Eichmann to house his Central Office for Jewish Emigration.

52. The traditionally Jewish residential section of Vienna.

53. Half Jews who were counted as Jews. Under the Nuremberg legislation, *Mischlinge* of the first degree (with two Jewish grandparents) who were also members of a Jewish religious community or married to a Jew (or both) were to be "counted as Jews," i.e., were *Geltungsjuden.*

54. When the Nazis occupied Rump Czechoslovakia in March 1939, they governed it as a so-called Protectorate of Bohemia and Moravia. Reinhard Heydrich served as its Protector until his death at the hands of assassins in June 1942.

55. The RMdI was in the odd position of having two secretaries of state, Pfundtner and Stuckart. Pfundtner was in fact superior to Stuckart.

56. The SS had its own terminology for its officer ranks. Eichmann's rank as *Obersturmbannführer* was the equivalent of an *Oberstleutnant* in the German army or a lieutenant colonel in the U.S. army.

57. When the Germans defeated France in June 1940, they occupied roughly its northern half. The unoccupied southern half remained formally independent with its capital at Vichy.

58. The reference is to a letter from Goering to Reinhard Heydrich, dated July 31, 1941, commissioning him to draft plans for "a final solution to the Jewish question."

59. After the war began, Germans who lived in conquered Eastern European countries were invited to "return to the Reich," usually in districts annexed to Germany. To make room for the returnees, Poles and Jews were evicted from their homes, businesses, and farms.

60. One of the German occupation districts of conquered Poland. Its capital was at Krakow.

61. On January 20, 1942, a conference of party and government officials was held at the Wannsee villa in suburban Berlin. Chaired by Reinhard Heydrich, it was called to coordinate the transport of Europe's Jews to the death camps being established in Poland.

62. Arthur Seyss-Inquart (1892–1946) was from 1940 to 1945 the Reich commissioner of the German-occupied Netherlands.

63. Hans Heinrich Lammers (1979–1962) was the chief of the Reich Chancellery from 1933 to 1935 and Hitler's closest legal adviser in matters pertaining to governmental affairs.

64. At the Wannsee Conference, Heydrich announced that the racial definitions formulated in the Nuremberg Laws would guide the selections of those to be sent to the camps in Eastern Europe but that *Mischlinge* of the first degree (two Jewish grandparents) were to be classified as Jews. The minutes record Stuckart's proposal that these *Mischlinge* be sterilized instead, thereby simplifying the administrative procedures involved in making selections for deportation. Loesener is suggesting that Stuckart made his proposal knowing both that it would spare many people from deportation and death and that the sterilizations might never be carried out.

65. Albert Speer (1905–1981) was an architect and one of Hitler's closest friends. In 1937, Hitler appointed him as inspector general of construction to oversee the rebuilding of Berlin and other major German cities. In 1942, Speer became responsible for supervising armament production.

66. The official name for the German army, as distinguished from the navy *(Kriegsmarine)* and air force *(Luftwaffe)*.

67. Loesener is referring to the "Law Regulating Rental Conditions for Jews" of April 30, 1939.

68. "When in doubt, favor the defendant."

69. Ludwig Gehre (1895–1945) was an officer in the counterintelligence section of the army command and an associate of Colonel Hans Oster, one of the central figures in the July 20, 1944, plot to assassinate Hitler.

70. Claus Schenk, Count von Stauffenberg, planted the bomb in Hitler's headquarters on July 20, 1944. He was captured and executed by the Nazis.

71. *Gestapo* headquarters in Berlin was at 8 Albrechtstrasse.

72. A revolutionary court established by the Nazis in 1934 to punish political crimes against the regime. Its notorious judge, Roland Freisler, presided over the sham trials of the leaders in the plot to assassinate Hitler.

73. The fierce Battle of Berlin was reaching its climax. Soviet armies had entered the city's outskirts on April 21.

74. Martin Bormann (1900–1945) headed the Party Chancellery after Hess's flight to England in May 1941. An impassioned Nazi ideologue, his role as Hitler's secretary gave him tremendous power during the war years.

3

BERNHARD LOESENER'S TESTIMONY BEFORE THE NUREMBERG TRIBUNAL

$\mathbf{F}$or several days in June 1948, Bernhard Loesener was called upon to testify before the United States Military Tribunal convening in Nuremberg in the trial of his former boss, Wilhelm Stuckart. Stuckart was one of 21 defendants charged with criminal conduct arising from their functions as officials of the Reich government.

Officially the trial was designated as the "United States of America vs. Ernst von Weizaecker, et.al. (Case 11)." Unofficially it quickly became dubbed as the "Ministries case." Count V of the indictment against Stuckart related to his activities as State Secretary in the Reich Interior Ministry. Stuckart was found guilty on Count V and three other counts and received a four-year prison sentence.

It is important to note that Loesener, was testifying for the Prosecution against Stuckart. A careful reading of his testimony, however, raises questions about whose side he was helping most. [The errors and misspellings in the transcript of Loesener's testimony appear in the original.]

OFFICE OF CHIEF OF COUNSEL FOR WAR CRIMES
MILITARY TRIBUNAL
No. IV
CASE No. XI
DOCUMENT No. NG-1944A
PROSECUTION EXHIBIT
No. 2500

Official Transcript of the American Military Tribunal IV Commission in the matter of the United States of America against Ernst von Weizsaecker, et al, defendants, sitting at Nurnberg, Germany, on 7 June 1948, 0915–1630. Commissioner Crawford presiding.

THE MARSHAL: The Commission of Tribunal IV is now in session.

MR. HARDY: May it please your Honor, this commission, this morning, for the benefit of the court reporters, is sitting for Case No. XI, that is the Ministries Case. I would like to call this morning, your Honor, the affiant of the prosecution, Dr. Bernhard Loesener, spelled L-o-e-s-e-n-e-r, to the witness stand.

THE COMMISSIONER: The Marshall will call the witness.

*   *   *

BERNARD LOESENER, a witness, took the stand and testified as follows:

THE COMMISSIONER: The witness will raise his right hand and repeat after me.

I swear by God, the Almighty and Omniscient, that I will speak the pure truth and will withhold and add nothing.

(The witness repeated the oath).

THE COMMISSIONER: Thank you. You may be seated.

Now, will you attorneys and the witnesses please speak slowly and distinctly and pause for the benefit of the interpretors and the court reporters.

DIRECT EXAMINATION

BY MR. HARDY:

Q. Witness, your name is Dr. Bernhard Loesener?

A. Yes.

Q. When and where were you born?

A. On the 27th of December, 1890, in Fuerstenberg on the Oder River.

Q. And what is your present address?

A. Berlin, Zehlendorf, Kronprinzenalleec 313.

Q. I am now handing you document No. NG-19-A, which is Prosecution Exhibit 2500. Is this an affidavit executed by you?

A. Yes.

Q. Did you execute this affidavit voluntarily?

A. Yes.

Q. Now, Witness, would you kindly read the affidavit through and tell me whether or not you have any changes to make therein?

A. I have read the affidavit repeatedly during the last weeks, and I see that it is an affidavit that I executed, and I have no changes to make.

Q. Now, Witness, would you refer to Document NG-2982, which is Prosecution's Exhibit 2505. I will have that given to you in a moment.

(The document was handed to the witness).

Q. (Continuing) Is this document also an affidavit which has been executed by you?

A. Yes.

Q. Now, Witness, in these two affidavits you now reaffirm everything contained therein to be the absolute truth?

A. Yes, I confirm that.

Q. Now, I notice in the first affidavit, that is NG-1944-A, Exhibit 2500, that some of the—in the Appendix No. 2—Would you give him a copy too, mimeographed, please? In Appendix No. 2, which is Page 10 in the original of the affidavit, do you have any changes to make in this appendix concerning the dates of the decrees?

A. The list of the decrees I have made out repeatedly. The first list I made in June of last year when Dr. Speyer was in Berlin and interrogated me for the first time. This list I put up on the basis of another list which was in English. This list later on was retranslated into German, and then by errors in translation and by misunderstandings it was distorted. When I was in Nurnberg the second time this February, I was asked by prosecution to write this list again in German with corrections, and I did so, and I have the list with me. It is a copy. This is the last version which is the only one which I recognize as correct, and is dated 27 February, 1948. The contents of this list is what I, according to my best knowledge and belief, consider as correct.

Q. Would you kindly refer to the mimeographed copy of this affidavit which is contained in Document Book No. 90?

A. Yes.

Q. Document NG-1944-A, Prosecution's Exhibit 2500?

A. Yes.

Q. Would you now indicate to me the changes which you wish to make in Appendix 2 thereof so that we can simply mark them in the record and then the document books can be altered accordingly?

A. I have put a short introduction to each one of the three appendices which explains what the following decrees are about. The text in the document book is not entirely in correspondence with the affidavit of 27 February that I made out. May I please just compare it for a moment?

Q. Yes, please.

A. This list as it appears in the document book is dated 24 February. The list which I have in another mimeographed copy and which is complete is dated 27 February. The text in Appendix I and the introduction which is contained therein is not quite correct, and I should like to read the corrected—may I read it in German please?

Q. Go right ahead. Witness, one moment please; could you read very slowly in German the corrected version of the document, and if you wait one moment, I will give the English copy to the interpreter now so that she can check it as she goes through.

A. May I start?

Q. Yes.

A. The decrees in Appendix I, on pages 2 and 3, to my knowledge, have been worked out in the Department of the Ministry of the Interior, which was headed by Stuckart, on his instructions, and were either signed by him or initialled by him in his capacity as Department Chief. Thus, in his capacity as Department Chief, he assumed not only formal, but also full material responsibility. This is also true of decrees, which because of their political significance, were signed not only by the Minister of the Interior, but by Hitler himself, etc.

Q. Now, that is the corrected version?

A. Yes.

Q. Now are there any other corrections you have on that list, Appendix I?

A. Yes, in Appendix I, the date of the last decree mentioned is not correct. In the document book the date is the 16th of November 1941, and it should read, 16 January 1941. That is the second decree concerning implementation of the law concerning the revocation of naturalization and deprivation of the German nationality.

Q. Any further corrections?

A. In Appendix I, there are no more corrections to make.

Q. Now, in Appendix II, have you any corrections, and deletions or additions to make?

A. Yes, there too, in Appendix II, the introduction is slightly different, and it should read—may I read it aloud?

Q. Yes.

A. "The following legal provisions set forth in Appendix II on pages 4, 5 and 6, were, according to my knowledge, drafted by another Ministry (or Supreme Reich Authority)", and that is a very important point, "and have therefore been signed in the first place by those. The Ministry of the Interior as participating Ministry, jointly signed them, and thereby shares the responsibility insofar as the decrees fell within its competence. For the following decrees Stuckart was the competent authority in the Ministry of the Interior." This is the introduction.

Q. Now do you have any changes to make into the list of the decrees that are cited thereunder?

A. In the column where it says, "signature", I have given the signatures as they are appended to the decrees, at least in the case of the more important decrees. Now, in Appendix II of this document book, one gets the impression as if the Ministry of the Interior had signed in the first place, which is not correct for all of the decrees listed in Appendix II. Now, to the first decree, the Third Decree to the Reich Citizen Law, it is signed by Frick (in first place). In the second decree mentioned there, which is the Fifth Decree to the Reich Citizen Law, the sequence of the signatures is, Hitler, Guertner, Frick, Hess and Reinhardt. Then I mentioned the Sixth Decree to th Reich Citizen Law, where the sequence of signatures reads as follows: Hitler, Guertner, Frick, Hess, and Schwerin von Krosigk.

The next one is the Decree concerning the implementation of the Law regarding the Legal Status of the Jewish Congregations (Kultur Vereinigungen). The signatures read: Hitler, Kehrl and Frick. In the first decree which follows, the text should be, "First decree concerning the implementation of the Law regarding the Legal Status of the Jewish Congregations." It should not be Denominational Communities von Jewish Cultural Associations, as it reads in the text of this document.

Then there are three decrees which I have forgotten. May I just give you the place for these.

Q. Go right ahead.

A. As Decree VII, the Decree regarding the elimination of the Jews from the German Economy is mentioned. And then there should be mentioned three decrees which I have left out, namely, the Decree on the implementation regarding the utilization of Jewish Property. The date is 16 January 1939, Reich Law Gazette I, page 37. The second is the Third Decree for the implementation of the Decree regarding the Utilization of Jewish Property. The date is 5 December 1940, contained in Reich Law Gazette I, Supplement No. 3, page 1564, and is very important, Law regarding Tenancy Contracts with Jews, dated 30 April 1939, Reich Law Gazette I, page 864; and then there are no further corrections to be made in Appendix II.

Then let us turn to Appendix III. There is a slight mistake in the date of the last decree mentioned, which is the Eighth Decree to the Reich Citizenship Law which is dated 18 January 1939, but should read 17 January 1939. That would be all I have to say concerning the appendices.

Q. Now witness, do you have any changes to make in your second affidavit, that is exhibit 2505. Would you read that over, please?

A. 2505? I cannot find this number. The number I have here is NG-2982. Is that the same document?

Q. Yes, NG-2982, exhibit 2505. That's correct.

A. Yes.

Q. Would you read that over, please?

A. Yes, the affidavit is correct. The copy that I have before me, the appendix is very long, but this is a copy of the letter, an official letter of Herr Dr. Stuckart which was drafted in September, 1942.

Q. Now then, the document attached to this affidavit in question, that NG-2982, exhibit 2505, is a letter which you received from Dr. Stuckart, is that correct?

A. No. This is a letter that Stuckart wanted to write to the Reichs-fuehrer-SS, Himmler, and he asked me to make the draft according to his very detailed oral instructions which he had given to me previously. This draft, as it stands here, I still had in my old files which I had saved during the collapse, and this is a copy of the draft I submitted to the Prosecution. The draft of this letter, as it is worded here, was submitted to Dr. Stuckart, and I suppose that he then signed this draft and sent it off. I, of course, have no way of knowing this, but if this letter had not been sent off, I would have known about it. If there were any changes that Dr. Stuckart made in the draft, that, of course, is beyond my knowledge because ordinarily one did not find out about that, in accordance with customary procedure in the ministry. The drafts, after being signed, were put into a final copy which in turn was signed again, and were then sent out. I never saw the final copy, nor was the final copy, the original, designated for the referents, but for the recipient.

Q. Now, witness, with those reservations and corrections, which you have made on these two affidavits, the affidavits are now in accordance with the truth and contain the facts as you know them?

A. Yes. I have sworn to these affidavits and they are correct.

Q. Thank you, witness.

MR. HARDY: *I have no further questions. In view of the fact that the defense counsel will ask questions concerning these two documents, I will give them to the court interpreter so that she can have them should they come up in the course of the questioning.*

THE WITNESS: *May I take off my earphones now?*

DR. STACKELBERG: *Yes.*

CROSS EXAMINATION

BY DR. STACKELBERG (for defendant Stuckart)

Q. Dr. Loesener, you became a member of the Nazi Party in 1930?

A. Yes.

Q. And in your affidavit, you said that you thought the radical attitude of the Party in Ethnic and racial questions were merely eccentricities of propaganda?

A. Yes.

Q. Dr. Loesener, would you please wait with your answer until the question has been translated, otherwise the answer won't be on record.

Dr. Loesener, do you wish to suggest by this statement that yourself did not approve of the radical attitude of the Party in racial matters?

A. Yes, that's what I wanted to say by that also.

Q. And did you, in addition, with to express by this statement that this radical attitude was, in your opinion, not a decisive part of National Socialism?

A. In the political election campaign, it was always customary that before an election took place, enormous exaggerations are voiced. I think it is like this all over the world, and it is also like this in Germany. The slogans on the platforms were exaggerated slogans which were mentioned again and again in order to get the voters over to the side of the Party and to appeal to their baser instincts, and it was customary that every voter who had a mind deducted a lot from the statements made by the electioneers during the election campaign. It has been our experience that after a Party got into power and became responsible for government it would then modify the slogans used during the election campaign. And it was like this that not only I, but many others, thought that the whole propaganda slogans in ethnic problems and racial questions was election propaganda. I myself never believed that these slogans then would be adhered to so literally later on.

Q. Thank you. Dr. Loesener, you also said that you did not approve of the law concerning officials and that because of the so-called Aryan paragraph that included those who had one Jewish grandparent. Were you the only one who held this opinion or were there many other party members who agreed with you on that point?

A. At that time I found out that my opinion was held by many others because that was the first proof that the Party men not only took their own slogans seriously, but went far beyond our expectations.

Q. Dr. Loesener, you yourself became a member of the Ministry on 27 April 1933?

A. Yes.

Q. And Dr. Stuckart entered the Reich Ministry of the Interior in the spring of 1935?

A. Yes.

Q. At that time your sphere of work was probably already the so-called Department for Jewish Affairs?

A. Yes. I had become head of that in the meantime.

Q. You certainly had to report on your sphere of work to Dr. Stuckart when he entered the Ministry, didn't you?

A. Yes.

Q. Now, in the report which you submitted you also expressed your own modified views?

A. I have to give a longer answer to this question. I said that I was horrified by the extent to which the Party followed up its racial persecution. I realized very soon that it would not be possible for the full-blooded Jews to obtain anything through the Ministry or through the government. The limitless hatred of Hitler and of the Party was too strong for that. However, what I did believe possible was to do something for the so-called "mischlings", the persons of mixed Jewish blood.

In 1933 already the trend of the Party was obviously to equalize the so-called "mischlings" (or persons of mixed Jewish blood) with those of pure Jewish ancestry as far as the laws were concerned. That meant, of course, that the Party would want to extend the laws concerning Jews in general to those with two Jewish grandparents and to those with one Jewish grandparent only. In this field, however, they were rather uncertain yet as to what they were to do and they still listened to arguments on the other side. With my resistance work against the Party, I started on this very point, but my activities were not very effective. My arm, in my capacity as referent, was not long enough. It did not reach far enough. I could only have influence on Party policy through private conversations, and of course, the field of activity was very limited. I could have had influence on party policy through official channels, but for that I needed the air of my superiors. Until the beginning of 1935 the situation was as follows:

My superiors, for instance, Ministerial Director Dammann and State Secretary Pfundtner were in complete agreement with my opinions, but they had no possibility to exert any influence with the Party because they did not have a very good reputation there. One of them was not a Party member and the other man, as a former German nationalist, was suspicious to the Party and was known as, and I would like to put that in quotes, a "bad National Socialist."

Or, many superiors were in good standing with the Party on the whole, but on the other hand they were not interested in my opinions. In the spring of 1935, the head of Department I, to which I belonged, was replaced. I was very curious then as to who would be the next head and of what political opinion this man would be. When Stuckart entered the office, all the referents reported to him about the situation in their various fields of work. At that time I had just been on leave, perhaps on sick leave, in any case, that was the reason that I was the last of the referents to report to him. I spoke to him a very long time. I had prepared my arguments in great detail for I had an interest in winning my superior over to my side, or at least to make him interested in my opinions, and I therefore put a great deal of emphasis into my statements.

As I remember correctly, I made an oral report to Herr Stuckart at that time which lasted about forty minutes. He listened to me with great attention and I was amazed that he did not interrupt me even once during this speech. I was, of course, prepared all the time to have him say, "Stop", and to tell me that my report was much too much against the Party. But that didn't happen.

I concluded with the request that the operation against the Mischlings—that is to say, people of mixed Jewish blood that had two Jewish grandparents or one Jewish grandparent—would have to be separated from the procedure instituted against the Jews; that they would have to be treated much more mildly and that if possible one would have to see that they would not be racially persecuted and that they should be treated in exactly the same way as the Aryan citizens. When I had finished, Stuckart told me, and he looked at me rather firmly and amiably, "Herr Loesener, I approve every word of what you have just said". I don't know whether we had any further conversation on this very day for I had stated everything I wanted to say, but in any case I was very pleased when I left the room for I had the certain conviction that now there was somebody who would aid me effectively in my work, which was directed toward opposing the aims of the Party.

In the time that followed this, proof was brought that my feeling had been correct. I thus had finally found a superior who not only approved of my attitude but who also had the necessary good standing with the Party and the necessary personal initiative in order to give effective support to these aims. That would be all that I have to say about this conference.

Q. Thank you. Dr. Loesener, you already said before that Dr. Stuckart had entered the Ministry as a department head.

A. Yes.

Q. The title "State Secretary" then was not in accord with the actual work he performed?

A. He was not State Secretary in our office. Stuckart had previously been State Secretary in the Ministry of Education. He left there after having had a quarrel with Minister Rust, as I heard—I don't know that from my own experience—and has then kept this title in his private life. We in the Ministry always called him, "Herr Staatssekretaer", Dr. State Secretary. His position was that of a Ministerial Director, and if I remember correctly, he also had this title in the list of ranks within the Ministry.

Q. Besides Department I, was Dr. Stuckart also the head of another department?

A. As long as I was working there, that is to say, until the spring of 1943, Herr Stuckart was only the head of Department I, and another Department, I-R, which was only a more or less sub-department of Department I.

Q. What was the relationship to State Secretary Pfundtner? Was Dr. Stuckart subordinate to State Secretary Pfundtner?

A. Yes.

Q. Department I at that time was probably titled, "Constitutional and Administrative Organization," is that so?

A. I don't quite remember what the exact title was. This was its field of tasks, anyway.

Q. Thank you. That is sufficient. Now within this field, the department participated in the drafting of laws and decrees?

A. Yes.

Q. Now who was the man who would give instructions to Department I concerning the detailed drafting of laws and decrees?

A. As in every other Ministry, the departments received their instructions from their superiors, and the next superior was the State Secretary, and the next step would be the Minister. The instructions were given by the Government Head, the Fuehrer, either immediately to the Minister, or the head of the Party would give instructions about which he would say that he received them directly from the Fuehrer. These instructions were regularly sent to the Minister, or if he was absent, to his deputy.

Q. And specifically, in Jewish affairs, who would give the instructions?

A. The same channel was used.

Q. Did these instructions also refer to the essential contents of the bills that were to be worked on?

A. Well, the essential content of course was the content of those instructions.

Q. Yes, of course. That means that it was the task of Department I to work out, in accordance with these instructions and in consideration of this technical legislative points of views, these drafts, is that so?

A. Yes.

Q. To whom did these law drafts have to be submitted?

A. The order to make the draft was given to the Referent in whose special field they fell and the Referent had to work out the details. Very often other ministries had to be included in the material content and then the Referent had to call the necessary conferences. He had to collect the documents in connection with that. If larger disputes would arise, he would report about them to the Department Head, and sometimes the State Secretary or the Minister, and then a larger meeting was called, in which all people who had a material interest and all ministries with their representatives would participate. The Party and the Reich Security Main Office, which is to say the Gestapo of course, or whatever Party agencies were interested in those things, would also participate. The drafts then were put into legal form by the Referent. They were discussed and corrected by his superior, and if they were approved in the Ministry they were signed and sent to the other Ministries and the Party so that they could put down their joint signatures.

Q. That is to say, within the Ministry, the drafts were submitted by the Referent to the Department Head, and he in turn would forward them to the State Secretary and to the Minister, and further than that if necessary?

A. Yes, every document that would leave the Ministry needed a final signature, and of course legal provisions would need that even more. This final valid signature for legal provisions was given by the highest ranking official.

Q. That is to say, the Minister?

A. Yes, the highest ranking official was the Minister. If he was absent, which happened frequently, it was then up to the State Secretary to give the signature, which is to say, the official State Secretary; that was State Secretary Pfundtner until the day I left who had the title of Acting State Secretary.

Q. Did it happen that the Referent of Department I or Dr. Stuckart, in his capacity as Department Head, had material objections against the laws that they were ordered to draw up?

A. Yes, that happened more than once.

Q. And did it then happen in such cases that Department I would submit the draft because it was ordered, but would at the same time write comments and point out the objections they had to it?

A. Yes, that would happen. If that happened, it was carried out just that way—or which was even more frequent—before the final draft was made, a huge discussion would arise and a battle was carried out about the content of this law or law draft.

Q. Now if these objections were submitted in written form did it ever happen that these drafts were signed by the Minister in spite of the objections?

A. Yes, if the objections that the department had were not approved by the Minister, then he would sign in spite of these objections. To that he was entitled according to the manner in which business was conducted.

Q. Did if also happen that drafts of Department I were changed by the Minister independently?

A. That happened too, for he too was entitled to that as the Chief of the Ministry.

Q. Did the Acting State Secretary, Dr. Pfundtner, perhaps also make changes?

A. Yes, he was entitled to that also.

Q. Did it not happen that questions which as such, were worked out in their details in other Ministries and were submitted to the Minister of Interior only for joint signature; that they were already initialed by the Minister or by the Acting State Secretary before Department I, or Dr. Stuckart, would see them?

A. That was not customary. As a rule, the gentlemen would forward the documents first to the department, but I do remember such cases in which that happened and that we had great difficulties about that. I know that in the various cases when decrees of the Economic Ministry which concerned the so-called utilization of Jewish property and so forth—I remember several cases where that was very uncomfortable for us.

Q. There the Minister had already made his decision before Department I had been consulted?

A. Yes. If he thought that he could survey the contents already and he made a mistake, then of course afterwards he was very obstinate and did not wish to lose face by taking back his signature. That was not very simple in such cases.

Q. You said before that the Minister was also away from Berlin at times. Did he have any influence on the business of the Ministry while he was absent, especially on these drafts for laws and decrees?

A. Yes, he had to do that because after all he gave the final signature, and we were very indignant about the fact that he was absent at times for very long stretches during the war, and because then every day in spite of the fact that there was a gasoline shortage, a courier plane had to fly back and forth.

Q. And if the Minister was not able to function, then he was represented by Dr. Pfundtner, the Acting State Secretary?

A. Yes, that was his first deputy.

Q. And Dr. Pfundtner really acted in this deputizing capacity?

A. Yes, of course.

Q. Which departments were there in the Reich Ministry of the Interior besides the Department I which was headed by Stuckart?

A. The arrangement varied somewhat, but in 1939 there was Department I, Dr. Stuckart; Department II, for Civil Service Laws, legislation for civil service, and personnel problems of civil service; Department III, if I remember correctly, was the Veterinary department, which had only a subordinate part; Department IV was a so-called public health department which was headed by Dr. Conti, who later on received the title State Secretary; Department V, for community matters, that is to say, administration of municipalities under Ministerial Director Dr. Suren; Department VI was a department which included various competencies. For the main part, it was matters of German folkdom that they dealt with, then matters of sports, real property surveying and several other matters, and that was headed by Ministerial Director Fellert. There was one more department headed by State Secretary Hierl concerning the Reich obligatory labor service, and I believe later on there was another department, but I don't remember.

Q. Probably a central department. And the police also was an independent sector within the Ministry, wasn't it?

A. Well, the position of the police was very peculiar. Originally, the police had been subordinate to the Ministry of Interior, and when Himmler became Chief of the German Police, his ambition would not permit him to have his department simply be among all the other departments of the Ministry of Interior. He called his police department "Main Office" and that was divided into the Main Office Security Police and the Main Office Regular Police. On the letterhead, the business address was "The Reich Ministry of the Interior," and underneath, "Chief of the German Police," and it may also have said, "The Chief of the German Police within the Reich Ministry of the Interior"; that I don't remember. Below that it said, "Main Office Security Police" or "Main Office Regular Police." This Main Office Police was only connected with the Ministry to an external view. Himmler did not take any instructions from Frick at all. I don't know whether Frick tried it, in view of the high position that Himmler had. Thus, the Main Office Security Police and Regular Police were a foreign body within the Ministry of the Interior, they were for us in any case, an enemy alien body, as we counted the Main Office as always with the Party group, that is the group with which we designated our enemies— that is the Party as such, the SS and Main Office Security Police, which was called Gestapo by popular parlance.

MR. HARDY: I trust that defense counsel realizes that the purpose for having this witness here is for cross examination of his two affidavits. He is going so far beyond the scope of these two affidavits now that I think it should be called to his attention. I do not want to register an objection on those lines; however, if defense counsel wishes to make Dr. Loesener his own witness for purposes of establishing organization of the SS and organization of the Ministry of Interior, the prosecution has no objection, but this is not the time nor the place for such development as that.

THE WITNESS: I beg your pardon. Would you just repeat this? I put on the headphones too late.

DR. STACKELBERG: Dr. Loesener, this was not a question meant for you; it was only a matter of procedure here.

THE WITNESS: Oh, I beg your pardon.

BY DR. STACKELBERG:

Q. In connection with the objection of prosecution, I would only like to say that the questions that I have asked are based on the affidavit and are caused by the affidavit, and the connection with the affidavit will immediately become apparent if I put my next questions.

Q. Dr. Loesener, now all these departments that you have just mentioned, besides Department I no other department was subordinate to Dr. Stuckart, not even the police?

A. No.

Q. Thank you; that is sufficient. Were there in the Ministry of Interior besides Dr. Stuckart other State Secretaries who had this title but actually were only department heads? You have already mentioned Dr. Conti. Do you remember any others?

A. Dr. Conti was one of them, the head of the Public Health Department; State Secretary Hierl, for the Reich Labor Service; and if I remember correctly, the Reich Sport Leader, von Tschammor-osten. He also, I believe, was State Secretary in the Ministry.

Q. Was it possible for Dr. Frick to firmly defend his point of view, that is the point of view of the Ministry as against that of the Party, or was he rather weak in going through with his opinions?

A. In my affidavit I have already characterized this situation with a few words. Frick was a weak man; he did try to push through the attitude of the Ministry of the Interior against party opinion but in any case he was not very successful with it.

Q. And he probably had just as little success in doing that with respect to Hitler?

A. Yes; to Hitler he only went very infrequently.

Q. But within the Ministry he was a severe superior?

A. He was always very charming and amiable towards me, but I know that at times he could be very disagreeable to others and that probably was very much subject to his momentary mood.

Q. You said before that he was very obstinate when he had a certain direction to follow.

A. Yes, especially in matters of form where he thought that it might be a question of lowering his prestige.

Q. Dr. Loesener, you have now confirmed for me that Frick was the decisive authority within the Ministry of Interior; that the deputy of Frick was not Dr. Stuckart but Dr. Pfundtner; that Frick was a rather severe superior within the ministry itself; and, that Dr. Stuckart only had Department I under his charge of all the many departments. I would then conclude from that that the direction of the Ministry of the Interior was certainly not in Dr. Stuckart's hands; isn't that so?

A. I should like to make one small addition. Herr Stuckart at times was also deputizing for the minister, if the minister was not able to function in his capacity, and also, if State Secretary Pfundtner was not present. Then State Secretary Stuckart was the next in line for deputizing in matters concerning his own department. I only want to say that in order to make the story complete, but of course, that was not the customary way but it was the exception.

Q. But this deputizing activity only referred to his own field of work; isn't that so?

A. Yes, I just said that.

Q. That is, Dr. Stuckart was not the directing authority of the Ministry.

A. No. The man who really directed the ministry was of course not Stuckart, not even in those cases where he deputized for someone. That would have been entirely against the procedural rules within the ministry.

Q. I wanted to ask these questions because you made a statement in your affidavit to the effect that Dr. Stuckart had been the actual acting minister. This statement you probably meant much more in connection with his general personality because he was more active and because he stood more behind the general opinions of the ministry, the clean-cut administration.

A. What is written in the affidavit is of course a condensation, an extract of a very detailed oral description. That of course, happens with every affidavit. What I meant by that is not that Stuckart was in any way formally active as minister or had in any way the functions of a minister. I only wanted to explain what I had suggested some other place, namely, that with Stuckart's entry at that time for the first time an active personality came in the ministry who was ready to risk something for the ideas that he had; he was very intelligent; and had a strong influence in party circles; at least people listened to his arguments even though the party would not approve of them; and, this was the reason that the significance of Department I again reached the level that it had formerly had, that it was the energetic leading department which again had a position.

THE COMMISSIONER: The Commission will recess for about twenty minutes.

(A recess was taken.)

THE MARSHAL: The Commission is again in session.

THE COMMISSIONER: You may proceed, Dr. Stackelberg.

Q. (By Dr. Stackelberg) Dr. Loesener, your affidavit contains a number of enclosures and you have already made a few corrections in these enclosures. I just want to ask you a few questions about the signatures which you mention in your affidavit. First of all the Reich Buerger Law, who, in your opinion signed that?

A. Hitler signed it. It will be seen in a minute who else signed that. Hitler and Frick.

Q. All right. In your affidavit you said that only Frick signed it so that that isn't complete.

A. I would like to refer to what I said before. As for the enclosures to my affidavit, something happened to them, and I am not responsible for at least one of the available versions. This was made evidently by a retranslation from an English text into a German text. The important one is the one of the 27th of February which I have in my hand.

Q. Yes, but we were not shown that so I have to stick to what is submitted in the document book. For example, the first regulation to the Reichsbuergergesetz according to my document, has only been signed by Frick, and that isn't right either.

A. In my document I wrote Hitler and Frick and Hess.

Q. The Blutschutz Law the law protecting German blood, is also supposed to be signed by Frick according to what you say. Perhaps you can tell me from what you have in your hand who signed it.

A. The Blutschutzgesetz was signed by Hitler, Frick, Guertner and Hess.

Q. In Enclosure 2 you mention the law concerning the Jewish religious communities of the 28th of March, 1938. According to your affidavit no signature is listed. On the one hand, the title isn't correct but I think you have corrected that.

A. Yes.

Q. And also the signatures?

A. I have it here, law about the Jewish Cultural Organizations, signed by Hitler; and secondly by the Minister for church Affairs, Kehrl; thirdly, Frick.

Q. Then you have a second regulation about the carrying out of the law about the adjustment of the Jewish cultural communities of the 4th of August, 1939. The title again needs to be corrected. They aren't religious associations, but cultural ones.

A. That is right, cultural associations.

Q. And who signed this regulation; who signed this decree?

A. I have no signatures on this document.

Q. Well, can I show you the Reich Law Gazette?

A. Reich Minister for Public Affairs, Dr. Muhs as his Deputy; the Reich Minister of the Interior, signed by Dr. Suren as his deputy. That was head of Department 5.

Q. Does this mean that Dr. Stuckart was absent, or how come that Ministerial director Suren signed it?

A. I can't explain that exactly. At least Suren somehow was involved in this.

Q. The communal department also had a legal department, is that right?

A. Yes, presumably it had its expert who examined the legal drafts, but I don't know.

Q. In Enclosure 2 you listed a decree of 14 November, 1940, to execute the decree about the investigation of Jewish businesses. This is only supposed to have been signed by Dr. Stuckart according to your affidavit.

A. Decree of 14 November 1940, Reich Law Gazette, 1520, and my text reads as follows: "Decree to carry out the law about the investigation of Jewish businesses signed by Stuckart (the second person to sign it)." This corresponds to my final version.

Q. The first one who signed it was Landfried of the Economics Ministry. When going through your affidavit and these three enclosures which you did not claim you made, I found that in eight cases the signatures were wrong and in all six cases the titles of the various laws and decrees are wrong. In Enclosure 2 the signatures are wrong in four cases.

A. I can only confirm those copies which I made out myself and not those which came to be put into these files. That is an error for which I am not responsible.

Q. And in Enclosure 3 the signatures listed by you are not correct in any case.

A. This is due to the fact that in the oral note it says that the matter was handled, or was signed by a different department in the Ministry of the Interior and that Mr. Stuckart also signed it, and therefore he took the responsibility as far as the decrees fell into his own jurisdiction, according to custom in the ministries. This does not mean that his signature was also published. He signed the draft in the corner for Department I with his initials, and in the Reich Law Gazette, in the printed form that is, that is not shown.

Q. But you can't say that for every single decree. Dr. Stuckart was perhaps absent occasionally, and then maybe a representative signed it.

A. Well, after all these years I can't tell you that. What I said here refers to the rule, the way it was accustomed. Of course, Mr. Stuckart could not have signed if he was not there, and someone deputized for him. That happened too, but I don't know, I can't say that for every individual case.

Q. At any rate let's say that the three enclosures, the way we have them in our document book, do not come from you and are not correct.

A. I do not take the responsibility for this version because it doesn't come directly from me.

Q. Now a few questions about other decrees. In Enclosure 2 of your affidavit, the decree to exclude the Jews from the German economic life is mentioned of 12 November, 1938, the 7th place in the affidavit.

A. Yes.

Q. Who signed that?

A. I didn't note that down here, and at the moment I couldn't tell you that from memory.

Q. I am showing you the Reich Law Gazette and will you please see who signed that?

A. Goering plenipotentiary for the four-year plan, and this does not contradict what I said in the introduction to Enclosure 2, because Enclosure 2 refers exclusively to decrees which were promulgated by some other ministry or some other Reich agencies, and therefore the latter usually signed it first.

Q. On the 12th of November, 1938, the date of this decree, the great conference about the Jewish persecutions of the preceeding days took place under the chairmanship of Goering.

A. Yes.

Q. Wasn't this regulation first suggested by the Economics Ministry in the conference?

A. I think probably that was so. I attended this conference but was relatively at the bottom of the list, and the tables were arranged in the shape of a horseshoe and at the head of it sat Goering. If I remember correctly Funk was sitting at his left, and then I think Minister Frick, and then a few other people, and Mr. Stuckart was on the left, and way at the end I was sitting. The people passed papers back and forth frequently, and they wrote something, and I don't know how this came to be made out.

Q. Therefore, you can't say that Mr. Stuckart also signed it?

A. Well, he was involved, objectively speaking, because this was a matter of the Jewish laws and this was one of the things that belonged to the competence of the Ministry of the Interior. Whether Mr. Stuckart also signed this decree I cannot confirm.

Q. Thank you. In the same Enclosure 2, in the 15th place, there is a police regulation about the marking of the Jews. At whose suggestion was this regulation formulated?

A. I will have to discuss this in more detail. The Party and its adherents, and I also say "Party" when I mean the totality of the Party, Gestapo, etc. for a long time had been pressing for an identification of the Jews. The public clamor was raised by the paper, "Der Stuermer", and once Gauleiter Mutschmann sent in a suggestion. That may have been in 1938. It was before the war. The Ministry of the interior always was against this thing. They knew on our opponents' side, that we could not be won over for this thing, and, therefore they just overruled us on it. The Propaganda Ministry invited us to a conference about marking the Jews. I was sent there as a representative of the Ministry of the Interior. I had assumed that as usual it would be a small conference of the participating experts. Such sessions usually were attended by six or seven people, but I came into a large hall filled with brown uniforms. State Secretary Gutterer of the proganda Ministry presided, and I was sitting exactly opposite him at the other end. In a very cynical manner Mr. Gutterer announced that the soldiers returning from the front-line and coming in on furlough were indignant about how well off the Jews still were back home, and these people on furlough had demanded severe measures against the Jews, since the Jews were supposed to be guilty for the war. I might add that I never heard anything like that from a soldier on furlough, but that was the reason that Mr. Gutterer gave for his speech.

Q. In other words, it was Mr. Gutterer who suggested this marking?

A. No, even more than that, he said these front soldiers on furlough had continually gone to see Goebbels and therefore Minister Goebbels had decided to go to the Fuehrer directly, and at that moment he had either returned or he was still with the Fuehrer, I don't know exactly, but in order to see to it that the Jews now be marked with the Star of David.

In this meeting, which was very informal, there was a discussion to and fro and everyone of these uniformed Party members tried to put his two cents worth in by making some sort of agitating speech. Then there was applause, not like on a conference, but as if it was an election campaign. As a representative of the Ministry of the Interior, I was allowed to say something only at the very end of the conference in spite of various requests for the floor. I could only object to the fact that the Propaganda Ministry here was intervening into something which belonged to the Departments of the Ministry of the Interior, and Mr. Gutterer answered that the Propaganda Ministry is always competent, as soon as popular opinion is getting excited and if it is a matter of calming down the people. Thus he expressly claimed the competence, in this question, for Minister Goebbels and he objected to the Ministry of the Interior being in charge of this. There was nothing left for me to do but to ask that at least we might be consulted in any future steps. That was necessary because Department I of the Ministry of the Interior constantly was on the guard in order to bring an exception for the privileged mixed marriages into any laws that might be prepared by another agency. These privileged mixed marriages, ever since the year that the law of the rents was passed, were considered exceptional cases and it meant that a Jew or Jewess who had an Aryan spouse would be excepted from the regulations of this discriminatory legislation. Not all of them, but almost all. And at least, if the marking could not be prevented, at least I wanted to see to it that an exception might be made for those Jews or Jewesses who were married to Aryans and that was done, but we couldn't prevent the marking itself any more.

Q. In other words, a colateral competence for this police regulation was not in existence here? You were completely taken by surprise?

A. A co-responsibility did not come about in the general sense. Afterwards we were forced to take note of a "fait accompli" because we had to give an approval of it by co-signing it because we had to bring in this exception and we had to sign for this exception. I emphasized that the responsibility was also taken over by Mr. Stuckart, *insofar* as the regulations fell into his jurisdiction.

Q. Alright, now, I understand you.

A. That's what it says up here in my introduction.

Q. You mean to say that the co-jurisdiction of the Ministry of the Interior referred only to these privileged mixed marriages?

A. The competence of Department I concerned the privileged mixed marriages because the main responsibility had been claimed by

Goebbels, and in the conference which I described, the representative of the RsHA made a very long and energetic speech and said that the Propaganda Ministry does not even have to draft any decrees, we are already working on it and in an hour, or this afternoon, it can be submitted.

Q. So that, in order to clarify it once more, the co-jurisdiction of the Ministry of the Interior referred only to the Privileged Mixed Marriages which were excepted from this regulation at your suggestion?

A. Yes, and I must add that until the last moment the Department I fought against it most strongly and that does not only mean that I raised every objection possible, but that Mr. Stuckart protested just as strongly to all agencies which he could reach, and Mr. Pfundtner was also very unfavorably impressed by this affair. I reported that this very bad proceedings was initiated by our opponents because they knew that they could not get any such regulation from us.

Q. And when you say "us", you include Dr. Stuckart?

A. Yes. I even emphasized this during my interrogations here, especially in the detailed interrogation by Mr. Beauvais, I said that Mr. Stuckart gave me his support in my efforts to save the mixed couples from the fate of the Jews and to protect those Jews who were married to German spouses. He gave me this support in spite of an increasing personal alienation until the last moment. In such matters, or on all occasions when the Jewish question came to a critical point, he always did something just as he used to do before. I always emphasized that here in Nurnberg.

Q. And you want to say that today?

A. Yes, that is my testimony.

Q. Another field now, Dr. Loesener. Did the Jewish Department I take up any special position or was it only one of many departments?

A. This was a section in Department I which called Office VII, for a certain period of time, later, it got a different number. It was one of seven or eight sections when Mr. Stuckart took over the department in 1935, and when I left at the end, it was one of very many more departments for because of the war emergencies new groups, or sub departments, and branches, had been created in Department I. I don't know how many experts we were in Department I.

Q. You said before that in Jewish questions, Hitler, Bormann, Heydrich, and similar people had the initiative and you designated them as your opponents?

A. Yes.

Q. Did these people exert any pressure on the Reich Ministry of the Interior?

A. I call these people the Party, briefly. The party was never hesitant if it was a matter of dealing with opponents. My position in the conferences in which I attended alone was always pretty dangerous because in the interests of the cause I never refrained from expressing my opinion very definitely, and I was very happy when in a large conference, Mr. Stuckart was present and he then did speak for the Ministry of the Interior, or at least for Department I. There was a state of continuous hostility which, of course, never resulted in open fights or disgusting incidents in official conferences because of my position, but in private conversations I was often called pretty bad names, and they weren't only meant for me, but also for Mr. Stuckart, because it was known that we were definitely of the same opinion in these matters. The expression "friend of the Jews" was often to be heard and it could have been fatal at that time.

Q. Dr. Stuckart then always resisted all radical demands?

A. If some large problem in my field arose, I of course was in close contact with Mr. Stuckart, especially in 1935, 1936 and 1938, and everything that had to be done was discussed and considered by us and of course, just as is done in a military campaign, there were periods when we said, "you can only go as far as this in your resistance. If you go any further, then you spoil the whole thing. Then you go too far. You break the camel's back. That was the well known border line to our resistance. But it was not fear of the Party which determined the limit—just objective considerations.

Q. Dr. Loesener, a few questions about the Nurnberg laws. In your affidavit you said that these Nurnberg Laws were the result of the urging of the Party, is that right?

A. Yes, I know. The Party made demands in the preceding years, especially this newspaper "Der Stuermer". It sent way beyond what was formulated later in the Nurnberg laws. The directives for the Nurnberg laws were given by Hitler himself. I described that in detail in my affidavit.

Q. Yes, you did. I just want to ask you a few questions. What were the actual conditions in Germany before the promulgation of the Nurnberg laws. I mean the independent actions of the Party when it tried to make the economic existence of the Jews impossible, for instance to exclude them from theaters and movies?

A. Up to the time of the Nurnberg Laws we did not have a single regulation which affected the Jews generally. That was one of my disappointments in 1933. This field was always handled piece-meal mostly in connection with the Jews in some kinds of profession. It became necessary to reconstruct the civil service law through which the officials, or the civil servants of Jewish blood were excluded from the Civil Service and this went on through all the professions; physicians, veterinarians, dentists— I don't want to list them all, it is a long list—but nothing had been said about the position of the Jews and the attacks of the Party became more severe all the time.

The Party clamored for anti-Jewish laws to suppress the Jews as much as possible, and we too had the desire that finally there should be a law so that we could resist the continuous excesses of the Party because we thought that once the name Hitler was on a decree, we would have an authority. That this did not become effective later we did not know beforehand.

Q. You say then that before 1935 the conditions in this field were not regulated but chaotic?

A. Yes. Excesses, etc. etc. Registrars were put under pressure not to conclude marriages between Jews and Aryans but they were threatened by the Party while the law did not forbid anything. The same thing happened in the Economy.

Q. Did the Nurnberg Laws at least create orderly conditions?

A. First of all, we were very happy that there was some basis provided, and for the first few years the authority of Hitler's name always gave us the possibility to say: now, this is regulated. Whatever the Nurnberg Laws don't expressly say, you cannot do, and in his speech before the Reichs Parteitag in Nurnberg which I heard, Hitler expressly emphasized that this is the definitive legislation for the Jews in the laws to protect German blood. We had inserted as the final paragraph with Hitler's approval that this law was valid only for full-blooded Jews. Hitler crossed this paragraph out immediately before the laws were promulgated and he added that it was only supposed to be published in Germany as a DNB telegram and this happened.

Q. You say then that the Nurnberg Laws, in some respect, brought about a correction of existing conditions in favor of the Jews?

A. Of course these were oppressing laws, and in their tendencies they were evil and shameful but they drew a limit which cut off a lot of things which the Party actually engaged in at that time. The Party actually prevented the Jews from carrying on their economic existence. They painted the windows with signs like "DON'T BUY IN JEWISH SHOPS". It forced the proprietors of restaurants to put up signs that Jews should not enter and similar things, and on the basis of the laws this could then be prevented for the next few years.

Q. Was the Party satisfied with the regulation regarding the Jewish question as provided by the Nurnberg Laws?

A. Never.

Q. And what was Dr. Stuckart's attitude towards that?

A. Dr. Stuckart was of the opinion which he had to hold as an official that these laws were supposed to be carried out the way they were published.

Q. In other words he resisted the more severe demands of the Party?

A. Yes. The worse job came up immediately after the promulgation of the Nurnberg Laws about the legal position of the mixed Jews, that is, the [fr 1/4] or [fr 1/2] Jews. Nothing was said about them in the Nurnberg Laws. This was supposed to be clarified in the first executive decrees to the Nurnberg Laws, and a very stiff fight began on this point. From the middle of September until the middle of November 1935, I, as an expert, and Mr. Stuckart hardly did anything but fight the Party about the position of the half Jews. The fight was very difficult because no one in the Ministry could approach Hitler directly. Frick who could have done so wasn't very familiar with these questions and didn't go there. Mr. Stuckart could not go there at that time. His position was not high enough for that, and the representatives of the Party kept coming, especially Dr. Gerhard Wagner, the head of the Reich Physicians, and he said, "I am just coming from the Fuehrer. The Fuehrer has decided that the half-Jews are to be given the same status as the Jews," or something like that which supported the demand of the Party, and if we had believed that, we would have had to give up the fight.

Stuckart was never satisfied with someone coming in and saying that the Fuehrer said such and such. During this period and often in my presence, he called up Mr. Lammers on the telephone in order to determine whether the Fuehrer actually had said something like that. If Lammers had confirmed something like that for us, then he would have had to be satisfied with it because we knew that Lammers was on our side. We never got a confirmation, but the Party, with its coarse methods, kept trying to get its point across. Mostly Dr. Stuckart and I together were sitting until late at night and our nerves were so tense that after signing the final version of the regulations in the middle of November, I had a nervous breakdown, and about four weeks later Dr. Stuckart had a similar breakdown.

Q. Do you remember perhaps the particularly characteristic statement on the occasion of such a conference with Party people? I mean a definite instance in which he hit his fist on the table?

A. Yes, I said that already here. Because of his work in that field he was not in the good graces of the Party, and the instance which you mean was the one when the Party people had left the office late at night and both of us had remained there by necessity. He hit his fist on the table in the greatest excitement, and said, "Don't these people know that there is a God?" or "Don't these people believe in any God?", something like that.

Q. Who took care of the later anti-Jewish legislations?

A. As usual, this came from the Party. Party agitators were used in Party gatherings, in the Party newspapers the most repulsive of which was the "Der STURMER" etc.

Q. Alright, that's enough. I just wanted to make sure that all these things came from the outside, that the initiative never lay with the Ministry of the Interior, that on the contrary, you were the clear opponents of these radical demands.

A. I want to stress with the greatest emphasis that the Ministry of the Interior and I, of course, and Mr. Stuckart, never urged anything like that in this respect.

Q. You mean against the Jews?

A. Yes, that's what I mean. As long as I was in the Ministry, that is until 1943, I can only testify that Dr. Stuckart always without exception tried to resist or to put a brake on the demands of the Party. I said this in detail and I emphasized this during the interrogation by Mr. Beauvais.

Q. There may be a few more examples. For example, the mixed people who were granted Reich citizenship. Were you and Mr. Stuckart responsible for this?

COMMISSIONER CRAWFORD: As soon as this witness answers the question we will recess until 1:30.

THE WITNESS: It was only, Mr. Stuckart and I, who were responsible for that.

COMMISSIONER CRAWFORD: The Commission will take a recess until 1:30.

(A recess was taken until 1330 hours.)

AFTERNOON SESSION

(The Commission reconvened at 1330 hours, 7 June 1948.)

THE COMMISSIONER: You may proceed with the examination of the witness.

DR. BERNAHARD LOESENER—Resumed

CROSS EXAMINATION—Continued
BY Dr. von STACKELBERG:

Q. Did Dr. Stuckart also intervene on behalf of free marriages between Aryans and Mischlings?

A. Yes, we held on principle the opinion that the Mischlings should be treated just as the German Aryans were treated. It was not possible to carry this opinion of ours into practice because of Hitler's and the Party's strong position on the contrary, and so we had to fight piece by piece for this whole question, and that also included the problem of marriages about which you have just asked me.

Q. Another question in connection with that. Was Dr. Stuckart successful in that the Jews and half-Jews were pensioned off with their full salary after they had been eliminated from public service after 1935? Was he successful in that endeavor?

A. Yes, he was successful there.

Q. Dr. Loesener, you said that Dr. Stuckart's field was enormously extended especially during the war. Then Dr. Stuckart was extremely overworked wasn't he?

A. Yes, he was extremely overworked.

Q. Now if, as you say in your affidavit, he did not have sufficient time at his disposal to help you in your field of work, couldn't the reason for this also be that he had so many other responsibilities?

A. Yes, that could be quite possible.

Q. You were also speaking about the Jewish persecutions of November 1938. Did Dr. Stuckart have anything to do with these events?

A. No, he had nothing at all to do with these incidents; on the contrary, he has expressed himself with words of the highest indignation and repugnance when he found out about that.

Q. Did Dr. Stuckart also take any practical steps in order to prevent the repetition of such incidents?

A. I am now referring to the meeting that I have mentioned before at which Goering was the chairman on the 12 of November 1938. During a recess in this conference, Stuckart came up to me and told me that we would have to cause Frick to issue a decree and we would have to do that immediately, if possible still during this meeting or immediately after—a decree by which other excesses of this kind should be prevented. We were successful in getting such a short decree and drafting it still in the meeting. It was signed, as far as I know, by Frick alone. Then we left the Luftfahrt Ministry—the Air Ministry—in Stuckart's car and went immediately to the Post Office No. 9 in Berlin. There I made a telephone call to the Ministry giving them the text of the decree, and I also called the Reich Printing Office—Oh, I have to correct myself; it was not the Reich Printing Office but it was the Editorial Offices of the Reich Law Gazette. It was not published in the Reich Law Gazette, but in any case it was immediately issued by teletype to all Minister Presidents and to all State administrative agencies. The content of this decree provided that further excess against the Jews would be opposed in a most severe manner. This was an instruction to the State agencies and authorities and we had no authority to give any other instructions.

After a short while, Frick called all the district governors and all the other officials in similar positions to Berlin and in a speech to them pointed out these incidents and also pointed out the damaging factor in such actions. In short, he tried in every way to see that all the administrative officers that were invited to attend: police presidents, district governors, etc., should within their competencies prevent such excesses from happening. The draft for the speech was made by Dr. Stuckart as far as I know.

Q. In your affidavit and in connection with the more severe situation of the Jews at the beginning of the war, did you not try to influence the Party to equalize the position of the Mischlings with that of the German population?

A. Yes, we did that. I drafted two decrees: one which was rather extensive and which aimed at complete equalizing the positions of all the Mischlings, that is to say, half-Jews and quarter Jews with that of the Aryan citizens, and another draft which was slightly more modified, which provided for the equalization of only the quarter Jews with the Aryan population, and the half-Jews, insofar as their conduct during the war was notorious, for I believe they were front-line fighters from the war before. In any case, it included a large group also of these half-Jews. These two drafts were submitted to the Minister. He immediately rejected the more extensive draft because he said it could not possibly come to any execution of this. The other draft then was discussed, but later on Hitler would not sign it. Whether it was really submitted to Hitler in actual practice, I don't know, but we did intend to let it go through the channels up to Hitler; however, the plan failed and was given up.

Q. In any case, Dr. Stuckart supported you in your aims and furthered your intentions?

A. Yes, Mr. Stuckart was the one who had to bring up these various drafts to the Ministers and to the other authorities.

Q. Dr. Loesener, you had already stated that in your department, Referat, the question of Mischlings was a very important one; besides that, there were two other questions that were also important; first, the so-called applications for exemption from the Nurnberg laws, and then the question of privileged mixed marriages. Did Dr. Stuckart intervene on behalf of people who had made applications for exemption from the Nurnberg law?

A. It was our intention to see to it that the Mischlings would be exempt from the provisions for the full Jews, and what we were not able to reach en bloc we tried to get through in as many individual cases as possible. Most of these cases were handled by myself and on my own responsibility; also because I could not go up to Herr Stuckart with every individual case, because that was not the job of the department head. But with very difficult cases in which I needed his advice and support, I went to him, or I would submit to him the draft of my decisions on cases where he would have to make a decision. He also signed these drafts of mine. I also know that Herr Stuckart himself also dealt with a number of individual cases that were submitted to him.

Q. What was the job of the Interministerial Committee for the Protection of German Blood and Honor?

A. That was only a very temporary organization. It was the first implementation law for the Protection of German Blood and Honor. This committee was to be established, but as far as I know, only very few meetings actually took place.

Q. Did this committee have any sort of authority to make decisions?

A. The committee only had the authority to work out the details of suggestions and drafts and to decide by a vote whether or not the application was to be submitted to the Fuehrer, that is Hitler. That is the reason why the procedure was slowed down. There was a lot of dispute in the committee for the opinions of these people representing the Party, and Dr. Stuckart's attitude or that of his deputy, could never be reconciled.

The committee was very soon made inactive and more simplified procedures were set up. The Ministry of the Interior was to contact a certain representative of Rudolf Hess and if these two gentlemen were in agreement, then the case in question should be submitted to Hitler so that permission for the marriage could be granted. In actual practice that also was ineffective because the plenipotentiary of the Party never agreed to anything. I believe there were two or three cases where it was possible by submitting the case to Hitler directly to get through the permission for this marriage, that is to say, not really through the ordinary official channels, but probably via Minister Lammers.

Q. That you and Dr. Stuckart did just to get the permission?

A. Yes, we had to do that because the representative of the party was so stubborn in his rejection.

Q. Now, the second biggest problem in your department was the establishment of privileged mixed marriages.

A. Yes.

Q. You spoke about that already. How was that a measure by which a large part of German full-blooded Jews were protected?

A. Yes, that was the idea. We could not change anything in the course fate took for the full-blooded Jews and in particular that could not be done by civil service which was generally held in contempt. A civil servant had no voice as far as Hitler was concerned. It is well known that he was contemptuous of legal experts and it was up to us to see and try to use different channels. We were well known for having intervened on behalf of the half-Jews. Therefore, we told ourselves the following: Every half-Jew must come from a marriage between an Aryan partner and a Jewish partner. We cannot exempt half-Jews from the Jewish laws if we don't go one step further and also protect his parents, and one parent of such a half-Jew was a full-blooded Jew. This simple argument was made even firmer by a whole series of individual points, in the course of which in view of the situation at that time, the real argument, namely, humane considerations, could not be mentioned because if anybody talked to Hitler about pity and human dignity, then the man who used the argument had lost from the beginning; he then was a bad National Socialist, and, therefore, we gathered up whatever we could get in the way of other arguments, that is to say, the damaging influence on the Aryan partner, and on the whole Aryan relations, etc.

Q. It is only important to me to know whether or not the establishment of this privileged mixed marriages of course meant an intervention of you and Dr. Stuckart on behalf of the great part of Jews.

A. Yes. There were about 12 to 14 thousand persons of full-blooded Jewish descent who were protected from the general fate of the Jews. We of course did not stop with that but we were successful in this field until the last moment.

Q. In your affidavit you also mention the beginning of deportations of Jews. Do you know when the evacuation of Jews started?

A. Just a moment; I have to think. We only found out about those things when there were rumors that something had happened. If I remember correctly, the first mass deportation sent was that of the Jews from Baden and Saarpfalz; that may have been at the beginning of 1941.

Q. Did the Reich Ministry of the Interior or Dr. Stuckart or you in person have anything to do with all those deportations?

A. Only insofar that we tried subsequently to save as many as possible; it was just as much a surprise to us as the pogroms or the marking of the Jews.

Q. You know that Dr. Stuckart at the Wannsee Meetings made the suggestion to sterilize the half-Jews even more extensively than Heydrich had originally intended. Do you know what he wanted to do and what he meant by having made such a suggestion?

A. I was fortunate enough to give you enough documents and proof of this. I have submitted them in evidence. The document you will find in my second affidavit as the appendix. This is the draft of a letter by Dr. Stuckart directed to Himmler. This letter was written half a year after the Wannsee Meetings. The instructions for this document, which had to be thought out very carefully because it was dangerous, were given to me by Stuckart before I took over this job and in oral form. These arguments were nothing new to me, for we had spoken about that before. Heydrich wanted to deport the half-Jews in exactly the same manner as the full-Jews, and it was now our problem to prevent that by all means. The half-Jews had to be kept within the confines of the Reich proper, so that they at least remained subject to Reich legislation and not to the arbitrary excesses of the SS. The situation was very dangerous, and it was important now to succeed in this endeavor through any means at our disposal; a simple objection to that would have been completely ineffective; and, therefore, we had to show Heydrich and Himmler that we had different intentions which had to be made rather tasty for Herr Heydrich. The sterilization of half-Jews is not something that had been suggested for the first time on that occasion. Already in 1935 before the Reich Party Day (Reichsparteitag), party members contacted us, for instance the Reich physician leader Wagner and a certain Dr. Paukel who was his deputy at the time, with the idea that half-Jews had to be sterilized. That was nothing new then, and that was how Stuckart again took up this old suggestion which had been suggested in party circles and had been renewed in a bill again and utilized it in order to reach his aim, namely to keep the half-Jews within the confines of the Reich. It was far less dangerous because Stuckart had found out from Conti, the head of Department IV, Public Health, how such a measure could be carried out and thereupon Conti answered that a sterilization program could not possibly be carried out while the war lasted. We already had too few physicians, he said; we did not have enough hospital beds and we could not possibly hospitalize 20, 30 or 40 thousand people on short notice, have them undergo surgery and to let them in hospital care for a while. This measure could at the very earliest point be carried out after the war was over; this information told us that we could reach what we wanted to reach; we had gained an indefinite period of time; at least until the completely uncertain end of the war.

Q. Was the sterilization program carried out?

A. No, nothing of the sort.

Q. Dr. Loesener, do you remember that in 1942 Dr. Stuckart wrote a letter to Lammers concerning the deportation of Jews; do you remember?

A. Yes, I know that he wrote such a letter. I don't remember any particulars about it. However, afterwards I saw Lammer's answer to that letter; that was about five or six lines only which clearly indicated that the Fuehrer did not want anything done in the program of mixed marriages, so that the people should not be subject to any further unrest about this problem, therefore, any further measures could not be carried out except those that were already provided for by law. I only want to say here that I have not seen this letter any more since 1943. It is possible that I am not giving you exact details here but that was the gist of it.

Q. Now, if I may summarize, I think one can say that Dr. Stuckart again and again intervened actively for a modification and measured attitude in the Jewish problem; isn't that so?

A. Yes, I can answer this yes to the fullest extent.

Q. That is to say Dr. Stuckart never was a Jew baiter, as he has been accused of having been.

A. No. Otherwise I would have asked for my resignation a long time ago.

Q. Now, just a few questions about this conference that you have just mentioned. Now, in the course of this conference, of 21 December 1941, did you tell Dr. Stuckart immediately at the beginning about this crime that happened in Riga or did you first give him various statements concerning your work during the last eight years?

A. Now, with this conference I had something in mind that was not quite usual for an official. I wanted to get rid of my department, and I therefore spoke about my whole position within the ministry. I told him that I was sorry about the fact that he did not trust me any longer as he did formerly; that our relationship was not the same as before; and, I told him I had the impression that my work was not adequate; that I had not been promoted when I should have been promoted and the sort of things an official would mention on an occasion like that.

Q. Did you also point out that your work had lost a great deal of practical value because the Reich Security Main Office had taken over a lot of the work?

A. Yes.

Q. And, wasn't your position which you had built up and defended for such a long time, through such hard work, damaged by the intervention of the Reich Security Main Office?

A. Yes, I once said that we were just "dying with our boots on." The initiative in the Jewish question had always lain with the Reich Security Main Office, but we still had had the possibility of exerting some influence upon it according to the legal provisions. Now, the Reich Security Main Office more and more disregarded this factor; they carried out their big operations without including us; we never could find out anything from them afterwards, and so, as time went on, it became more and more silly to risk anything.

Q. So your conference really was very strongly colored by an attitude of resignation.

A. Well, if an official working in a ministry, during war time, in a totalitarian state, goes up to his superior and tells him he doesn't want to play ball any more, then, of course, that carries with it a great deal of resignation for further cooperation and further collaboration.

Q. What I mean is, wasn't there also on Stuckart's part a lot of resignation because he would miss you as a collaborator? And, it would hinder his work?

A. Yes, of course that followed from it, what I myself could not be successful; with Stuckart could not be successful either, and vice versa.

Q. You said Dr. Stuckart in connection with your report about the crime in Riga had told you that that happened on supreme orders; did he also make this statement in a resigned tone of voice?

A. You have to take into consideration that, as can be well understood, I was rather excited in the course of this conversation and for Stuckart the situation was not very agreeable either. Now, that conversation of course went very fast, just as if we had been throwing tennis balls at each other. Whether or not this special statement was made in a very definite resigned tone of voice I can't say of course; I am not denying of course, but I just don't remember.

Q. Did not also the deportation of Jews play some part in your conversation?

A. Yes; that of course was the main subject of the conversation following.

Q. Did this statement of Stuckart's, that that happened on supreme orders, perhaps refer to the deportations that you were talking about?

A. This statement which Stuckart made was made at the end of our conversation concerning this special field; I had given him a description of the events; I was rather upset; I also told him very clearly what I thought about it. I told him that these things were disgusting or something like that. I probably used a stronger expression. I told him "Now just look what is going to be the result of these deportations", or something like that; and then, finally, he told me: "Well, don't you know that that happened on supreme orders?"

Q. Then you expressed your disapproval very sharply?

A. Yes, I certainly did; I was in the habit of saying very clearly what I thought.

Q. And, Dr. Stuckart of course on principle approved of this attitude, didn't he?

A. My experience was that I was able to say things to Dr. Stuckart that I could not say to anyone else, and at least I could completely rely on the fact that he would never use these things against me or perhaps even report me to the Gestapo. I said things to Stuckart that would not have only brought me to the concentration camp, but right in front of gun muzzle if he had reported me. And I can give examples.

Q. Then Dr. Stuckart did in no way express his approval of this crime in Riga, did he?

A. No, certainly not.

Q. Did you draft the letter of 16th March 1942, which was also directed to Heydrich and which was submitted by Prosecution in Volume 90,II Document 2586-I Prosecution Exhibit 1454; do you have Volume 90-II?

A. Yes.

Q. I shall give you the page in a minute. Page 428; that is the German page; you have it before you?

A. Yes. NG-2586-I, 16 March 1942; is that it?

Q. Yes. In this document something is contained like this: "Their high intelligence, and high education in connection with the Germanic hereditary map makes the half-Jews outside of Germany into born leaders but also into very dangerous enemies."

A. Yes, that was a standing argument of Herr Stuckart which he had already used and advanced in 1935 on the occasion of the fight for the content of the first implementation decrees.

Q. There were some similar statements submitted contained in other documents. I only wish to conclude from that that your premise was that the deported Jews would remain alive outside of the Reich?

A. I can't say yes to this question if it is held in such a general way. I myself was very pessimistic. It was a matter of course for me to try and see the truth, and I tried to get information wherever I was able to get it. I, of course, do not necessarily mean that I got my information only through the propaganda organs of the Party, that is the press, but I tried to get it where they were credible, these informations, and in the circles in which I moved, since 1936 I belonged to a resistance group, the attitude was generally current that the Jews would be liquidated, and I mean to say bodily liquidated, and I came to see their point and share it. Later on it was also confirmed by the fact that I heard very cynical remarks by Geestapo representatives during the meetings, etc. Sometime it was even sufficient for us to look at the facial expression of these people. If such a problem was touched upon there was either arrogant mockery or something like that, so I was especially upset when I got my first confirmation that deported German Jews were murdered in huge numbers. That was the High case. I was extremely upset, and the effect upon me was that I immediately went and—

Q. But you also advanced as an argument the fact these Jews would remain alive. That was a very important argument, and that is why I say your basic premise could not possibly have been that all would now be subject to liquidation.

A. Now with such arbitrary action, of course, confusion would result.

Q. Oh, you mean those were arbitrary actions?

A. Yes, these deportations, etc.

Q. Dr. Loesener, one more question. The letter to Himmler mentioned in your Exhibit 2505, that certainly took a lot of courage at that time, didn't it?

A. It was no small matter to send such a letter, that is true, and it is also certain that Himmler probably didn't get very many letters like that, and with full signature, too.

Q. In conclusion, did Dr. Stuckart in any way try or render his support that Jews or Mischlings were damaged?

A. No.

Q. You mean quite the contrary that he did everything he could in order to protect them, didn't he?

A. Yes. I only want to give you an example here. We had heard that in Vienna catastrophe was about to happen. A huge number of children had been rounded up. These children were, according to their descent, half-Jews, but with this confusing and intricate legislation they were supposed to be treated like Jews because they were brought up in the Jewish faith. We heard that the Gestapo in Vienna was going to transport and deport these children to the east. There were several hundred, perhaps two hundred, two hundred and fifty, three hundred, I have forgotten. Stuckart immediately intervened with all his strength, and he did it in the following way, that by way of Lammers he saw to it that this deportation was not carried out.

Q. Thank you. Now today in retrospect couldn't we say that Stuckart has helped that a great many Jews who were living in mixed marriage and a great many Mischlings had remained alive, isn't that so?

A. Yes, that is the result of my activity in the Reich Ministry of the Interior, and I am proud of it, even though today I am not in a very happy position. And I could never have been successful in these endeavors if my superior, Dr. Stuckart, had not risked his life in exactly the same way I did so that this thing was successful to the end.

DR. von STACKELBERG: No further questions, thank you.

DR. SIDEL: Dr. Seidl for the defendant, Dr. Lammers.

CROSS-EXAMINATION

BY DR. SEIDL:

Q. Mr. Witness, I have only a few questions to put to you in connection with the two affidavits that you have executed. First a question in reference to the affidavit of the prosecution which was submitted by prosecution as Exhibit 2500. That is the long one, and that has the number, NG-1944-A. In this affidavit you describe the establishment of the so-called Nurnberg Laws, and I should like to ask you, Mr. Witness, did the State Secretary of the Reich Chancellery, Dr. Lammers, at the time have anything at all to do with the establishment of the Nurnberg Laws or did the agencies of the Reich Chancellery participate in the drafting of the legislation or participate in any other way in the issuing of these laws?

A. Nobody of the Reich Chancellery participated in the drafting and in the conferences for the Nurnberg Laws, neither Herr Lammers nor any other gentlemen.

Q. My next questions then are concerned with the affidavit, No. NG-2982, which is Exhibit 2505 submitted by prosecution. This is the affidavit, an important part of which is the draft of a letter which in September, 1942, was written by the Reich Minister of the Interior to the Reichfuerer-SS and Chief of the German Police, in 1944. Now I would like to point out the end of this letter to you, Mr. Witness, in Paragraph 2 there. It says that a copy of this letter went to the Reich Minister and Chief of the Reich Chancellery. That is correct, isn't it?

A. Yes.

Q. It further says in Paragraph 2, Re, "your letter of 22 May 1942, I am herewith forwarding you a copy of letter which has been signed by me today directed to the Reichsfuerer-SS and Chief of the German Police. Please take cognizance of it." Now, Mr. Witness, this letter of 22 May 1942, is that identical with the letter you had mentioned before when you were asked by defense counsel for Dr. Stuckart, and when you said that the most important content of this letter was a statement by the Reich Minister and Chief of the Reich Chancellery according to which no further steps were to be taken in the problem of Mischlings and in the Jewish question because of the Fuehrer's decision?

A. I can't say that with complete certainty any more. The letter that I find under the documents here was still in my hands, and I submitted that to prosecution. That is why I know so much more about that one, but I think that it is extremely probable that that was the letter since the date would be correct, and also the motive of this letter would be in agreement with the cause. Besides, we always thought of Lammers as one of our people in this question and, therefore, tried to give him further material we had as soon as and as generously as was possible for us, for it could always be possible, it could always happen, that Lammers went to Hitler once, just after such a letter had arrived, and that then at last would try to present some of the arguments to Hitler.

Q. But you know positively, Mr. Witness, that Lammers did cause a decision from Hitler and that Lammers then forwarded this decision to the highest Reich authorities?

A. Yes.

Q. May I then conclude from the answer that you gave before that the reason for the fact that Dr. Lammers received a copy of this letter, which is an essential part of your affidavit, that the reason for this forwarding was that you and Stuckart knew that Dr. Lammers also was an opponent of further measures against Mischlings or persons of mixed Jewish blood and that Dr. Stuckart and you had an ally in him in this endeavor to prevent any further steps against Mischlings?

A. Yes, I said that already. That is the truth. If I may add, I myself did a lot of things and carried out a lot of things by way of the Reich Chancellery without telling Dr. Stuckart about it, and I did that through a friend of mine in the Reich Chancellery, Reich Cabinet Counsellor Killy, and he again dealt with it on his own initiative or responsibility, or wherever it was necessary, trying to get the things through by way of Minister Lammers.

Q. Do you know, Witness, that Dr. Killy, the Reich Cabinet Counselor in the Reich Chancellery, was a Mischling himself?

A. Yes.

Q. Dr. Loesener, you also mentioned that exemptions had to go through the Reich Chancellor in the Reich Chancellery in view of the opposition of the Party. Did I understand you correctly?

A. Yes, these exceptions, permissions for individuals, that is to say, exceptional provisions always had to go by way of Lammers in order to be submitted to Hitler. A lot of people were there who tried to get the audience time at Hitler's office for themselves, and that of course, would have modified the effect. That is why we tried to put in the background all the other people who wanted to change anything in this procedure, for of all the people who were in Hitler's confidence and whom Hitler trusted, Lammers was the only one who did not distort the facts but who reported entirely within our intent.

MR. HARDY: *Your Honor, I think the witness should be instructed that he perhaps could answer those questions yes or no. Some of them he has elaborated on to such an extent that I think it is unnecessary, this last question particularly. I don't think the witness has to go to such an elaboration on each question.*

THE COMMISSIONER: *Yes, he should answer them as simply as possible.*

Q. (By Dr. Seidl) I did have one more question, Mr. Witness. Now, in case of these exemptions by way of the Reich Chancellery, did they try to use rather generous standards and to grant applications for as many applicants as possible, or what else can you say in this respect?

A. Of course, I have a lot to say about this, but I can't very well tell that here. That was simply a question of diplomacy and the politics of the moment. Once it was possible to report a lot of cases at the same time and some other time one had to keep back all the others at a long time because it was not the right moment for doing it.

Q. You are talking about Hitler's audiences?

A. Yes, if he had won a victory once then of course he would try it again, but if he was in a bad spot once, then, of course, it was difficult. Lammers sometimes left these things on his desk for months, because he simply said "Hitler just isn't interested in that right now. That is impossible. We would have no chance. I have to wait until the psychological moment has arrived."

DR. SEIDL: *No further questions. Thank you.*

MR. HARDY: I have one or two questions, your Honor, before we dispose of this witness.

REDIRECT EXAMINATION

BY MR. HARDY:

Q. Dr. Loesener, is it my understanding that the appendix to your second affidavit, that is Exhibit 2505, originated because of the fact that the defendant Stuckart felt that the only way that he could save these half-Jews from extermination was to propose sterilization of these Jews?

A. I already stated that Stuckart did not really want to see the half-Jews sterilized but he only made this suggestion after he had made sure that a sterilization was not possible at all until the end of the war.

Q. Now, did he make any suggestions as to full Jews, being sterilized rather than extermination?

A. The fate of the full-blooded Jews at the time when this question came up, had already been decided by deportation. I emphasized repeatedly that nothing could be done in the case of full-blooded Jews. The only thing that could possibly be done and was successful was to protect those Jews who were living in privileged mixed marriage.

Q. Now, when you state that none of these so-called half-Jews were sterilized, did you state that as a known fact?

A. Yes, of course that is established.

Q. Do you know whether or not any of the full Jews were sterilized?

A. I don't know that.

Q. Do you know whether or not any of the foreign workers who were not necessarily Jewish were sterilized?

A. No, I don't know. I had nothing to do with the question of the foreign workers and have nothing to say about it. I can only talk about things that I had learned after the war from press notices, but that would not be of interest here. At the time I didn't know anything about it.

Q. Would it surprise you to know that a large sterilization unit had been set up at Auschwitz Concentration Camp for the purpose of sterilizing Jews at a period of time very near the date of this letter, sent to the Reichsfuehrer-SS by Stuckart?

A. I can't testify to that in any way because I have not ever found out anything about that, and as I said, after the war I had found out from press notices just what happened, but from the time about which I have to testify here I know nothing.

Q. Then you do not exclude the possibility that this letter from Stuckart was one of the many modifying factors behind Himmler's order that Jews were to be sterilized?

A. This letter referred to the sterilization of half-Jews, and has nothing to do with the other problem.

Q. Of course, Witness—Just a moment. Of course, Witness, a half-Jew or a full Jew made no difference to Heinrich Himmler, did it?

A. That is not impossible, because if that had not been the case, we would not have attempted to write this letter. With all these people nobody could know whether at some time or other an argument would not be successful, and in this meeting at Wannsee, as I found out later, the only talk was about the sterilization of the half Jews. When I drafted this letter I did not know anything but that it was only a matter of sterilizing half-Jews. Otherwise, all the arguments that I advanced in here would not have been applicable. These arguments do not apply to full-blooded Jews.

Q. And yet it was common knowledge that whether they were one-quarter Jews or one-half Jew or three-quarter Jew, or what have you, that made no difference whatsoever to Heinrich Himmler, isn't that true? Himmler, the only thing he was interested in was whether or not you had Jewish blood, isn't that it?

A. Well, there was some difference, of course, for if it had made no difference to him, then Himmler would have deported the half-Jews, but after all they were not deported until the end of the war, and that certainly proves that our intervention on behalf of the half-Jews had been effective and that Himmler actually made a distinction. Finally, different measures were taken against half-Jews. They were put into labor squads, etc., but actually the police did make a distinction because otherwise the half-Jews would not be alive today.

Q. And once a half-Jew became attached to a labor squad, was he under the jurisdiction, in any way whatsoever, of the Ministry of the Interior?

A. At the time when the labor squads were established I was no longer in the Ministry. I was then working with the Reich Administrative Court in a different activity, and on purpose I kept away from this matter. I know no details about it, and I can't answer your question.

Q. Now, at this conference where Stuckart made this proposal on the 29th of December, 1941, were you yourself also present at the conference?

A. May I ask you which meeting do you mean, you mean the 21st of December, 1941?

Q. Pardon me, 21st of December, yes, 1941.

A. Yes, of course, that was a conference between myself and Stuckart alone. I am sure you must have made an error.

Q. Pardon me. I meant the January 1942 conference where Stuckart made the statement that the Jews should be sterilized, and the half-Jews should be half sterilized. Were you at that conference?

A. No.

MR. HARDY: I have no further questions. Any further questions by Defense Counsel?

RECROSS EXAMINATION

BY DR. von STACKELBERG:

Q. Dr. Loesener, you said that you were not present at this conference, but you knew Dr. Stuckart's motives for his proposal as described by you before?

A. The motives as they are put down in the draft of my letter to Himmler, did not originate at the moment when I was supposed to take this draft, but as I said before, those were motives that were no longer new because the Party had already started a long time ago to try to eliminate the Jews by way of sterilization.

COMMISSIONER CRAWFORD: The witness may be excused from the stand.

MR. HARDY: I have one announcement to make before we recess, your Honor. The witness Schmelter whom we intended to call here this afternoon for cross examinating by Defense Counsel has been waived by Defense Counsel. After the recess Mr. Peterson and the Prosecution will make available for examination four affiants of the Prosecution by Berger's Defense Counsel. Tomorrow we would like also to have the Marshal bring Oswald Pohl here at 9:30, in addition to the affiants who have not been examined this afternoon by Defense Counsel for Berger.

Also for the remainder of the time tomorrow and Thursday, the Defense Counsel have brought eight to ten witnesses to appear for direct examination and also possible cross-examination.

I thought I would let your Honor know the schedule.

COMMISSIONER CRAWFORD: The Commission will recess for about (text ends)

APPENDIX
NAZI LEGISLATION

The laws in this appendix represent the major milestones in the Nazis' legislative assault upon Jews in German society. Dr. Gerhard Wagner, the radically anti-Semitic head of the League of National Socialist Medical Doctors and Loesener's nemesis, called the Nuremberg Laws "the racial constitution of the German people." A basic issue in drafting this "racial constitution" centered on how the Jew was to be defined. Wagner believed that having one Jewish great-grandparent was sufficient to be considered a Jew. Julius Streicher went even further, claiming the sufficiency of "even one drop of Jewish blood." The first official definition of the Jew came in the "Aryan Paragraph" of April 11, 1933, which was part of a supplementary decree attached to the Law for the Restoration of the Professional Civil Service. The Aryan Paragraph established that one Jewish grandparent was sufficient to make someone a non-Aryan. The radicals, Wagner and Streicher among them, had hoped for a more far-reaching definition.

The question of definition came up again, as we have seen, in the drafting of the Nuremberg Laws in 1935. Loesener's account of the bitter wrangling over defining the Jew is instructive of how the Nazi system addressed the problem. Once again Wagner and Streicher took the extreme position, this time against the presumed "laxity" of Loesener. The compromise they eventually reached received legal formulation in the First Supplementary Decree to the Reich Citizenship Law of November 14, 1935. The new definition of the Jew clearly stipulated that someone with three or four Jewish grandparents was unequivocally a Jew. Someone with two Jewish grandparents, however, might or might not be classified as a Jew. The answer was yes—if he or she was married to a Jew or held membership in a Jewish religious congregation. If neither of these applied, however, the person with two Jewish grandparents was classified instead as a *Mischling* of the first degree. The person with one Jewish grandparent, who in 1933 had been classified as a non-Aryan, was now deemed to be a *Mischling* of the second degree. These definitions held until the end of the Third Reich. In the case of the *Mischlinge*, this classification usually offered protection from the harshest of the Nazi measures.

It is noteworthy that the Nazi legislative assault against the Jews very often took the form of decrees that were supplementary to a basic law. The Reich Citizenship Law of September 15, 1935, eventually had thirteen decrees attached to it; the Law for the Protection of German Blood and German Honor, also of September 15, 1935, had one very important decree attached; even the April 1933

Aryan Paragraph came in the form of a supplementary decree to the Law for the Restoration of the Professional Civil Service. The decrees were usually more important than the law to which they were attached. Loesener explained why: Given the pace of Nazi legislation, he said, "the number and importance of 'decrees' . . . soon outweighed legislation in the formal sense. Henceforth the simplest and most convenient means for bringing into being legal measures against the Jews, took the form of a 'Supplementary Decree' attached to the Reich Citizenship Law. This law's Paragraph 3 provided the basis for ordering a range of directions for its implementation and extension."[1] The range of those directions is evident in decree after decree as we see them order, step-by-step, the removal of Jews from virtually every area of German life and culture.

THE "ARYAN PARAGRAPH"

LAW FOR THE RESTORATION OF THE PROFESSIONAL CIVIL SERVICE (April 7, 1933)

Paragraph 3.

Civil servants who are not of Aryan extraction are to be retired. Honorary civil servants *(Ehrenbeamte)* are to have their titles rescinded.

The above does not apply to civil servants who have been in the civil service since August 1, 1914, or those who fought for the German Reich at the front during the World War, or those who had a father or son killed in action during that war.

FIRST SUPPLEMENTARY DECREE TO THE LAW FOR THE RESTORATION OF THE PROFESSIONAL CIVIL SERVICE (April 11, 1933)

Paragraph 2.

A non-Aryan is defined as any person who descends from non-Aryan, and especially Jewish parents or grandparents. It suffices if one of the four grandparents is non-Aryan.

Civil servants who entered the civil service after August 1, 1914, are required to prove that they are of Aryan extraction or were soldiers at the front.

THE REICH CITIZENSHIP LAW OF 15 SEPTEMBER 1935

The Reichstag has unanimously adopted the following law, which is promulgated herewith.

Article I.

A "subject of the state" *[Staatsangehöriger]* is anyone who enjoys the protection of the German Reich and who, in return, has particular obligations to the Reich.

The status of subject of the state is acquired in accordance with the provisions of the Reich and State Law of Citizenship.

Article II.

A "citizen of the Reich" [*Reichsbürger*] is only that subject who is of German or related blood and who, by his conduct, demonstrates that he is both willing and suited to serve faithfully the German people and Reich.

Reich citizenship is acquired through the granting of a certificate of Reich citizenship (*Reichsbürgerbrief*).

The Reich citizen is the sole bearer of full political rights in accordance with the provisions of the laws.

Article III.

The Reich Minister of the Interior in agreement with the Deputy of the Führer issues the legal and administrative decrees required for the implementation and supplementation of this law.

Nuremberg: September 15, 1935

At the Reich Party Congress of Freedom

The Führer and Reich Chancellor
Adolf Hitler.

The Reich Minister of the Interior.
Frick.

FIRST SUPPLEMENTARY DECREE TO
THE REICH CITIZENSHIP LAW (*November 14, 1935*)

Article I
Paragraph 1.

Pursuant to Paragraph 3 of the Reich Citizenship Law of 15 September 1935, the following is decreed:

Until further regulations concerning the certificate of Reich citizenship papers are issued, subjects of German or kindred blood who possessed the right to vote in the Reichstag elections at the time the Citizenship Law came into force shall for the time being possess the rights of Reich citizens. The same shall be true of those to whom the Reich Minister of the Interior, in agreement with the Deputy of the Führer, has granted provisional citizenship.

The Reich Minister of the Interior, in agreement with the Deputy Führer, can revoke the provisional Reich citizenship.

Paragraph 2.

The regulations in Article I also apply to Reich subjects of partial Jewish descent (*Mischlinge*).

A Jewish *Mischling* is anyone who is descended from one or two grandparents who are racially full Jews, insofar as he or she is not considered to be a Jew according to Article V, Paragraph 2. A grandparent is considered a full-blooded Jew if he or she belonged to the Jewish religious community.

Paragraph 3.

Only the Reich citizen, as the bearer of full political rights, may exercise the right to vote on political matters or hold public office. The Reich Minister of the Interior, or any agency empowered by him, can make exceptions during the transition period, with regard to the admission to public office. The affairs of religious organizations are not affected.

Paragraph 4.

A Jew cannot be a citizen of the Reich. He has no right to vote on political matters and he cannot hold public office.

Jewish civil servants will retire by 31 December 1935. If these officials served at the front during the World War, either for Germany or her allies, they will receive, until they reach retirement age, the full pension to which they were entitled according to the salary they last received; they will, however, not advance in seniority. After reaching the age limit, their pensions will be calculated anew, according to prevailing salary schedules.

The affairs of religious organizations will not be affected.

The conditions of service of teachers in Jewish public schools remain unchanged until new regulations for the Jewish school system are issued.

Paragraph 5.

A Jew is anyone who is descended from at least three grandparents who are racially full Jews. Article II, Paragraph 2, second sentence, will apply.

Also deemed to be a Jew is a Jewish *Mischling* subject who is descended from two fully Jewish grandparents, (a) who belonged to the Jewish religious community at the time this law was issued, or joined the community at a later date, (b) who was married to a Jew when the law was issued or marries one subsequently, (c) who is the offspring of a marriage with a Jew as defined in Section 1 of this paragraph and which was entered into after the Law for the Protection of German Blood and Honor became effective, (d) who is the offspring of an extramarital relationship with a Jew as defined in Section 1 of this paragraph, and was born out wedlock after 31 July 1936.

Paragraph 6.

Requirements for the pureness of blood as laid down in Reich law or by orders of the NSDAP and its echelons—which exceed Article V—will not be affected.

Any additional requirements for the pureness of blood, which exceed Article V, can be made only by permission of the Reich Minister of the Interior and the Deputy Führer. If any such requirements exist, they will be void as of 1 January

1936, unless they have been approved by the Reich Minister of the Interior in agreement with the Deputy Führer. Requests for approval must be made to the Reich Minister of the Interior.

Article II
Paragraph 7.

The Führer and Reich Chancellor can grant exemptions from the regulations laid down in this supplementary decree.

The Führer and Reich Chancellor
Adolf Hitler

The Reich Minister of the Interior
Frick

The Deputy of the Führer R. Hess.

SECOND SUPPLEMENTARY DECREE
TO THE REICH CITIZENSHIP LAW (December 21, 1935)

Pursuant to Article III of the Reich Citizenship Law of 15 September 1935 the following is decreed:

Paragraph 1.

Civil servants *[Beamte]* within the meaning of Article IV, Paragraph 2 of the First Supplementary Decree to the Reich Citizenship Law are those directly or indirectly employed by the Reich—with the exception of notaries who are directly compensated by the fees they charge—and those directly or indirectly employed by the federal states and by the local municipalities and communities, including those employed by agencies incorporated in public law. Also included in this definition of civil servant are those public employees of the social insurance agency who possess the rights and duties accorded to civil servants.

Included in the definition of civil servant in accord with Article IV, Paragraph 2 of the First Supplementary Decree to the Reich Citizenship Law are those civil servants who draw their incomes either in their entirety or in part from the position they occupy, the teachers in the public schools and the teachers in the institutions of higher education, insofar as they are not excluded on the basis of their official duties.

Also to be defined as civil servants according to Article IV, Paragraph 2 of the First Supplementary Decree to the Reich Citizenship Law are Honorary Professors, university lecturers and private lecturers at the institutions of higher learning. For all of them, their retirement will include the revocation of their licenses to teach; the same stipulation applies to all others released from their official duties as teachers at institutions of higher learning.

The regulations of Article IV, Paragraph 2 of the First Supplementary Decree to the Reich Citizenship Law apply also to those in the armed forces.

Civil servants awaiting retirement and who during the World War served on the front lines for the German Reich or one of its allies are to receive their retirement incomes instead of their regular incomes until such time as the regulations governing their official retirement would otherwise have been fulfilled

If formal disciplinary measures are pending against a civil servant (Paragraphs 1 through 4), they may proceed with the objective of depriving that person of his or her retirement income and official title.

Paragraph 2 (omitted).

Paragraph 3.

On the basis of Article IV, Paragraph 2 of the First Supplementary Decree to the Reich Citizenship Law and Article II of this [Second] Supplementary Decree, the Reich Bank and the German Railway Association are authorized to issue the appropriate decrees.

Paragraph 4 (omitted).

Paragraph 5 (omitted).

Paragraph 6.

1. The stipulations regarding tenure in public office as stated in Article VI, Paragraph 1 of the First Supplementary Decree to the Reich Citizenship Law apply also to medical doctors holding leading positions in public hospitals and clinics as well as other hospitals and clinics open to the general public and to those making disability recommendations to the state health insurance panels.

2. Jewish head physicians at public hospitals and clinics and in other hospitals and clinics open to the general public and those who make disability recommendations to the state health insurance panels are to be removed from their positions as of 31 March 1936. Existing contracts will be dissolved as of that same date.

3. Jewish hospitals are not affected by these regulations.

4. Doubtful cases are decided by the Reich Minister of the Interior after consultation with the Reich Medical Chamber.

Berlin, 21 December 1935

The Reich Minister of the Interior
Frick

The Deputy of the Führer
R. Hess

The Reich Minister of Justice
Dr. Gürtner.

THIRD SUPPLEMENTARY DECREE
TO THE REICH CITIZENSHIP LAW *(June 14, 1938)*

Pursuant to Article III of the Reich Citizenship Law of 15 September 1935, the following is decreed:

Article I
Paragraph 1.

A business enterprise is considered to be Jewish if the owner is a Jew (see Article V of the First Supplementary Decree to the Reich Citizenship Law of 14 November 1935).

A general or limited partnership is considered to be Jewish if one or more of the personally liable partners are Jews.

A business enterprise qualifying as a juristic person is considered to be Jewish:

if one or more of the persons appointed as legal representatives or one or more of the members of its supervisory board are Jews,

if Jews have a controlling capital or voting interest. Controlling participation is defined as ownership of 25 percent or more of the capital or when the voting shares of Jews have reached 50 percent.

The provisions of Subparagraph 3 above apply also to enterprises subject to the laws and statutes on mining *(bergrechtliche Gesellschaften)* which are not recognized as juristic persons before the courts.

Paragraph 2.

If, as of 1 January 1938, a joint-stock company or a company with limited liability had no Jews on its board of directors it will be assumed that Jews did not have a decisive influence in its affairs either by way of capital investment or by virtue of voting power (Article I, Paragraph 3, Letter b). The opposite assumption will be made if, on that same date, one or more members of the board of directors were Jews.

Paragraph 3.

A business enterprise will be considered Jewish if it is in fact under the controlling influence of Jews.

Paragraph 4.

1. Branches of a Jewish enterprise will also be considered Jewish enterprises.
2. Branches of a non-Jewish enterprise will be considered Jewish if its principal or one or more of its higher officials are Jews.

Paragraph 5.

The Reich Minister of Economics can, until 1 April 1940, grant exceptions to those enterprises defined in Article I, Paragraph 3, Letter a.

Paragraph 6.

The provisions of Articles I, III, and IV are appropriately applied also to associations, foundations, institutions, and other organizations which are not business enterprises.

Article II

Paragraph 7.

1. Jewish business enterprises will be listed in an official directory. The Reich Minister of the Interior will determine the governmental agency which will maintain this directory.
2. The registration of business enterprises in which Jews of foreign citizenship are participants requires the approval of Reich Minister of Economics.

Paragraphs 8–16 (omitted).

Article III.

At a time still to be determined, the Reich Minister of Economics is authorized, in cooperation with the Reich Minister of the Interior and the Deputy of the Führer, to require a special identifying mark for those Jewish enterprises which are to be recorded in the official directory.
Berlin, 14 June 1938

The Reich Minister of the Interior
Frick

The Deputy of the Führer
R. Hess

The Reich Minister of Economics
Walther Funk

The Reich Minister of Justice
Dr. Gürtner.

FOURTH SUPPLEMENTARY DECREE
TO THE REICH CITIZENSHIP LAW (July 25, 1938)

Pursuant to Paragraph 3 of the Reich Citizenship Law of 15 September 1935, the following is decreed:

Paragraph 1.

The licenses of Jewish doctors to practice medicine will expire on 30 September 1938.

Paragraph 2.

The Reich Minister of the Interior or the authority empowered by him may, upon the recommendation of the Reich Medical Chamber, permit doctors whose licenses have expired to continue their practice until further notice. This permission may be conferred publicly.

Paragraph 3.

1. Jews whose licenses to practice medicine have expired and who have not received permission to continue practicing according to Paragraph 2 are forbidden the practicing of medicine.
2. A Jew who according to Paragraph 2 is permitted to continue his practice of medicine is, except for his wife and legitimate children, allowed to treat Jews.
3. Whoever intentionally or out of negligence violates the provisions of Paragraphs 1 or 2 will be sentenced to a jail term of up to one year and a monetary penalty, or either one of them.

Paragraph 4.

The granting of a license to practice medicine to a Jew is prohibited.

Paragraph 5.

1. Doctors whose licenses have been revoked in accordance with the provisions of this decree may, in the case of need or in recognition of their front line service, and upon recommendation of the Reich Medical Chamber, be granted a temporary living allowance.
2. Details regarding administration of the above provision will be determined by the Reich Medical Chamber in cooperation with the Reich Minister of the Interior and the Reich Minister of Finance.

Paragraphs 6 and 7 (omitted).

Paragraph 8.

The Reich Minister of the Interior is authorized to make appropriate amendments to Reich Medical Ordinances of 13 December 1935.

The Führer and Reich Chancellor
Adolf Hitler

The Reich Minister of the Interior
Frick

The Deputy of the Führer
R. Hess

The Reich Minister of Justice
Dr. Gürtner

The Reich Minister of Finance
[signed for] by Reinhardt.

FIFTH SUPPLEMENTARY DECREE TO
THE REICH CITIZENSHIP LAW *(September 27, 1938)*

Pursuant to Paragraph 3 of the Reich Citizenship Law of 15 September 1935, the following is decreed:

Article I.
The Exclusion of Jews from the Legal Profession

Paragraph 1.

The law profession is closed to Jews. Insofar as Jews are still practicing law, they will be excluded in accordance with the following procedures:

a)   In the territory of the Old Reich:
Admission of Jews to the legal profession is revoked effective November 30, 1938.
b)In Austria:

Jewish lawyers are upon orders from the Reich Minister of Justice to be stricken from the register of lawyers.

For the time being Jews listed with the bar association in Vienna may, if their families have been in Austria for at least fifty years and if they fought at the front, have their exclusion temporarily delayed. In that case the timing of their exclusion will be determined by the Reich Minister of Justice.

Until the decision for exclusion from the list of those practicing in the legal profession is made, the Reich Minister of Justice may place preliminary prohibitions upon the right of individuals to practice in the profession.

Paragraphs 2–6 (omitted).

Article II (omitted).

Article III.

Legal Counsel and Representation for Jews

Paragraph 8.

For legal consultation and representation of Jews, the justice administration admits Jewish legal counselors *[Konsulenten]*.

Paragraph 9.

Jewish legal counselors will be admitted only to the extent that a need for them exists.

Admission to [the status of legal counselor] may be revoked without notice. Admission to the status legal counselor may be limited to the needs of a single client.

Jewish legal counselors and their representatives are to be drawn as far as possible from the Jews excluded from legal practice by Paragraph 1 of this supplementary decree. Those who saw front line service are to be given preferential consideration.

Paragraph 10.

Jewish legal counselors may provide legal services only to Jews and to Jewish business enterprises, Jewish associations, foundations, institutions and other Jewish organizations; they alone may provide judicial or extra-judicial advice and representation, be it in court or outside of court.

Paragraph 11.

Jewish legal counselors will be assigned a specific location in which to exercise their professional activities. The establishment of branch offices, office hours held elsewhere, or similar arrangements at other offices can be made upon securing permission from the judicial administration.

Insofar as Jewish legal counselors are permitted to deal with legal matters, they are allowed to practice with full powers in districts assigned to them by the judicial administration and appear before all courts and administrative bodies, including the higher courts and justice officials, and in representation of their client against an opposing party. This obtains only insofar as legal counselors may participate in a legal proceeding in the particular court to which they are admitted. Further restrictions that exist also apply.

Finally, professional activities of the Jewish legal counselor are not to be subject to any geographic restrictions.

Paragraphs 12–14 (omitted).

Article IV Paragraphs 15–18 (omitted).

Paragraph 19.

The Reich Minister of Justice is authorized to order whatever supplementary measures may be required to implement this decree. To the degree that these measures affect the Reich Minister of Finance, he is to be consulted.

The Führer and Reich Chancellor
Adolf Hitler

The Reich Minister of the Interior
Dr. Frick

The Deputy of the Führer
R. Hess

The Reich Minister of Finance
[signed for] by Reinhardt.

SIXTH SUPPLEMENTARY DECREE TO
THE REICH CITIZENSHIP LAW *(October 31, 1938)*

Pursuant to Paragraph 3 of the Reich Citizenship Law of 15 September 1935 the following is decreed:

Paragraph 1.

1. Jews are excluded from the profession of patent attorney.
2. Jewish patent attorneys who are still registered with the Reich Patent Office or its Austrian branch office are to be stricken from the registration lists of as 30 November 1938.

Paragraph 2.

If on the day this decree takes effect, a Jewish patent attorney is still involved in a legal matter with the Reich Patent Office or its Austrian branch . . . he may continue his representation until 31 December 1938.

Paragraphs 3–7 (omitted).

Paragraph 8.

1. A front line soldier in the sense of this decree is someone who fought in the World War (from 1 August 1914 to 31 December 1918) on the side of the German Reich or one of its allies in a battle, a skirmish or in the trenches, or took part in a siege. It is insufficient if someone never confronted the enemy, even if he was serving in a battle zone.
2. Equivalent to having fought in front lines in the World War is participation afterward in the battles in the Baltic, against the enemies of the national uprising and for the defense of German soil.

Paragraphs 9–12 (omitted).

The Führer and Reich Chancellor
Adolf Hitler

The Reich Minister of Justice
Dr. Gürtner

The Reich Minister of the Interior
Frick

The Deputy of the Führer
R. Hess

The Reich Minister of Finance
Count Schwerin von Krosigk.

SEVENTH SUPPLEMENTARY DECREE
TO THE REICH CITIZENSHIP LAW *(December 5, 1938)*

Pursuant to Paragraph 3 of the Reich Citizenship Law of 15 September 1935 the following is decreed:

Paragraph 1.

Paragraph 4, Sentences 2 and 3 of the First Supplementary Decree to the Reich Citizenship Law of 14 November 1935 and Paragraph 1, Section 5 of the Second Supplementary Decree to the Reich Citizenship Law of 21 December 1935 are abolished.

Paragraph 2.

1. The pensions of Jewish civil servants who,
   a) according to Paragraph 4, Section 2, Sentence 1 of the First Supplementary Decree to the Reich Citizenship Law of 14 November 1935, with the expiration date of 31 December 1935, or
   b) according to Paragraph 2 of the Law Regarding Measures in the Former District of Upper Silesia of 30 June 1937, with the expiration date of 31 August 1937,
2. have retired and have received either a full or provisional pension on the basis of general regulations effective for group a) as of
   a) 31 December 1935, and for group b) as of
   b) b. 31 August 1937
   c) are, as of 1 January 1939, to have their pension payments recalculated [reduced].
   d) Pensions already paid out are not to be affected.

The Reich Minister of the Interior
Frick

The Deputy of the Führer
R. Hess.

EIGHTH SUPPLEMENTARY DECREE TO
THE REICH CITIZENSHIP LAW *(January 17, 1939)*

Pursuant to Paragraph 3 of the Reich Citizenship Law of 15 September 1935 the following is decreed:

Paragraph 1.

The licenses and diplomas of Jewish dentists, veterinarians and pharmacists are cancelled effective 31 January 1939.

Paragraph 2.

1. Jews are forbidden the practice of medicine, including dentistry and veterinary medicine.
2. Jews in any of the professions of medical assistants (as defined in Paragraph 1 of the Law for the Regulation of Nursing) may only practice their profession on Jews or in Jewish institutions.
3. Jews are forbidden the practice of veterinary medicine.

Paragraph 3.

1. The Reich Minister of the Interior or the administrator appointed by him may allow dentists whose licenses have been cancelled as per Paragraph 1 to practice their profession on a temporary basis, although such permission may be revoked without notice.
2. Paragraph 1 applies to dentists as defined in Paragraph 123 of the Reich Insurance Regulations and the Austrian Dental Technicians Law.

Paragraph 4.

A Jew who is authorized as per Paragraph 3 may, with the exception of his wife and legitimate children, treat only Jewish clients.

Paragraph 5.

1. Whoever intentionally or negligently acts in violation of Paragraph 2, Section 1 or Paragraph 4 is subject to a maximum jail term of one year, a monetary fine, or both.
2. Whoever acts in violation of Paragraph 2, Section 2 or 3 will be fined up to 150 Reichmarks or receive a jail sentence.

Paragraphs 6–8 (omitted).

The Reich Minister of the Interior
[signed for] by Pfundtner

The Deputy of the Führer
R. Hess.

NINTH SUPPLEMENTARY DECREE TO
THE REICH CITIZENSHIP LAW (May 5, 1939)

Pursuant to Paragraph 3 of the Reich Citizenship Law of September 15 the following is decreed:

According to Paragraph 5, Section 2b of the First Supplementary Decree to the Reich Citizenship Law of 14 November 1935, it is not considered being married to a Jew if the spouse is a Jewish *Mischling* subject *[Staatsangehöriger]*—descended from two fully Jewish grandparents—whose Austrian marriage could not be dissolved under Austrian Law, provided that as of 16 September 1935 he or she was legally separated and since then has not been reunited with that spouse.

The Reich Minister of the Interior
Frick

The Deputy of the Führer
R. Hess.

TENTH SUPPLEMENTARY DECREE
TO THE REICH CITIZENSHIP LAW *(July 4, 1939)*

Pursuant to Paragraph 3 of the Reich Citizenship Law of 15 September 1935 the following is decreed:

Article I

Paragraph 1.

1. All Jews will become members of a Reich Association *[Reichsvereinigung].*
2. The Reich Association is a legally recognized entity. It bears the full name of "Reich Association of Jews in Germany" *[Reichsvereinigung der Juden in Deutschland]* and has its headquarters in Berlin.
3. The Reich Association makes use of the local branches of the Jewish Religious Community Associations *[jüdische Kultusverinigungen].*

Paragraph 2.

1. The Reich Association has as its purpose the promotion of Jewish emigration.
2. The Reich Association is also responsible
   a) for a Jewish school system
   b) for Jewish welfare work
3. The Reich Minister of the Interior may assign other duties to the Reich Association.

Paragraph 3.

1. All Jews who are state subjects or are stateless and have their place of domicile or permanent residence within the territory of the Reich are members of the Reich Association.
2. In the case of a mixed marriage only the Jewish partner is a member
   a) if the Jewish partner is the man and the marriage has produced no children, or
   b) if the children are legally Jewish.

3. Jews of foreign citizenship and those living in a mixed marriage who are not already members on the basis of Section 2 are free to join the Reich Association.

Paragraph 4.

The Reich Association is supervised by the Reich Minister of the Interior; its statutes and by-laws must meet his approval.

Paragraph 5.

1. The Reich Minister of the Interior is authorized to dissolve Jewish associations, organizations and foundations or order their integration into the Reich Association.
2. In the case of a dissolution, the liquidation will proceed according to the provisions of the civil code. The Reich Minister of the Interior may, however, nominate liquidators or relieve them from office and determine that the liquidation depart from the provisions of the civil code. Upon conclusion of a liquidation, the property of the Jewish organization is transferred to the Reich Association.
3. In the case of an integration the affected property of the Jewish entity is transferred to the Reich Association. A liquidation in this case does not take place. The Reich Association assumes responsibility for all the obligations of the integrated entity.
4. The Reich Minister of the Interior may abolish or revise the constitutions and decisions of any Jewish association, organization or foundation if it departs from any of these guidelines. Jews who on the basis of any retroactively cancelled statutes or decisions make a profit or make gains are required to turn over these undeserved riches to the Reich Association.

Article II.

Jewish School System

Paragraph 6.

1. The Reich Association of Jews bears responsibility for the schooling of Jews.
2. For this purpose the Reich Association must establish and maintain a sufficient number of elementary schools. It may also conduct middle and higher schools as well as professional and occupational schools or any other schools or courses that serve to promote the emigration of Jews.
3. The Reich Association bears responsibility for conducting training schools for those who will teach in its institutions.
4. The schools established and maintained by the Reich Association will be private schools.

Paragraph 7.

Jews may attend only those schools that are under the administration of the Reich Association. They are subject to the general rules regarding compulsory school attendance.

Paragraph 8.

1. Existing Jewish schools, public and private, as well as Jewish teacher training institutions and other Jewish educational institutions will be disbanded if they have not been taken over by the Reich Association at a time to be stipulated by the Reich Minister for Science, Education and Public Instruction in agreement with the Reich Minister of the Interior.
2. The Reich Association is empowered to appropriate Jewish owned property that is necessary for the maintenance of its school system. The Jewish property owners are to be compensated for their losses by the Reich Association. Cases of dispute concerning compensation are to be decided by the School Administration Authority without access to the courts.

Paragraph 9.

The teachers in Jewish schools who still have civil service standing will be retired as of 30 June 1939. They are obligated to accept positions offered them by the Reich Association to teach in one of its schools. If they reject such an offer they lose their right to receive a pension.

Paragraph 10.

Abolished herewith are existing Reich and regional regulations regarding the schooling of Jews, especially regarding their admission to schools, and those regarding the establishment and maintenance of their public schools, including the appropriation of public funds for the purpose of supporting religious instruction in Judaism.

Paragraph 11.

The Jewish school system is under the supervision of the Reich Minister for Science, Education and Public Instruction.

Article III.

Jewish Welfare Services

Paragraph 12.

As the responsible bearer for welfare services for Jews, the Reich Association must adequately support needy Jews so that they do not become public charges. For those Jews requiring institutionalization, the Reich Association must provide facilities exclusively for them.

Article IV.

Concluding Regulations

Paragraph 13.

No compensation is to be provided for disadvantages produced by the implementation of this decree.

Paragraph 14.

1. The Reich Minister of the Interior will enact the regulations governing the implementation of this decree.
2. Insofar as the Jewish school system is concerned, regulations will be enacted by the Reich Minister for Science, Education and Public Instruction. The same applies for measures based on paragraph 5 if the Jewish facility falls under the jurisdiction of the Reich Minister for Science, Education and Public Instruction.

Paragraph 15.

The right to enforce this decree in Austria is reserved.

The Reich Minister of the Interior
Frick

The Deputy of the Führer
R. Hess

The Reich Minister of Science, Education and Public Instruction
Rust

The Reich Minister for Church Affairs
Kerrl

ELEVENTH SUPPLEMENTARY DECREE
TO THE REICH CITIZENSHIP LAW *(November 25, 1941)*

Pursuant to Paragraph 3 of the Reich Citizenship Law of 15 September 1935 the following is decreed:

Paragraph 1.

A Jew who resides permanently in a foreign country cannot be a German subject. Permanent residence *[ständiger Wohnsitz]* abroad is defined as residing abroad under circumstances which indicate the residence is not temporary.

Paragraph 2.

A Jew loses the status as a German subject

a) if at the time this decree becomes effective, he has his permanent residence abroad,

b) or, or if after this decree takes effect, he takes up permanent residence abroad.

Paragraph 3.

1. Pursuant to this decree, the Jew who loses his status as a German subject, therewith forfeits his property to the Reich. Also forfeited to the Reich, pursuant to this decree, is the property of stateless Jews who, upon the date this measure takes effect, possessed the status of German subject.

2. The forfeited assets are intended for the promotion of measures that contribute to the solution of the Jewish problem.

Paragraphs 4–13 (omitted).

The Reich Minister of the Interior
Frick

The Leader of the Party Chancellery
M. Bormann

The Reich Minister of Finance
[signed for] by Reinhardt

The Reich Minister of Justice
Dr. Schlegelberger.

TWELFTH SUPPLEMENTARY DECREE
TO THE REICH CITIZENSHIP LAW (25 APRIL 1943)

Pursuant to Paragraph 3 of the Reich Citizenship Law of 15 September 1935 the following is decreed:

Paragraph 1.

1. State subject status *(Staatsangehörigkeit)* may be granted provisionally and is revocable at any time. This brings into existence a separate group of people bearing the status of provisional state subjects.

2. In addition to state subject status there is the additional status of "protected subject" *[Schutzangehöriger]*; someone with protected subject status cannot simultaneously possess state subject status

Paragraph 2.

State subjects may have this status revoked either by a general edict or by individual decision in specific cases and will be designated as having provisional state subject status.

Paragraph 3.

Protected subjects of the German Reich are residents of Germany who do not belong to the German people *[Volk]* and who by general edict or by individual decision in specific cases have been granted this status.

Paragraph 4.

1. Jews and Gypsies cannot become state subjects. Neither can they become provisional state subjects or protected subjects.
2. Jewish *Mischlinge* of the first degree are to be considered Jews if they do not possess the status of state subjects, and if the other provisions of Paragraph 5, Section 2 of the First Supplementary Decree to the Reich Citizenship Law of 14 November 1935 apply to them.

Paragraph 5.

The Reich Minister of the Interior, in agreement with the Leader of the Party Chancellery and the Reich Führer of the SS and Reich Commissioner for the Strengthening of Germandom, issues the legal and administrative orders necessary to implement this decree.

Paragraph 6.

This decree applies also to the Protectorate of Bohemia and Moravia.

The Reich Minister of the Interior
Frick.

THIRTEENTH SUPPLEMENTARY DECREE TO THE REICH CITIZENSHIP LAW (July 1, 1943)

Pursuant to Paragraph 3 of the Reich Citizenship Law of 15 September 1935 the following is decreed:

Paragraph 1.

1. Breaches of the law by Jews will be punished by the police.
2. Poland's Criminal Law Procedures of 4 December 1941 will no longer apply to Jews.

Paragraph 2.

1. Upon the death of a Jew, his property is forfeited to the Reich.
2. The Reich can grant a settlement to the deceased's non-Jewish heirs or dependents who are residents of Germany.
3. The compensation can take the form of a capital sum. This grant cannot exceed the sales value of the transferred property which is under the control of the German Reich.

4. The compensation can take the form of transfer of materials and rights which are part of the property. There are to be no legal fees for this property transfer.

Paragraph 3.

The Reich Minister of the Interior, in agreement with the appropriate Reich officials, will issue the legal and administrative guidelines necessary for the implementation of this decree. In this connection he will also determine the extent to which this order applies to Jews of foreign citizenship.

Paragraph 4.

This decree takes effect on the seventh day after its publication. In the Protectorate of Bohemia and Moravia it is applicable within the area under German administration and jurisdiction; Paragraph 2 is applicable also to the Protectorate's Jews.

The Reich Minister of the Interior
Frick

The Leader of the Party Chancellery
M. Bormann

The Reich Minister of Finance
Graf Schwerin von Krosigk

The Reich Minister of Justice
Dr. Thierack.

LAW FOR THE PROTECTION OF GERMAN BLOOD AND GERMAN HONOR OF SEPTEMBER 15, 1935

Convinced that the purity of German blood is essential to the survival of the German people, and inspired by the uncompromising determination to safeguard the future of the German nation, the Reichstag has unanimously adopted the following, which is herewith promulgated:

Paragraph 1.

1. Marriages between Jews and nationals of German or related blood are prohibited. Marriages concluded in violation of this law are void, even if, for the purpose of evading this law, they are concluded abroad.
2. Proceedings for annulment may be initiated only by the Public Prosecutor.

Paragraph 2.

Extramarital relations between Jews and nationals of German or related blood are prohibited.

Paragraph 3.

Jews are not permitted to employ in their households female nationals who are of German or related blood and who are under the age of 45.

Paragraph 4.

1. Jews are forbidden to display the Reich and national flag or the colors of the Reich.
2. They are, on the other hand, allowed to display the Jewish colors. The exercise of this right is protected by the state.

Paragraph 5.

1. Anyone who acts in violation of the prohibition in Paragraph 1 is subject to punishment by incarceration.
2. Anyone who acts in violation of the prohibition of Paragraph 2 is subject to punishment by imprisonment or hard labor.
3. Anyone who acts in violation of the provisions of Paragraphs 3 or 4 is subject to punishment with imprisonment of up to one year and a fine, or with either one of these two penalties.

Paragraph 6.

The Reich Minister of the Interior, in agreement with the Deputy of the Führer and the Reich Minister of Justice, will issue the legal and administrative regulations required for the implementation and supplementation of this law.

Paragraph 7.

This law will become effective on the day after its promulgation; Paragraph 3, however, not until 1 January 1936.

The Führer and Reich Chancellor
Adolf Hitler

The Reich Minister of the Interior
Frick

The Reich Minister of Justice
Dr. Gürtner

The Deputy to the Führer
R. Hess.

FIRST SUPPLEMENTARY DECREE TO THE LAW FOR THE PROTECTION OF GERMAN BLOOD AND GERMAN HONOR
(November 14, 1935)

Pursuant to Paragraph 6 of the Law for the Protection of German Blood and German Honor of 15 September 1935 the following is decreed:

Paragraph 1.

1. Subjects of the state *[Staatsangehöriger]* are German subjects as defined in the Reich Citizenship Law.
2. The Jewish *Mischling* is defined in Paragraph 2, Section 2 of the First Supplementary Decree to the Reich Citizenship Law of 14 November 1935.
3. The Jew is defined in Paragraph 5 of the same decree.

Paragraph 2.

Among the prohibited marriages according to Paragraph 1 [of the Law for the Protection of German Blood and German Honor] are those between Jews and subjects of the state who are *Mischlinge* with one fully Jewish grandparent.

Paragraph 3.

1. Subjects of the state who are *Mischlinge* with two fully Jewish grandparents who wish to marry someone of German or related blood, or a subject of the state who is a *Mischling* with one fully Jewish grandparent, must acquire the permission of the Reich Minister of the Interior and the Deputy to the Führer or his delegated representative.
2. In reaching a decision special attention is to be paid to the physical, psychological and character qualities of the petitioner, the length of his family's residence in Germany, his or his father's role in the World War, and the nature of his family history.
3. The petition for permission to marry is to be presented to the higher administrative authorities in the town of the petitioner's residence.
4. The procedures in this matter are to be regulated by the Reich Minister of the Interior in agreement with the Deputy of the Führer.

Paragraph 4.

To be disallowed are marriages between state subjects when each are *Mischlinge* with one fully Jewish grandparent.

Paragraph 5.

Marriage restrictions because of Jewish blood are fully covered in Paragraph 1 and Paragraphs 2–4 of this decree.

Paragraph 6.

No marriage shall be concluded if it is feared that its offspring will endanger the purity of German blood.

Paragraph 7.

Before a marriage can be concluded, every engaged couple must present a Marriage Fitness Certificate (Paragraph 2 of the Marriage Fitness Law of 18 October 1935) demonstrating that no hindrance to the marriage exists.

Paragraph 8.

1. An annulment of a marriage concluded in contravention of Paragraph 1 of the Law for the Protection of German Blood and German Honor or of Paragraph 2 of this decree can only be effected by way of a petition of annulment.
2. For marriages concluded in contravention of Paragraphs 3, 4, and 6, the consequences of Paragraph 1 and of Paragraph 5, Section 1 of the Law for the Protection of German Blood and Honor do not apply.

Paragraphs 9–10 (omitted).

Paragraph 11.

Extramarital relations in the sense of Paragraph 2 of the Law for the Protection of German Blood and German Honor means sexual relations. Punishable also under Paragraph 5, Section 2 of this law are sexual relations between Jews and subjects of the state who are *Mischlinge* with only one fully Jewish grandparent.

Paragraph 12.

1. A household is to be considered Jewish [Paragraph 3 of the Law for the Protection of German Blood and German Honor] if a Jewish male is head of the household or a member of the household.
2. An employee of the household is a person who is taken into the household within the guidelines of a working relationship or who on a daily basis does household work or undertakes other duties related to the household.
3. Female subjects of the state who are of German or related blood and who at the time of the promulgation of the Law for the Protection of German Blood and Honor were employed in a Jewish household may continue that employment if on 31 December 1935 they will have been at least 35 years old.
4. Foreigners who are not permanent residents of Germany are not subject to these regulations.

Paragraph 13.

Whoever acts in violation of Paragraph 3 of the Law for the Protection of German Blood and German Honor or Paragraph 12 of this decree is punishable, according to Paragraph 5, Section 3 of the Law, even if he is not Jewish.

Paragraph 14.

Whoever acts in violation of Paragraph 5, Sections 1 and 2 of the Law for the Protection of German Blood and Honor is to be brought before the High Criminal Court.

Paragraph 15.

To the extent that the regulations of the Law for the Protection of German Blood and German Honor and its supplementary decrees apply to subjects of the German State, they apply also to those who are stateless if the latter have their permanent residence in Germany. Stateless persons who have their permanent residence abroad are subject to these regulations only if they have at one point possessed German citizenship.

Paragraph 16.

1. The Führer and Reich Chancellor may grant exceptions to the regulations stated in the Law for the Protection of German Blood and German Honor and to its supplementary decrees.
2. Criminal prosecution of a foreign citizen requires the permission of the Reich Ministers of Justice and the Interior.

Paragraph 17.

This decree takes effect the day following its publication. Paragraph 7 will take effect on a date to be determined by the Reich Minister of the Interior. Until then the Marriage Fitness Certificate will be required only in doubtful cases.

The Führer and Reich Chancellor
Adolf Hitler

The Reich Minister of the Interior
Frick

The Deputy of the Führer
R. Hess

The Reich Minister of Justice
Dr. Gürtner.

LAW REGULATING RENTAL CONDITIONS FOR JEWS (April 30, 1939)

The Reich government promulgates the following:

Paragraph 1
Easing of Rental Protection.

A Jew cannot seek redress under the rent control law if the landlord terminates the rental agreement and submits certification from the municipal authority that an alternate accommodation has been secured for the tenant. This does not apply if the landlord is a Jew.

Paragraph 2
Premature Cancellation.

If one party to the rental agreement is a Jew, it may be cancelled at any time within the prescribed time limit. The landlord may, however, only terminate prior to the contractual period of notice if he can submit certification from the municipal authority that alternate quarters have been secured for the tenant for the period following the conclusion of the rental relationship.

Paragraph 3
Subtenancy.

Jews may only conclude subtenancy agreements with Jews. Permission of the landlord is not required in case he is also a Jew.

Paragraph 4
Accommodations.

1. A Jew is required to accept Jews as tenants or subtenants, if so requested by the municipal authorities, in living accommodations which he owns or holds on basis of the right of usage, or which he has leased from a Jew. In case the conclusion of such an agreement is denied, the municipal authorities can order that a contract with the conditions they determine is agreed upon. The extent of the compensation for the cession of premises and any sublease supplement is set by the municipal authority, insofar as it is not itself the price authority, in agreement with the competent price authority. Local authorities may exact fees for their establishment of rental contracts.
2. For the determination of leases and sublease agreements, the local authority may charge fees.

Paragraph 5
New Rentals.

Jews may lease vacant or about-to-become vacant premises only with the authorization of the municipal authority. The provisions of Paragraph 4 apply specifically to these accommodations.

Paragraph 6 (omitted).

Paragraph 7
Mixed Marriages.

Should the application of this law depend on whether the landlord or tenant is a Jew, the following applies in the case of a mixed marriage (Mischehe) of the landlord or the tenant:

1. The provisions are not applicable if the woman is a Jew. The same is true if there are offspring from the marriage, even if the marriage no longer exists.
2. If the man is a Jew and the marriage has no offspring, the provisions of the law apply without consideration of whether the husband or the wife is landlord or the tenant.
3. Offspring that are counted as Jews receive no consideration.

Paragraphs 8–13 (omitted).

Paragraph 14

Reservations, Authorizations.

1. The right to apply this law in Austria and in the Sudeten German territories is reserved.
2. The Reich Minister of Justice and the Reich Minister of Labor are authorized, in agreement with the Reich Minister of the Interior, to issue provisions for enforcement of this law and to introduce appropriately similar measures in Austria and in the Sudeten German areas.

The Führer and Reich Chancellor
Adolf Hitler

The Reich Minister of Justice
Dr. Gürtner

The Reich Minister of Labor
Represented by Dr. Krohn

The Deputy of the Führer
R. Hess

The Reich Minister of the Interior
Frick.

POLICE DECREE REGARDING
THE IDENTIFYING MARK FOR JEWS (September 1, 1941)

Pursuant to the Decree of the Reich Minister of 14 November 1938 Regarding the Police Decrees and the Decree Regarding the Law-Making Authority *(Rechtsetzungrecht)* in the Protectorate of Bohemia and Moravia of 7 June 1939, and in agreement with the Reich Protector, the following is decreed:

Paragraph 1.

1. Jews over the age of six are forbidden to appear in public without displaying the Jewish star *(Judenstern)*.
2. The Jewish star must be palm-sized, have six points, be made of yellow cloth outlined in black, with the letters *JUDE* (JEW) written on it in black.

Paragraph 2.

Jews are forbidden to
a)   leave the local community in which they reside without the written permission of the local police
b)   wear or display any medals, decorations or other badges.

Paragraph 3.

Paragraphs 2 and 3 are not applicable to
a)   a Jewish husband living in a mixed marriage *(Mischehe),* when there are offspring who are not considered to be Jews, even if the marriage no longer exists, or if the only son has been killed in action in the current war.
b)   the Jewish wife of a childless mixed marriage for the duration of the marriage.

Paragraph 4.

1.   Whoever deliberately or through negligence acts in violation of Paragraphs 1 and 2, will be fined 150 RM or sentenced to a six-month prison term.
2.   Additional police security measures and guidelines for more severe punishment are not precluded.

Paragraph 5.

This police decree applies also in the Protectorate of Bohemia and Moravia with the proviso that the Reich Protector in Bohemia and Moravia may adapt the provisions in Paragraph 2 to meet local conditions in Bohemia and Moravia.

Paragraph 6.

This police decree takes effect 14 days after its proclamation.

The Reich Minister of the Interior Represented byHeydrich.

SELECTED BIBLIOGRAPHY

General Treatments

Benz, Wolfgang. *The Holocaust: A German Historian Examines the Genocide.* Translated by Jane Sydenham-Kwiet. New York: Columbia University Press, 1999.

Botwinick, Rita Steinhardt. *A History of the Holocaust: From Ideology to Annihilation.* Upper Saddle River, NJ: Prentice-Hall, 1996.

Burrin, Phillipe. *Hitler and the Jews: The Genesis of the Holocaust.* Translated by Patsy Southgate. London: Edward Arnold, 1994.

Dawidowicz, Lucy S. *The War Against the Jews, 1933–1945.* 10th anniversary ed. New York: Free Press, 1986.

Fein, Helen. *Accounting for Genocide and Jewish Victimization During the Holocaust.* New York: Free Press, 1979.

Friedlander, Saul. *Nazi Germany and the Jews.* Vol. 1, *The Years of Persecution, 1933–1939.* New York: HarperCollins, 1997.

Gilbert, Martin. *The Holocaust: A History of the Jews of Europe During the Second World War.* New York: Holt, Rinehart and Winston, 1986.

Hilberg, Raul. *The Destruction of the European Jews.* Rev. ed., 3 vols. New York and London: Holmes and Meier, 1985.

Katz, Steven T. *The Holocaust in Historical Context.* Vol 1, *The Holocaust and Mass Death Before the Modern Age.* New York: Oxford University Press, 1994.

Landau, Ronnie S. *The Nazi Holocaust.* Chicago: Ivan Dee, 1994.

Levin, Nora. *The Holocaust: The Destruction of European Jewry, 1933–1945.* New York: T. Y. Crowell Co., 1968.

Marrus, Michael R. *The Holocaust in History.* Hanover and London: University Press of New England, 1987.

Mayer, Arno J. *Why Did the Heavens Not Darken? The "Final Solution" in History.* New York: Pantheon Books, 1988.

Schleunes, Karl A. *The Twisted Road to Auschwitz: Nazi Policy Toward German Jews, 1933–1939.* Urbana: University of Illinois Press, 1970.

Yahil, Leni. *The Holocaust: The Fate of European Jewry, 1932–1945.* Translated by Ina Friedman and Haya Galai. New York and Oxford: Oxford University Press, 1990.

Encyclopedias and Dictionaries

Edelheit, Abraham J., and Herschel Edelheit. *History of the Holocaust: A Handbook and Dictionary.* Boulder: Westview Press, 1994.
_____. *A World in Turmoil: An Integrated Chronology of the Holocaust and World War II.* New York: Greenwood Press, 1991.
Encyclopedia of Genocide. 2 vols. Edited by Israel W. Charney. Santa Barbara, CA: ABC-CLIO, 1999.
The Encyclopedia of the Holocaust. 4 vols. Edited by Israel Gutman. New York: Macmillan, 1990.
The Encyclopedia of the Third Reich. 2 vols. Edited by Christian Zentner and Friedemann Beduerftig. Translated by Amy Hackett. New York: Macmillan, 1991.
Epstein, Eric Joseph, and Philip Rosen. *Dictionary of the Holocaust: Biography, Geography, and Terminology.* Westport, CT: Greenwood Press, 1997.
Fischel, Jack R. *Historical Dictionary of the Holocaust.* Lanham, MD: Scarecrow Press, 1999.
Snyder, Louis L. *Encyclopedia of the Third Reich.* New York: McGraw-Hill, 1976.

Bibliographies

Edelheit, Abraham J., and Herschel Edelheit, eds. *Bibliography on Holocaust Literature.* Boulder: Westview Press, 1986.
_____. *Bibliography on Holocaust Literature: Supplement.* 2 vols. Boulder: Westview Press, 1990, 1993.
Szonyi, David M., ed. *The Holocaust: An Annotated Bibliography and Resource Guide.* New York: KTAV Publishing House, 1985.

Document Collections

Arad, Yitzhak, Yisrael Gutman, and Abraham Margoliot, eds. *Documents on the Holocaust.* Translated by Lea Ben Dor. Jerusalem: Yad Vashem, and Oxford: Pergamon Press, 1981.
Friedlander, Henry, and Sybil Milton, eds. *Archives of the Holocaust: An International Collection of Selected Documents.* 22 vols. New York and London: Garland Publishing, 1989.
Hilberg, Raul, ed. *Documents of Destruction: Germany and Jewry, 1933–1945.* Chicago: Quadrangle Books, 1971.
Mendelsohn, John, ed. *The Holocaust: Selected Documents in Eighteen Volumes.* New York and London: Garland Publishing, 1982.

The "Jewish Question" Background

Bacharach, Walter Zvi. "Antisemitism and Racism in Nazi Ideology." In Michael Berenbaum and Abraham Peck, eds., *The Holocaust and History: The Known, the*

Unknown, the Disputed and the Reexamined, pp. 64–74. Washington, DC: USHMM, Bloomington and Indianapolis: Indiana University Press, 1988.

Bein, Alex. *The Jewish Question: Biography of a World Problem*. Translated by Harry Zohn. Rutherford, NJ: Fairleigh Dickenson University Press, and London and Toronto: Associated University Presses, 1990.

Housden, Martyn. *Helmut Nicolai and Nazi Ideology*. New York: St. Martin's Press, 1992.

Weiss, John. *Ideology of Death: Why the Holocaust Happened in Germany*. Chicago; Ivan Dee, 1996.

Public Opinion in Nazi Germany

Bankier, David. *The Germans and the Final Solution: Public Opinion Under Nazism*. Oxford: Blackwell Publishers, 1992.

Kershaw, Ian. *Popular Opinion and Political Dissent in the Third Reich: Bavaria, 1933–1945*. Oxford: Clarendon Press, 1983.

Welch, David. *The Third Reich: Politics and Propaganda*. London and New York: Routledge, 1993.

Wollenberg, Joerg, ed. *The German Public and the Persecution of Jews, 1933–1945: "No One Participated, No One Knew."* Translated by Rado Pribic. Atlantic Highlands, NJ: Humanities Press, 1996.

The Nazi System/Bureaucracy

Browning, Christopher R. *The Final Solution and the German Foreign Office; A Study of Referat D, Abteilung Deutschland 1940–43*. New York: Holmes and Meier, 1978.

_____. "The Government Experts." In Henry Friedlander and Sybil Milton, eds., *The Holocaust: Ideology, Bureaucracy, and Genocide*, pp. 183–197. Millwood, NY: Kraus International, 1980.

_____. "Referat Deutschland, Jewish Policy, and the German Foreign Office." *Yad Vashem Studies* 12 (1977):37–73.

Caplan, Jane. *Government Without Administration: State and Civil Service in Weimar and Nazi Germany*. Oxford: Clarendon Press, 1988.

Gellately, Robert. *The Gestapo and German Society: Enforcing Racial Policy*. Oxford and New York: Oxford University Press, 1990.

Mommsen, Hans. "The Realization of the Unthinkable: The 'Final Solution of the Jewish Question' in the Third Reich." In Hans Mommsen, *From Weimar to Auschwitz*, trans. Alan Kramer and Louise Wilmot, pp. 224–253. Princeton: Princeton University Press, 1991.

Legislation and the Judiciary

Büttner, Ursula. "The Persecution of Christian-Jewish Families in the Third Reich." *Leo Baeck Institute Yearbook* 34 (1989):267–289.

Grenville, John. "Neglected Holocaust Victims: The Mischlinge, the *Judischver-sippte*, and the Gypsies." In Michael Berenbaum and Abraham Peck, eds., *The Holocaust and History*. Bloomington: Indiana University Press, 1998.

McKale, Donald M. *The Nazi Party Courts: Hitler's Management of Conflict in His Movement, 1921–1945*. Lawrence, Manhattan, and Wichita: University of Kansas Press, 1974.

Miller, Richard Lawrence. *Nazi Justiz: Law of the Holocaust*. Westport, CN: Praeger, 1995.

Moser, Jonny. "Depriving Jews of Their Legal Rights in the Third Reich." In Walter H. Pehle, ed., *November 1938: From "Kristallnacht" to Genocide*, trans. William Templer, pp. 123–138. New York and Oxford: Berg, 1991.

Müller, Ingo. *Hitler's Justice: The Courts of the Third Reich*. Translated by Deborah Lucas Schneider. Cambridge: Harvard University Press, 1991.

Noakes, Jeremy. "The Development of Nazi Policy Towards the German-Jewish 'Mischlinge,' 1933–1945." *Leo Baeck Institute Yearbook* 34 (1989):291–354.

Stolleis, Michael. *The Law Under the Swastika: Studies on Legal History in Nazi Germany*. Translated by Thomas Dunlap. Chicago and London: University of Chicago Press, 1998.

Note

1. Loesener Memoir (see p. [000] here).

INDEX

Printed in the United States
85067LV00005B/82-114/A